Investing in Residential Income Property

by Douglas M. Temple

U.S.NEWS & WORLD REPORT BOOKS

ESTATE PLANNING

by William C. Clay, Jr.

A division of U.S. News & World Report, Inc.   WASHINGTON, D.C.

U.S.NEWS & WORLD REPORT BOOKS

Directing Editor: Joseph Newman

Editors for this Dual Edition:
Roslyn Grant and Judith Gersten

Dual Edition Books, arranged with the original publishers and the authors, are created and abridged especially for the U.S.News & World Report Money Management Library.

Investing in Residential Income Property
Henry Regnery Company
Copyright © by Douglas M. Temple

Estate Planning
Dow Jones-Irwin, Inc.
Copyright © by William C. Clay, Jr.

Copyright © 1976 by U.S.News & World Report, Inc.
2300 N Street, N.W., Washington, D.C. 20037

ISBN 0-89193-424-3

Library of Congress Catalog Card Number 76-46687

Printed in the United States of America

Contents

Contents

Editor's Note

To build an estate and then to manage it to your satisfaction is no easy matter. But it is by no means an impossible goal, even in this inflationary era. Assistance is at hand for those who would like to join the ranks of Americans who have succeeded in this undertaking. Each book in this Dual Edition is devoted to one aspect of this two-part goal.

Employed persons seeking to supplement their paychecks and to protect their estates against the pernicious effects of inflation will learn from the first book in this volume that adopting the role of landlord may solve their financial problems. For many people the words "apartment house owner" evoke a vision of a tough-minded individual who enjoys a large income collected by his agents in the form of monthly rents from hundreds of tenants. While many landlords fit this description, another type is the person who, as a sideline, owns and manages a small building containing perhaps four apartments. This latter type of landlord is the role seen as suitable for the novice by Douglas M. Temple, author of *Investing in Residential Income Property.*

While there are many books devoted to real estate investment, this one provides the rarely available step-by-step approach essential for those seriously considering an investment in this field. Addressing himself to those who have only a small amount of cash to invest, Professor Temple carefully covers every factor involved in becoming a landlord on a part-time basis.

Those who have never before visualized themselves as landlords quite possibly also have never thought of themselves as being in need of an estate plan. The popular image of an estate plan limits its use to rich persons who take every possible step to protect their vast holdings. This concept is far from the reality. There is no one who does not need an estate plan, regardless of how small the amount of one's possessions and savings. This is because few, if any, persons are unconcerned about the custody of their children, the support of their surviving spouse, the disposition of their property, and the minimizing of their taxes. Although such concerns are universal, relatively few people plan for these contingencies, most likely because they have not been sufficiently informed about the uses of an estate plan.

Estate Planning should help to remedy this situation. In language that is easily understood by the layman, attorney William C. Clay, Jr., provides the fundamental information one should have before obtaining the assistance of a legal advisor in designing a plan that will ensure the best use of one's estate now and in the future.

As in all volumes in this Dual Edition series, our editors have preserved the greater part of the original texts; only less essential material has been trimmed to bring the essence of the books into sharper focus. This enables the reader to save time and money while acquiring useful knowledge about money management.

Investing in
Residential Income
Property

Introduction

In the search for financial security the individual is faced with a multitude of alternatives. The problem of finding a way to build an estate to provide that security is probably more difficult now than it ever has been in the past. Inflation is the villain.

Many informed investment advisers have concluded that the owner of real estate probably has a somewhat better than average chance to beat inflation. But the problem is not solved simply by purchasing the first piece of real estate you come across. Many people have achieved substantial wealth through real estate but they have worked hard at it. It is important to know how to determine value and, hence, the maximum price to pay. You must be familiar with how to arrange the best financing and how to maximize the benefits of income tax regulation. You have to have an investment strategy geared to your objectives. You then must be prepared to search for, buy, and manage the property that will be the most suitable for *you*.

This book has been written to provide a guide to the amateur investor—the person who wants to try to find his financial security through real estate investing. There are many ways to invest in real estate, and they are explained, discussed, and compared. The information and ideas will make it easier for you not only to decide what you want to do but also give you step-by-step guidance in making an investment in residential income property, the type of real estate investment considered to be extremely suitable for the investor wishing to be active in handling his own affairs.

There are two basic investment objectives: to maximize current income to replace or supplement employment income, and to maximize long-term capital appreciation, particularly for retirement. Here are some of the reasons why an investment in residential income property may appeal to you as you try to achieve these objectives.

Maximum income from your investment in an apartment building will be generated by skillfully managing the property to minimize operating expense, obtain maximum rents, and use as little borrowed funds as possible. A well-situated and managed property can return an after-tax rate in excess of that obtainable from investments with comparable risk. Because income tax rules permit charging not only all cash expenditures but also depreciation against income, the ultimate income tax payable on the return is much less than on, say, bonds, business profits, or other income-producing investments. And because depreciation is a noncash expense, the actual cash return is greater than the after-tax income. Even for owners who buy an apartment to provide current income, there also is the possibility of long-term capital appreciation to be "cashed in" when the property is sold.

Many types of investments can be made with partly borrowed funds, thus employing leverage—the technique of using someone else's money to earn a return greater than the cost of the borrowing. The advantage of the real estate investment is the relatively lower cost of using leverage. The property is used as security for the loan—and mortgage rates are lower than for loans for many other types of investments.

What investment can offer the greatest hedge against the future reduced purchasing power of the dollar? The investor needs a vehicle that will increase in value at at least the inflation rate or else he is losing ground. At least in the past, much real estate has tended to increase in value over time and so to the extent that that will continue in the future, it has the necessary characteristic.

In fact, the factors that cause increased prices for goods and services act on real estate values in the same manner. Long-term capital gains are taxed on a favorable basis.

Many people have discovered that it is desirable to shelter their current income from income taxes and thus there are many investment opportunities offered as tax shelters. Real estate—and in particular, residential income property—is highly suitable for the investor seeking to minimize income to be shared with Uncle Sam. A unique characteristic of residential income property is the investor's ability to have an operating loss for tax purposes, largely because of depreciation expense, yet have enough cash from rents to cover the cash expenses. Under these conditions the loss can be charged against other income, thus reducing the total amount of income taxes payable. For certain types of residential income property accelerated depreciation is permitted, thus increasing the tax-sheltering benefits.

Just how do you measure the return from an investment? With a savings account the interest earnings, when left to compound, give an illusion of growth—your ending balance is greater than the beginning. Realize, of course, that as long as the inflation rate exceeds the after-tax interest rate, you are actually losing money by using a savings account as an investment. Well-managed apartment houses return for their owners a current income rate in excess of interest rates even on savings certificates.

There may be some opportunities to buy corporate bonds at a discount. If you hold them to maturity and they are redeemed at face or par you may have achieved what is thought of as a capital gain. The problem is that the reason for the discount is the relatively low annual yield rate and the appreciation in part offsets it. And there is no opportunity for appreciation beyond the redemption value.

In real estate your investment return may come from as many as three sources: current income (net of rents and operating expenses), long-term appreciation in value, and mortgage reduction (equity buildup) if you have used borrowed funds and the debt is repaid out of income. The tenants truly may buy the property for you.

It is not practical to make any statement of overall yield from an investment in real estate that can be compared directly with alternative opportunities. The matter is too complex. But the various yields for a specific property can be calculated. To show how is a major purpose of this book.

A possible disadvantage to investing in real estate is its relative lack of liquidity. Residential real estate in particular is most suitable for long-term investing. It is difficult and expensive to get your money out of this type of real estate on short notice after you have invested. For the long term, however, the demand for multiple-unit housing appears strong; and recovering an original investment plus realizing the capital gain should be relatively easy. There is an effective market mechanism for buying and selling—real estate brokers—providing the investor with ample assistance in making and liquidating investments.

There are no guarantees of success offered here. By following the ideas and suggestions presented, however, you should have a better than otherwise chance of success in achieving financial security through investing in residential income property.

CHAPTER 1

Investing in Real Estate

Underneath everything is the land. There is a finite supply of land, yet there is a continuing increase in the population and demand for land. With that built-in advantage, real estate obviously has something "extra" going for it that most other investment vehicles do not.

But not all kinds of real estate investment are right for all people all of the time. How do you choose?

In this chapter we will look at several kinds of real estate investment vehicles: owning your own home, vacant and raw land, industrial and commercial property, condominiums, syndication, real estate investment trusts, and residential income property.

After considering the special features of each real estate investment vehicle from an investment point of view, including income tax considerations, the conclusion will become inescapable: for the small, private investor, residential income property — the small apartment building — is the best real estate investment vehicle.

What is real estate?

A piece of land defined and designated by a description of boundaries or other form of legal description is known as real estate or real property. When a structure is placed on the land, it becomes a part of the realty. It is possible legally to treat land and structure separately, but most of the time the term, real estate, means land and any and all things attached to it.

Because real estate is an asset, title to which can be transferred, modified, and so on, there needs to be an orderly way to describe a particular piece of real property. There are two basic systems of describing land and its improvements: by *metes and bounds* and by *lot and block number* in a subdivision.

In colonial times tracts of land were described in writing by using topographical features such as rivers, trees, rocks, fences, and structures as points of reference. Even today in many states, land descriptions may include such things. This is the metes and bounds method.

As towns were developed, land was divided into blocks, then into smaller units on which houses and commercial buildings were built. In the process, surveyors prepared maps showing the area divided into uniform-sized segments. Each segment was numbered for ease of reference, and a copy of the map was filed as a public record. Today it is legally customary to describe a piece of real estate by its lot and block number in a subdivision of a particular name. This system is further tied into a federal system of land identification, and it is from this federal system, the so-called Government Survey, established in 1785, that we get such terms as *principal meridian, township,* and *range.*

The legal description of a piece of property is a matter of public record, and all changes and transfers of title are recorded by a county recorder or registrar of deeds or similarly titled public official. We will discuss additional aspects of this later when we cover escrows and title insurance.

Under ordinary circumstances no mention whatever is made of buildings or lots. *Title* to the property is transferred, and that, unless stated to the contrary, automatically includes anything that is a part of the realty—not only buildings, but mineral rights and rights to the airspace above the land.

In theory the owner of the land could erect a building without limit of height, as the ownership is limited only by the horizontal boundaries of the parcel. The use of property is, however, subject to building codes and zoning ordinances as well as potential court action by neighbors objecting to a structure that would infringe on their rights to a view or for esthetic considerations. An owner may grant permission to, say, a governmental agency to construct an elevated road or railway over his land, through his "airspace."

Advantages to real estate investment

There are, of course, several ways in which real property can be used for investment purposes, but the following characteristics apply across the board. First, there is utility. A building can serve as housing for people, for a commercial activity, or for government service. Land by itself can be used as a park, to grow agricultural products, or to be held for conversion to another purpose. In short, land and buildings can always be *used* (and the use will dictate the economic value).

When land is used for an economic activity, the owner will either gain the return represented by the value of the use or will be paid a rent geared to the utility value. The owner's goal should be to put his land to the highest and best use in order to command the maximum return. If you own land, you can use it yourself or you can realize an income from it.

If you own land and change its use to increase its utility, you increase its economic value. But the opposite may also occur. Thus the sound management of property requires that it be put to the highest and best use. Many types of real estate lend themselves to the making of changes that may lead to increased value both currently and in the future.

In general over the past forty years, the money value of real estate has been increasing—and at a rate greater than the rate at which the value of money has been decreasing. In other words, there has been a *real* gain. The increased demand for real estate by a burgeoning population, the increased cost of construction, and inflation have all caused the value of much real property to appreciate. Moreover, although all physical assets, including buildings, have a tendency to wear out—to depreciate—in the case of buildings in the recent past such depreciation has been more than offset by appreciation. A two-bedroom home bought in 1946 for $5,000 now may sell for $20,000. Not every piece of property has increased in value in this way or to this extent, but enough have to support the generalization that, in the past, appreciation has exceeded depreciation and there has been a long-term gain for the owner of real estate.

This gain is *not* automatic and depends on many factors, some of which are quite beyond the control of the owner-investor. Other kinds of assets—shares of stock, for example—at various times in the past have also appreciated in value (the converse has also occurred). The difference, however, is that the owner of real estate may be in a position to *influence* the change in value of his asset, whereas a stockholder, who does not hold a controlling interest in the ownership of the corporation, is essentially powerless to do anything about the changes in the value of his investment.

Thus the second advantage to real estate investment is its potential for long-term capital appreciation.

Real estate investments also can produce significant *income*, from lease or rental income that exceeds expenses or from interest income from making loans secured by real estate.

Real estate, in short, can provide means to the realization of both basic investment objectives—income and long-term gain.

Investment in other vehicles may also produce current income and/or long-term gain. But only real estate provides massive *tax advantages*. Thanks to Congress's recognition of the need to provide tax benefit incentives to achieve socially desirable goals, income and gain from certain types of real estate investments are treated beneficially under the income tax laws. This generally holds true also for state income tax regulations.

By the use of the options granted, depreciation expense can be charged against rental income, for example, and thus serve to convert current income to long-term capital gain. Long-term capital gains are taxed generally at 50 percent of the rate applicable to current income.

Real estate investment qualifies for these tax breaks because it is designed to contribute to the social good (as well as to make money for the investor). There is a clear need for new housing in virtually all parts of the country. It has been government policy to leave the job to the private sector. But the private sector works best under maximum profit incentives, the mainstay of our free enterprise system. By allowing depreciation to be charged against current income, thus reducing income tax payable on earnings and minimizing the tax payable on long-term gains, government has made real estate projects attractive to investors. The "loopholes" are not really loopholes at all. The rules were deliberately devised to achieve specific objectives. Those capable of creating housing, are, in fact, encouraged to utilize the tax regulations to their full advantage.

Real estate investors consider this factor very carefully; it is of major concern. But it is equally important to realize that even if the tax advantages currently available to investors are eliminated, the fundamental advantages of a real estate investment will still apply.

There probably is some form of real estate that is the right investment for you. At this point, do not worry about whether your investment nest egg is adequate. In the meantime, let us look at the real estate investment choices available to you.

Owning your own home

We have said there are two ways in which to invest in real estate: to buy it and to lend money on it. The first choice involves your personal living accommodation. The great American dream is to own your own home; nonetheless, it is a real estate investment.

The single-family home you own and occupy does not produce rental income, but your cost for housing is reduced by the amount you can deduct on your income tax return for property taxes, uninsured physical property damage or loss over a minimum, and mortgage interest, if any. Too, if you own the property long enough and keep it in reasonable repair, you stand a good chance of selling the property for more than you paid for it, thus realizing a long-term gain. Moreover, you may have an additional advantage because of the favorable income tax treatment of that gain. Indeed, the income tax advantage to home ownership is one of the prime reasons for the widespread development of condominiums, because you do not have to own and occupy a single-family dwelling to qualify for these benefits. You can buy an apartment created with condominium ownership features and treat it, for income tax purposes, as a single-family home. When you own a condominium unit, your ownership boundaries stop at the underside of the paint on the interior walls. You also have an undivided interest in all the common ways of the structures and the outside areas. All other condominium unit owners share this ownership with you. In effect you have bought the airspace in your unit. As a consequence you share in the property taxes and can make the appropriate income tax deduction. If you have a mortgage, the interest is likewise deductible. The purchase of condominium units is financed in the same way as single-family dwellings as far as individual unit buyers are concerned.

A cooperative apartment provides much the same benefits, except that there is less flexibility in disposing of your apartment investment than in the case of the condominium. With the latter you can sell the unit virtually as you can a single-family home.

Your cooperative ownership interest is in the form of shares in the association and the purchaser must meet the membership requirements of the association. In effect the purchaser must be passed on by other members. This does not necessarily pose a problem, but it may. Investment in a cooperative, in short, has less liquidity.

If you live in a portion of a multiple-family dwelling that you own, such as a duplex, the tenant is helping to buy the building for you. Here again the tax laws help. To reduce your taxable income, you can deduct all of the property taxes, the mortgage interest, and, with respect to the portion rented out, depreciation, and operating expenses. You declare the rents as income, of course. When you dispose of the property, your taxable long-term gain will be determined by the amount of depreciation charged against income during the time you owned it.

Closely related to an investment in your home is that of a vacation or second home. Here too you have the opportunity for long-term gain if the property appreciates. If you choose to rent it out for the time you do not wish to use it, you have the potential for rental income. The accounting becomes slightly more complex in such cases because you have to separate the time you use it for yourself from the time it is used by others for a charge. You must prorate the depreciation and perhaps some of the operating expenses to arrive at the amounts to be deducted from your taxable income.

There recently has been a development in second-home or vacation property ownership involving partnership. Let's assume you would like to have the use of a house or apartment at a resort but do not want to own the property completely. Rent is too expensive. Your need would be met if you could use the property for one month in the year. Find eleven others with the same idea, form a partnership, buy the property, and agree as to which month each partner will have the use of the building. In this way, each partner can charge against his other income one-twelfth of the property taxes and mortgage interest. No depreciation could be charged unless you rented out your month. Then you would report the rental income received and charge expenses, including your share of the depreciation. The net result is to minimize the cost of using the vacation accommodation. There would also be the potential for long-term gain on the resale. We have described here the basics of a limited partnership or syndicate.

Some creative real estate and title insurance people have come up with another way of doing what has just been described.

Instead of forming a partnership to own real estate, they have found a way to write a deed so that during a stated *period of time* each calendar year the titleholder owns the property. He is free to sell his ownership interest, arrange financing, and so on. This provides more flexibility than the partnership-syndicate plan. The technique is *interval ownership* and its development is credited to Interval Incorporated, Coral Gables, Florida. The Lawyers Title Insurance Corporation assisted in setting up this imaginative plan.

Speaking further of real estate you might own, we should look at mobile homes. Today there are luxurious mobile-home parks where you can have all the benefits of the latest in housing comforts at relatively low cost. You can spend large amounts, too. In many mobile-home communities you rent the space and buy the mobile home. From a tax point of view, the only deduction you may have is interest expense and a motor-vehicle tax. It is possible to set things up so you can have the advantages a nonmobile-home owner has. Buy the lot and finance the mobile home much the way you would obtain a home mortgage. Some mobile-home parks are simply land subdivisions where lots are for sale subject to rules concerning the installation of mobile homes. Lenders now will make loans for terms up to fifteen years and there is even federal mortgage insurance available. When you want to take a trip, rent the mobile home to someone and charge depreciation in addition to property taxes and loan interest against your taxable income.

Finally, let's look at the advantages of buying a home site for a second home. There has been substantial development of vacation areas to make small plots of land available to those who, while they may use it at first to camp on, ultimately build a cabin or year-round second home. There is more to say about buying raw land as a speculation; for the present we are concerned with those planning to use and build for themselves. Once you take title, or enter into a sales contract under which you are to pay the property taxes, you can charge as a deductible expense the amount of those taxes. Any financing expense is also deductible. Here again, you have a real estate investment. There is also a potential for long-term gain, and certainly the land salesman wants you to believe that. Regrettably, in every part of the country there have been abuses and purchasers have been disappointed, though some have, in fact, done quite well. In some cases the potential is clearly there.

In terms of future financial security, you should seriously consider *owning* the place where you live. Even for situations where, in the past, it has been normal to rent, arrangements now can be made to be an owner-occupant. But now that it is clear your first investment in real estate should be for your own personal living accommodation, we are ready to look at some additional opportunities to build future values.

Investing in land

Why not go out into the country, find some acreage for sale at a few dollars an acre, hold it for a few years, and sell it to a sub-divider at thousands an acre? It can be done. It has been done. What are your chances of making a success of it?

This is predevelopment land and the expectation is that there will be development in the future; that is, the property will be sub-divided, built on, or put to some use that will increase its economic value. Guessing where development will come is a risky business.

It is possible, if you are going to get involved on a big scale, to have feasibility studies made by experts in the field. Such experts are not always correct in their projections; all you really have for your money is an educated guess as to the possible future of your land. If you are involved on a small scale, you will have to trust your own judgment. And that is a risky business. In short, while there are large profits to be made in speculating in raw pre-development land, commensurate with such profits is considerable risk.

Along with the risk are expenses. During the time you hold the raw land, you will have to pay property taxes. If the land is such that you can rent it for agricultural or storage purposes, that income might offset the expense. But never forget that when it comes to investing, your funds can *always* earn, as a minimum, the interest rate on a risk-free savings account. Unless you can be reasonably assured that your land investment is growing in value at least the savings account rate, think more than twice about getting involved. There are other, better places for your money.

On the other hand, all presently developed property was once predevelopment land. Timing of your investment is more important. Buy acreage shortly before there is a need for it to be subdivided.

Zoning and land-use laws

You may find it profitable to subdivide it yourself. But be careful: subdividing is no longer an activity for amateurs. Most states have laws that govern the subdividing of land and sale of the parcels to the public. The basic requirement applicable to most situations is that a subdivision report, disclosing all pertinent facts about the property, be prepared, approved by the state commission, and made available to prospective purchasers. There are also local zoning and land-use laws to consider and comply with before subdivided land can be offered. As a subdivider you will incur expense for land surveying, legal advice, and probably financial assistance. In most areas it is almost as complicated to divide a large lot into two or three smaller pieces as it is to create a thousand home sites from acreage.

But there is substantial profit potential, and you should not be discouraged from investigating what would be required in a particular instance. If you are a prospective purchaser of a plot in a new subdivision, you should insist that the seller give you all of the information required by the local subdivision regulation.

Is the purchase of a vacant city lot a sound real estate investment? Perhaps. The owner will receive a property tax bill and that expense must be considered as an additional investment in the project even though there may be some income tax benefit. Having a tax-deductible expense does not *automatically* mean you are making money. No matter what tax bracket you are in, the expense is reduced only by the income tax saved; you still will have paid out some money. For example, you buy a lot for $10,000 and plan to hold it for resale at a higher price because you see that property of this type is scarce and you have good reason to expect that the lot will be very attractive a few years hence. You get a property tax bill of $250 for a year, and you are in a 40-percent tax bracket. Your actual out-of-pocket expense for property taxes on the lot is $150. To determine whether the lot was a good investment, add the net tax expense each year you owned it to the original cost and then deduct that total from the net proceeds.

Another factor to consider when investing in vacant land is zoning. Virtually all communities today have master plans and zoning and building ordinances. Property will be zoned or approved for specified uses; that means that some uses are forbidden. It may be possible to have the zoning changed, but it would be unwise to count on being able to persuade a planning commission and, perhaps, the adjacent property owners to approve the changes. One hedge in such circumstances is to offer to buy *subject to* obtaining appropriate zoning modifications, thus sharing the risk with the seller.

An important characteristic of residential income property is the fact that a multiple-dwelling unit—say, a fourplex—often can be erected on land otherwise used for a single-family dwelling, actually quadrupling the land use. That is one of the major reasons for the attractiveness of a small apartment as a real estate investment. The cost of the land is spread over several units. As a prospective investor in vacant city lots, watch for opportunities to buy land that is or can be zoned for multiple-family use. Aim to purchase land that is not being used for its highest and best use and for a price that does not reflect such use. Be sure that you can obtain the necessary approval to put it to the highest and best use and realize a return commensurate with your risk and ingenuity.

A final word about vacant land. Up to this point we have talked mostly in terms of land being subdivided and used for dwelling purposes. There are other uses. In days gone by, much industrial and commercial activity was located according to considerations that did not include much land planning. In recent times, land planners have applied some of the basic principles of residential subdividing to the creation of industrial parks and shopping centers.

If you are aware of a community that is underdeveloped as far as shopping centers are concerned, that might mean an investment opportunity for you. Industrial parks often receive preferential local tax concessions in order to attract jobs and payrolls. It might be that your talent and resources are needed right where you are to create such a project.

Investing in commercial property

Some prospective investors in real estate are attracted to store and office property where, they feel, getting tenants who would always pay their rent would not be too difficult. For many situations this observation is quite sound, but what frequently happens is that the tenant becomes successful in his business, decides to retain for himself the benefits of owning property, and becomes an ex-tenant. On the other hand, businessmen are often better off retaining their capital in the business and charging rent expense on a fully tax-deductible basis.

How would you like to have a large nationwide food chain ask you to build a building to its specifications and agree to sign a long-term lease, particularly when you found that your bank would lend you money on the strength of the lease? The tenant will offer to pay for the insurance and property taxes. Large corporations often erect buildings, sell them to investors, and lease them in order to minimize their investment in real estate because they can make more on those funds in their business. (This is known as *lease-back*.)

Although the companies will want an option to renew the lease, they are not under any obligation to do so. If at that time the property is no longer suitable for their use, perhaps because of neighborhood deterioration, they simply walk away. The owner-investor is then faced with finding a new tenant, and that might be difficult — and expensive.

Meanwhile, he will have experienced a relatively trouble-free investment in real estate. The technique of "sale and lease-back" is widely used in many different situations, including federal, state, and local government projects.

The areas of real estate investment discussed thus far generally have involved the owner-operator. That is to say, you have done the investing and managing yourself. And there are some distinct advantages to that: you can exercise control and your own judgment and take action you think will be in your best interest. You can also become involved in a real estate investment without personal activity and active participation in the managing of the investment.

Nonparticipative investing

Here, by definition, we mean that it is solely your money that is put to work, not yourself. The most passive role is that of the person who lends money on property by way of mortgages and trust deeds. The person who puts up the money can hire a manager to take care of the bulk of activity, and that additional expense may be well worth it — depending on the likes, talents, and obligations of the owner. But there is one step further removed from day-to-day involvement: the *syndicate.*

Syndicate is the term applied to a limited partnership formed for the purpose of owning and operating a real estate investment. There are two main objectives to this form of ownership: it allows owners to have the income tax benefits of operating gains or losses as their own and avoids double taxation of business profits that takes place, for example, in corporations; and it permits the owners to avoid personal involvement in day-to-day operation. The syndicate device is widely used outside the field of real estate, too.

The syndicate will consist of a general partner, who often is a real estate management firm or building contractor, and the individual investors, who are limited partners; that is, the individual's liability is restricted to the amount of his investment or contribution to the partnership. Established properly, the limited partnership itself pays no income tax. Operating gains or losses are reported by each investor; this device has been widely used for tax sheltering.

A limited partner in a real estate syndicate enjoys all of the advantages of current income or tax sheltering, *plus* long-term capital-gain benefits without having to find the investment or tenants, or manage or sell the property to realize the gain. Obviously the people who perform these functions must be paid, and that cost is borne by the limited partners. In theory, however, through management expertise, volume buying, and other economies of scale, the cost should be minimized. A major objective is to run the syndicate in such a way that the individual partner-investor makes more profit than he would if he were to do everything himself. Some syndicates have achieved that objective; many have been serious failures.

Another form of nonparticipative investing is provided by the real estate investment trust—REIT. One of the disadvantages of the snydicate is that a limited partner may have trouble liquidating his investment because there normally is not a market for partnership interests. This problem is overcome, in theory, by the REIT, an organization formed to invest in various forms of real estate and to hold in trust the assets of those who put up the money. The investors buy shares of beneficial interest in the trust; a group of experienced and reputable persons serves as trustees. Once the trust is off the ground, the shares may be marketable in a manner similar to shares of stock. Many REITs obtain listings on the major stock exchanges for that purpose. Under federal income tax laws, if the income of the trust comes from specified forms of investment—primarily ownership of real property or mortgage loans—and each year at least 90 percent of the income is distributed to shareholders, there is *no* tax assessed on the trust. In turn, the shareholders declare income from the trust, and such income is taxed to the individual on a current or long-term, capital-gain basis, according to the way in which the money is earned by the trust. Thus double taxation is avoided as long as the trust continues to qualify.

Both investment objectives—current income and long-term capital gain—may be achieved through investment in a REIT. Some REITs are operated primarily for current income and concentrate the use of the investors' funds in long-term real estate mortgages. Others buy and operate income-producing properties and expect capital appreciation. However, the REIT may not be as suitable for tax sheltering as a syndicate because of the restriction on passing tax losses as freely through to the investor.

The trustees of a REIT contract for services to be provided by specialists in property management and mortgage servicing. As a general rule, it is not the function of the trust to do other than provide the funds for purchase or lending, make the decisions with respect to the investments, and supervise the independent contractors who take care of the day-to-day activity of running the trust properties or investments. The closest the shareholder of the trust gets to the action is when he votes on the election of the trustees, who are his representatives much the way directors of a corporation represent the stockholders. The REIT appeals to the investor who wants to have his money work in real estate but who does not want to be involved personally with the actual process.

Is a REIT a good investment? The REIT is as good as the people operating it, a truism applicable to all situations. Note that the investor has little or no opportunity to influence the nature of the investments made by the trustees or the decisions concerning contracts for services or the disposition of assets. Further, it is essential that the investor understand the objectives of the REIT and match them with his own. If he wants only long-term gain and no current income, only a few REITs currently in operation are suitable. Many have been established to obtain relatively high yields for current income in competition with other types of lenders such as life insurance companies and banks. One risk REITs run is that of becoming locked into fixed-return investments that fall in value relative to alternative forms of investment. There is little opportunity for capital appreciation for REITs operating as lenders; that happens only if the REITs buy mortgages at a discount and they are paid off without loss — and this is not customary REIT practice.

Most REITs established for capital appreciation invest in properties from which current income, or at least no operating loss, is expected. The expectation is that the trust will ultimately sell the asset for more than its cost, thus obtaining the long-term gain. The proceeds would then be distributed to the shareholders.

Complex real estate projects require large sums of money. The purchase and conversion of a large acreage into a regional shopping center or the construction of a fifty-story office building involve cash requirements that far exceed the capacity of most financial institutions operating by themselves. Often several banks or life insurance companies may put up together the needed resources. A REIT that has amassed fairly large sums by widespread sale of its shares may have the ability to finance projects too large for institutions on their own or in concert. But not all REITs are that large, and even if a particular REIT is, it is unlikely to concentrate too heavily in single projects.

All the same, the REIT device has made it possible to finance larger developments than have generally been possible without it. Extra earnings often are possible because of size, and some REITs will make them; this quality, therefore, gives the individual investor an opportunity to participate in huge projects. Conversely, the larger a project, the further it has to fall if things go wrong. The extra profit potential carries with it extra risk.

A final note on nonparticipative investing: either a syndicate or a REIT may allow you to meet your investment objective without getting your hands dirty. But perhaps you would prefer a middle-ground position that allows you to make more decisions with respect to the operation. In that case, you should employ a manager or property management service to do the work while you maintain the major decision-making authority.

The costs of professional management are easily ascertainable. Often the charge is based on a percentage of the rents collected, but the precentage will vary with the services to be rendered, which vary according to the contract you enter into. We will go into more detail on this subject later when we discuss what an owner does for himself. For the present we can list the following areas:

Find tenants. Your goal will be to reduce to zero the time elapsing between the departure of one tenant and the arrival of the next. There is no way to recover rent for vacancies. This requires that you know in advance when a tenant plans to leave, a matter usually taken care of by the terms of the lease or rental agreement requiring notice of termination. Then you need to know where to find prospective tenants. If the property management service is also in the real estate business, it may have a ready source of prospects. If you do this work yourself, you will have to advertise and do whatever is necessary to bring the property to the attention of those who might rent or lease it.

Not every property is automatically rented to the first prospect. Showing property can be a time-consuming and even frustrating job. On the other hand, many people enjoy that type of contact and challenge. Property management services may be employed to find a tenant, in which case they would show the property and arrange for the paper work as well. The fee for this in some areas is paid by the tenant; in others, by the owner. It may also be lumped into an overall management charge. Check for local conditions.

Collect rents. The majority of tenants pay their rent on time with checks that do not bounce. Even a few bad tenants present a problem, however. Some tenants respond better to pressure applied by a third-party property manager as opposed to the owner. When contracting for property management services, specify whether the rent collection responsibility includes getting the rent regardless of difficulty or just collecting the rents the tenants offer.

Repairs. In some states, if the property is large enough, a resident manager is required by law. In addition to being a rent cashier, the manager will ordinarily be expected to fix leaky faucets, have broken windows replaced, and so on. Otherwise, the owner must respond to requests from tenants for items of this nature. There is also the matter of decorating. You can redecorate on a regular basis—all units once every three years, for example—maintaining the property on a high level; at the end of each lease (especially before re-renting the accommodations); or only when tenants complain. You can also advise the tenant that you will buy the materials if he will do the work.

Under your property-management service contract you should specify all the above, as well as anything else you want settled. Then problems not covered will be referred to you.

Lending on real estate

Perhaps the foregoing has led you to conclude you want no part of directly managing property. You are attracted to the non-participative aspects of the syndicate or REIT but still feel either device does not give you enough control. You want control but no involvement with those using the property. There are other ways.

The traditional real estate loan is a mortgage. When a lender puts up funds and the borrower offers an interest in real property as security, the *note*, which is the evidence of the debt, is secured by a mortgage, the document in which the borrower agrees that the lender has a security interest in the property. Title to the property is vested or recorded in the name of the borrower. The lender does not acquire title and cannot sell or transfer title in the absence of a default by the borrower. As long as the indebtedness is paid off according to the loan agreement, the lender has a passive role. He collects the payments, watching to make sure that they are made on time if the loan is to be repaid in installments, or that the principal is repaid on the date agreed upon. Borrower and lender are free to agree on repayment terms; there may be a statutory limit on interest rates, late charges, and repayment penalties. For our purpose we will consider only the typical mortgage to be repaid in monthly installments that cover repayment of principal and interest on the unpaid balance.

Perhaps you have spent a good part of your life up to now paying off a mortgage. Consider how much interest you have been paying. That was income to the lender. Why not be a lender yourself?

From the lender's point of view, the risk is that of potential default—nonpayment by the borrower. Necessarily, therefore, the loan must be secured so you will be able to obtain the amount of the unpaid balance of the loan. The mortgage provides you with a legal right to force the sale of the real property, with as much of the proceeds of the sale going to you as the debt is outstanding. If the proceeds are less than the amount needed to settle the debt, the chances are you will be out of pocket for the balance. This involves a *deficiency judgment*—getting the court to allow you to go after the borrower to recover the balance of the indebtedness over and above what was obtained from the sale. In most states the law holds that the creditor has *only* the value of the property as security, and you should realize that many things can happen to cause the value of an asset to sink below the unpaid balance of a mortgage.

Your goal, therefore, is to lend money and to have the security of a piece of property that can always be sold for enough to pay off the debt, but never to have to foreclose on the mortgage. The interest you charge is simply the rent for the use of your money.

The best kind of mortgage is a *first* mortgage, because the first charge on the proceeds of a foreclosure sale, after delinquent state and local property taxes, if any, have been paid, is to the unpaid balance of the first mortgage. If the sale does not produce enough to cover that and the expenses, there is nothing left for a second mortgagee or any other creditor. It is therefore best to be first in line, though relative to other mortgages, the first mortgage carries the lowest rate of interest because the risk is smaller than for *junior*—meaning "coming after the first"—mortgages. To lend your money for mortgages, although you can handle the advertising and, far more important, checking on the prospective borrower yourself, you may be better off going to a mortgage loan broker. This businessman, who specializes in matching those having funds to lend with those who want to borrow funds, charges a fee, often to the borrower, for his services. Alternatively, you can make arrangements instead with real estate brokers to call on you when loans are required in real estate deals.

Because conventional lenders such as banks, savings associations, and life insurance companies are the regular market for many types of real estate loans, the private investor may have to accept more risk; but to compensate he usually can charge a higher rate of interest. Private investors also can qualify as lenders under the Federal Housing Administration (FHA) and Veterans Administration (VA) mortgage insurance programs. For these loans interest rates generally are lower than for noninsured loans, but of course the risk is reduced.

A private lender may be able to arrange with a savings association or bank to act as a collection agent for the mortgage payments. The borrower is then instructed to make his payments accordingly. As a general rule, if payments become delinquent, the lender will need to establish his own procedure for learning when he should take action either to collect delinquent payments or institute foreclosure proceedings. The cost, if any, for the collection activity will simply be a charge against the investor's income, and after expenses the rate of current income on a first mortgage loan will likely exceed less risky investments. Hence, mortgage loans are attractive, particularly to those wishing to maximize current income.

Increase the risk and you can increase the rate of return. There is considerable activity in second and third mortgages. Remember: foreclosure could wipe out the junior mortgages. Yet those who invest in second mortgages may realize not only higher interest rates but also a gain from purchase of the mortgage at a discount.

An additional risk factor and profit potential in all mortgages is prepayment. The basic goal of a lender is to have a safe, secure investment with repayment on a timely basis. There is expense incurred in obtaining the loan, and as long as the payments are being made the lender usually does not want the loan to be paid off in advance. If it is, he must set about to find another investment, and he may not be able to earn as much in a new situation. (The reverse of that may also be true.) The risk is there. To compensate, it is customary to include in the mortgage terms a penalty to be paid by the borrower if the loan is paid off in advance. This is the prepayment penalty. It may appear in any mortgage—first, second, and so on—and it usually is a percentage of the original loan or of the balance at the time of payoff, ranging from, say, 1 to 3 percent. In other cases, the lender may have a sliding scale with the penalty reduced as the regular termination approaches. Others may allow for limited repayment of principal each year without penalty and charge one only if the entire loan is paid off at one time. As a borrower you will want to avoid a prepayment penalty; as a lender you'll have a different attitude. As a lender you may obtain, in addition to interest income, a lump-sum amount of income or profit if the loan is paid off and a prepayment penalty exacted.

Assume you become concerned that the borrower will repay the money early. At that point you may decide you would like to get rid of this prospective bad debt by selling the note and mortgage to another investor. You would be willing to sell it for less than the outstanding balance because you are eliminating the risk. The purchaser would buy if he felt that the amount of the discount was enough to make the risk of nonpayment attractive. He would then hold the mortgage, expecting the borrower ultimately to settle the debt. The excess of payments to principal over the cost of the purchase of the mortgage would be his extra gain. There are some investors who specialize in buying mortgages at discount. Because the rewards are higher than for other types of investment, the risks are greater and you really need to know what you are doing.

In all cases, all mortgages should be filed with the county recorder or registrar so their existence is a matter of public record. The lender is then protected to the extent that the title holder cannot pass clear title and thus defeat the mortgagee. He may be able to pass title—that is, sell the property—but the title will be subject to the outstanding loans. The lender may insert in the mortgage agreement a provision calling for accelerating the payment of the balance if the original borrower conveys title to someone else; the unpaid balance then becomes due and payable in full at the time the sale occurs. This device gives the lender the opportunity to evaluate the new purchaser and to decide whether he wants to have him take over the loan.

Up to this point we have spoken in terms of you putting up funds as a loan on real estate. You may do something of the same thing, but by means other than a mortgage. Assume that you own some property, perhaps your home, and you plan to sell it; but you don't want all cash from it, preferring to use it as your real estate investment as a lender. As described, you could take back a mortgage from a purchaser. But, also, you could sell on a sales contract. The purchaser would agree to a stipulated purchase price, cash down payment, and balance in monthly payments for a designated term and rate of interest. This agreement would be in the form of a sales contract and you, the seller, would retain title to the property. In this case the buyer would record the sales contract so you could not pass clear title subsequently. At such time as the contract is fully paid you would then execute a deed to pass clear title to the contract purchaser. Generally the contract purchaser has the same rights of redemption as a mortgagor and it would take just as long to get rid of a defaulting contract purchaser as a mortgagor. The sales contract does, however, give some psychological benefit for the contract seller and, other things being equal, that might be reason enough to be an investor-lender.

Parties agree, at the time the loan is made, that if there is a default, the lender will be able to recover the property. This agreement is incorporated into a deed, which is held by a disinterested trustee, such as a title insurance company or corporation set up for the purpose. If the debtor pays his obligation, the trustee then reconveys title to him. If there is a legal default, the trustee then allows the deed to be used to convey title to the lender, who can do whatever he wishes with the property to recover his unpaid balance. As a practical matter, the trustee may be employed to make the sale and give the proceeds to the lender.

Apart from the legal technicalities that separate the two—mortgage and deed of trust—they are really the same thing. In fact, in some states, at least for first liens or encumbrances on real property, only the deed of trust is used, not a mortgage. The trust deed was invented to overcome difficulties lenders felt they had with mortgages. In those states where trust deeds rather than mortgages are used, lenders still must allow for redemption by defaulting borrowers; thus as far as protecting borrowers is concerned, state laws have equalized the two devices. For our purpose, mortgage and trust deed are interchangeable terms.

Risks involved in real estate investment

Basically, an investment in real estate—whether you function as owner or as lender—is a long-term proposition. It is not reasonable to expect a profit from turning over the investment in a few days, weeks, or months. That is a characteristic of other forms of investment, but not of real estate. The prospective investor who must have liquidity should stay away from real estate. Once the investment is made, freeing up the funds in the short term will ordinarily involve a loss.

Although an owner, as opposed to a lender, carries the major portion of the risk (because in theory, the borrower is obligated to pay off the debt even if the project is a disaster), from a practical point of view a lender should consider all of the risks inherent in the investment even though he may have some protection against loss by way of the mortgage.

First, before *investing*, find out about zoning, planning commission regulations and plans, environmental controls, potential annexations, presence of easements, and availability of utilities. A major expense is property taxes. The property may be overdue for reassessment. The tax rate for the next year may be substantially higher than before. The extra rental unit in the basement, garage, or attic may not be legal. You may not be able to get a permit to remodel the large, single-family building into a pair of flats. The vacant land may not in fact be served by water and power, and the cost to extend such facilities in order to develop the land may exceed the value of the improved property. The seller may not be able to pass clear title. The local government may plan to condemn the property and obtain it under its rights of eminent domain. Will the appraised value under these circumstances be in line with your investment? The attorney fees to protect your rights may turn the investment into a financial nightmare. The building may need a new roof, new plumbing, and new wiring, all waiting to be installed at your unplanned expense. In many areas the building code requires bringing older properties up to code even if only modest repairs are to be made. The owner and his lender face any number of surprises. In-depth checking before buying or lending is essential to successful investing.

Second, assuming that all possible precautions have been taken, other matters must be taken into consideration:

For *rental* property the key is avoiding vacancies. It is impossible to recover lost time. Being able to fill vacant units promptly is vital. But how about the tenant who is happy to keep your property occupied but somehow just can't pay the rent? He is not much of a bargain. You must be prepared to eliminate the credit risk. This will require checking references, getting rent deposits, and being tough on the day when the rent is due. It takes time to evict a tenant who does not want to leave. Repairs can be expensive, particularly those you cannot do yourself. To have a satisfactory return on the investment, operating expenses must be carefully controlled. Rents must be set to allow for maintenance (and be realistic as far as the marketplace is concerned).

Having a tenant bound to a lease has some advantages. On the other hand, in the absence of an escalation clause—rare in most leases—the owner is caught in a bind if expenses increase, and he has no way to raise rents. Property taxes can increase, and the owner has little or no control over that expense. He may not be able to have his assessed value reduced if he feels it is too high. He may even wake up some morning to find that rent controls have been imposed either by Uncle Sam or by a local municipality. Mortgage payments and other costs must be met regardless of what has happened to his income. If he abandons the property to the lender, he sacrifices his equity.

Third, in the case of investments for tax sheltering, the spread between income and expenses must be watched. The spread becomes undesirable when the actual expenses, as opposed to paper (depreciation) expenses, get out of line. When there is an operating loss requiring more cash to be paid out than comes in, without regard to the taxable income, the investor will have to provide the cash and increase his investment. That may not be what he had in mind. Particularly in tax shelter investments, the balancing of cash income and outgo is a delicate operation.

Fourth, the aim of real estate investment is the long-term gain to be realized on disposition of the investment. You are counting on the asset's appreciating in value. This plan may be interfered with by a number of factors.

Timing of the resale is important. If you are forced to liquidate the investment, it may come at an inappropriate time insofar as the market is concerned. It may happen that when you want to sell, there are a large number of similar properties, all apparently more attractive than yours, available on the market at ridiculously low prices. You may find that by the time you allow for the cost to fix the place up, to put it on the market, and to sell it (payment of real estate commission), the sales price is not going to be high enough to give you any gain over your original cost. Economic conditions beyond your control may serve to eliminate the appreciation you were counting on. If other owners have allowed their property to go to ruin, you can be sure that factor will have a depressing effect on the value of yours. You may find that you overlooked a strenuous prepayment penalty in your financing.

Finally, experts are not always right. Real estate syndicates and REITs all face precisely the same problems. The people who operate them are expected to be expert enough to avoid unsatisfactory results. But before giving them his money, the investor must assure himself that they are, in fact, expert. What has been their track record in other projects? If they had failures, why? If they are new at the job, what has been the business experience of the organizers? Are the prospective benefits reasonable? Don't let your desire for an above-average return interfere with your judgment. Outrageous returns are not available, except by luck, which you cannot count on. And there is always a problem in interpreting rates of return. There are several ways to measure returns, but *any* syndicate, REIT, or individual real-estate investment offering to provide, say, 15 to 20 percent annual returns is hardly to be believed. Extravagant claims need to be recognized, though it is also true that you can make satisfactory investments in real estate through a syndicate or REIT.

Let's assume you do want to try your hand. You investigate investment opportunities, make arrangements for the financing, prepare a financial plan for the operation, estimate your current and long-term results, and undertake to manage the property yourself. You might even have a good set of tools and are ready to answer a tenant's call for help with a leaky faucet or sticky window. It is further assumed you intend to continue to be employed and this property investment project will require only spare time. Your goal is to take a sum of money and, through this venture, generate an attractive current return and be in the position to reap a capital gain some years hence.

You will need to decide what type of residential income property you should buy. There are several to choose from: single-family, duplexes, and larger multiple units. What are the considerations?

The larger the property, the greater will be the amount of money needed to buy it. The more tenants, the more property management effort will be required. As long as you are going to be a part-time manager while holding down a job, there is a limit on how big the project should be. Rate of return is also an important matter. Which type yields the most?

For the beginning, amateur, income property investor, the smaller the project, the less frightening the problems appear and presumably the smaller the financial risk. That might lead you to conclude you should start with a single-family house. Let's look at that possibility.

This type of income property investment, except under the most unusual circumstances, will provide the least satisfactory return. The income, relative to land and other costs, is at the minimum. To demonstrate this point, consider a single-family dwelling for which the fair rental value is, say, $200 per month. If you could convert the building to two rental units, would you expect the rental income to remain the same? It is likely you could rent each unit for $125 so now you have two times $125 to equal $250 gross income per month. You will find that the additional costs to operate, apart from the conversion expense, would not increase in the same proportion as the increase in income. Property taxes might go up slightly if it was reassessed as income property. If the rents included utilities, two families would incur greater expense than one, but only perhaps. The single-family property would be rented to a family, whereas two apartments under these conditions would be more suitable for adults. The value of income property is determined basically by the amount of net income available from it, so if that income is increased, its value will increase.

If, on the other hand, you have lived in a single-family home for many years and have either paid off the mortgage, or the mortgage payments are modest, you might obtain an attractive return by renting it. Realize that this is possible only because you have a significant equity; otherwise the mortgage payments for a large loan, plus the other expenses, would preclude you from having a surplus from the maximum rent you could get. And, if you have a big equity, why not release those dollars and use them in conjunction with borrowed funds and use leverage to maximize your return?

Faced with investing today in residential income property, you can invariably do better with multiple units than with single-family dwellings.

The case for the fourplex

Frequently a fourplex is built on a lot originally intended for a single-family home. A fourplex typically uses relatively little land and as a consequence, on a per-rental-unit basis, there is a minimum cost for land and a maximum return from the land value. The proportionate share of property taxes per unit is also at a minimum. Yet the rental charge is not subject to reduction, because each unit is complete—living, dining, sleeping—and justifies an appropriate charge. By spreading land cost and other expenses over four units, the maximum return is possible.

By applying what has just been said, you might conclude the maximum return would be available from the largest possible residential building—not so. As the size of the project increases, there are additional expenses for management, for example, that serve to offset some of the advantages. As you move from the fourplex to, say, six units, the lot size must increase and then you find that you are not making the most use of it. Larger properties will have swimming pools and other amenities that add to their desirability but also increase cost and reduce, relatively speaking, the return. On the other hand, while you could expect to have a minimum of trouble in managing a fourplex yourself, it is not economical for a commercial property management firm to operate several small, scattered properties when compared with the large-scale project.

2

Financing a Real Estate Investment

The purchase price of property generally will govern the amount of cash needed; Lenders determine the amount they will lend on the basis of the appraised value of the property. These percentages vary with the supply and demand for money as well as with the nature of the borrower and type of property.

Most real estate investors start at what is probably the wrong end—they find a piece of property, learn how much can be borrowed and then scramble for cash to make up the difference. This way works, but there is a more scientific way to approach the problem. Determine first the maximum amount of money you can scrape together for the investment; then go looking for property.

First, however, a general rule: unless you have at least $5,000 in cash, beyond the liquid assets needed to cover any personal emergencies, you should not consider making a *purchase* investment in real estate. You may be able to put smaller amounts to work in real estate syndicates, REITs, and second mortgages—but not as a purchaser of income property. You may be able to buy a small plot of underdeveloped land for less than $5,000, but to realize a return it probably will require a further investment.

This does not mean that you could invest with a *down payment* of $5,000. There are costs associated with the purchase that must be met at the time it is made. Your cash must be enough to cover these costs as well. The down payment is the difference between the sales price and the total amount to be borrowed for which the property is used as security. For example, take a piece of property going for $60,000:

Sales	$60,000
Mortgage	$50,000
Down payment	$10,000

Up to this point $10,000 cash will be needed. Then there are the closing costs: loan fees, title insurance, prorated expenses. The total will vary from one transaction to another. Whatever they amount to, they must be paid at the time the deal is closed. If, in this example, the closing costs amount to $1,500, the total cash needed is $11,500. As far as raising cash is concerned, we will not distinguish between money needed for down payment and for closing costs. It is the total number of dollars needed that we are after.

Cash—your own

You probably have some money in a savings account, having accumulated it with the idea that some day you would put it to good use. That day may be close at hand.

Timing of the withdrawal may be important. If you have a regular passbook account, you probably are earning interest to the day of withdrawal. If you have a bonus or certificate account, there may be a penalty or deduction of earned interest if you withdraw before a due date. This is not necessarily a large amount, nor should it be a factor causing you to give up a project; you simply should check into the situation. Delaying a withdrawal by a few days might make a difference.

An alternative to withdrawal is to borrow on the account, using the passbook or certificate as security. Many savings institutions make this type of loan and charge 1 percent over the savings rate. Your interest cost is 1 percent of the amount borrowed. If the money goes into a good investment, it certainly will earn more than the 1 percent. If you repay the savings account loan out of the earnings from the real estate investment, you will recapture the funds and have both the asset and the savings account balance.

For an example, assume you have $15,000 in a savings account. Where else can you raise money?

What is the market value of your home? What is the present balance of your mortgage? Chances are very good that you have an equity in your present property that can be tapped to provide money for your next real estate investment. Then you face two basic choices: refinance the present loan or borrow by way of a second mortgage.

The most desirable choice probably involves not increasing your monthly cash outlay for housing. If that is the case, forget the second mortgage route. To refinance the present mortgage you need to find a lender—maybe the lender who made the present loan—to reappraise the property and make a loan in an amount greater than the current unpaid balance, giving you the difference in cash.

A word of caution: if you now have a very favorable interest rate, perhaps because the loan was obtained many years ago, in all probability the new loan will be at a much higher rate. To borrow anew you probably will have an additional cost that will have to be recovered out of the investment to be made with the cash. There may also be a prepayment penalty, though this sometimes is waived if the new loan is made by the original lender. There also will be the costs of a new title search as well as an appraisal. Therefore, *before* refinancing, get all your costs lined up so you can see what expenses will have to be recovered from the investment.

Let's assume you obtain $6,000 in cash from refinancing. If for some reason, getting a new first mortgage is not feasible, you can explore the second mortgage alternative. For this loan there will be expenses for appraisal, title search, and title insurance. The interest rate will be higher and the term, shorter. The monthly payment will have to be met either by way of increased living expenses or from the real estate investment; do not forget this aspect if you raise part of the cash for the project from this source. Finally, as with all loans of this nature, they have to be repaid even if the investment is not profitable.

For well-situated property, owned by persons with satisfactory credit records, second mortgage money is generally available. It costs more than many other alternatives; we won't use it here in our continuing example.

How about getting out your life insurance policies? Unless you bought the no-cash value of term life insurance, your life insurance policy has a cash surrender value, on which you can obtain a policy loan. If you bought the policy many years ago, the policy loan rate, which is stated in the contract, will startle you—it will be quite low in comparison to current interest rates.

In view of this you may wish to consider raising some cash by borrowing on your life insurance. Again, you will incur an interest cost, to be recovered from your investment. But you will not have appraisal and title costs. Usually the loan can be paid off in amounts and at times you choose; monthly repayment of principal is not usually required. Interest is often paid annually. If you are confident about paying the interest out of other income and having the amount of life insurance payable reduced by the amount of the loan, then you should seriously consider raising cash in the manner outlined.

If you want the full amount of life insurance protection restored, the loan will have to be paid off. Otherwise, in the event of the death of the life assured, the beneficiary will receive the amount of insurance *less* the unpaid balance of the loan and accrued interest. If the policy is allowed to lapse, the loan balance and accrued interest will be charged against the cash surrender value. The balance will then be available to be withdrawn in cash; it might automatically be used as a loan of premium to keep the policy in force until that amount is used up.

For our example, assume you do not use your life insurance as a source for cash to invest.

You may have other investments for which the outlook is not as favorable as for a real estate venture; for example, shares, especially shares of a stock or of a mutual fund that, if sold, would give you a loss for income tax purposes.

An investment in real estate, as is the case with every investment, should be made only after you have taken a good look at your investment objectives, what you have in current investments, and what the outlook is for your future. It is a mistake to make any investment, forget it, *and* expect to make a handsome profit when you pull it out—at retirement, say. Investments must not be neglected; they need to be reevaluated periodically.

In our example, so far you have raised $15,000 from liquidating a savings account and a further $6,000 by refinancing your home, for a total of $21,000—well beyond the minimum. But what if you could raise only $2,000 or $3,000 this way? Where else can you raise money?

You can get together with a few other people who are in the same boat. Obviously, troubles can arise when two or more human beings try to make decisions about handling money, but it may be practical for a small group to pool their resources. The easiest way to handle the contractual arrangements would be for one person or couple to represent the group. The other investors could have a contract with the representative, spelling out the obligations. The alternative method is to form a partnership and have all parties named in deeds, mortgages, and so on executed in connection with the investment. This latter route is more secure, but it is cumbersome.

If you find your present housing has outlived its usefulness, how about selling it? The cash raised could then be invested. In turn, you could rent an apartment. Whether you rent from someone else or use a part of your own income property, selling your present home will give you cash to invest. As stated earlier, if you live in part of a building and rent the balance to others, you will lose a small part of the income tax advantage but that is not a serious consideration.

There are, then, many ways of raising cash. We will assume you can raise at least $5,000 and thus have enough to make a purchase on your own. How do you finance the balance needed for the project?

Borrowing on real estate

If your investment objective is to maximize long-term gain and minimize current income subject to income tax, you should utilize *leverage*. As a general rule, the maximum investment return is obtained when you secure the largest possible—in terms of dollar value—property for the cash dollars you invest. This involves borrowing the balance needed to make the purchase, using the property itself as security for the loan.

When you borrow money at a fixed interest rate and invest it in a project where the prospective return is not limited or guaranteed, you hope for a good spread between what it costs in interest expense and what your realized profit is. If you borrow at 8 percent and earn 12 percent, you earn 4 percent on the funds invested. This is one example of leverage. However, if the venture does not fare well, the borrower will still have to pay the fixed interest cost even though there is little or no return from the investment to cover it.

An example of the foregoing involves borrowing $20,000 at 8

percent and investing it; the investment turns out very well and we earn 15 percent:

Earnings	$3,000
Interest cost	1,600
Gain	$1,400

You usually are not able to borrow 100 percent. Let's assume you make a $50,000 investment that actually produces a profit of 12 percent, $6,000. If you borrow half, $25,000, at 8 percent, your interest cost is $2,000, leaving $4,000 profit on your half, or a 16-percent return on your investment.

If you can borrow 80 percent or, conversely, invest as little as 20 percent of your own funds, interest cost at 8 percent on $40,000 would be $3,200. If investment earnings are $6,000, the net profit is $2,800. But the $2,800 is profit on an investment of only $10,000, or 28 percent.

The idea of leverage involves borrowing as much as you can at the lowest interest cost and investing it to produce the greatest return. The greater the proportion of borrowed funds, the greater will be the percentage return on your invested cash, assuming the rate of return exceeds the fixed interest cost. The motivation to invest in the largest possible project in terms of dollars cost comes from the fact that rates of return tend to increase as the size of the project increases. For example, the rate of return from a $25,000 duplex generally will be smaller than from a $500,000 apartment complex.

Factors in borrowing
A mortgage lender recognizes how leverage works. He does not begrudge your 12 percent and 15 percent return potential. He is glad to lend, say, 8 percent if he is assured that no matter what happens you will pay off the loan. He is not your partner, sharing in gains and losses. He only wants his interest. With much of the risk removed, the interest rate represents simply the charge made for the use of money.

A real estate mortgage is typically a long-term proposition. Terms of up to thirty years are not uncommon. With repayment spreading over that length of time the lender may want some hedge against inflation. When the prospects for continued inflation are good, long-term interest rates will be higher than for the short term; they include some allowance for the future reduction in value of dollars.

The interest rate will also be influenced by the cost of the money to the lender. A savings institution may be paying 5 percent on passbook accounts. If it can lend those funds on mortgages at 8 percent, it has a 3 percent spread. Lenders understand leverage. If the passbook rate goes up, or the demand for commercial loans increases, mortgage rates will go up, too.

Lenders, however, must make loans to stay in business, so there may be substantial competition to lend on real estate from time to time. The situation is dynamic, and a borrower should shop around for the best terms.

Let's look closely at each of the factors: interest rates, borrower's credit, nature of the security, proportion to be lent, and appraisal policies.

Generally, mortgage interest rates are set simply on the basis of supply and demand, but there is more to it than the casual observer sees. We have already noted that the length of the loan term may affect the rate. When the supply of lendable funds is less than the demand, lenders may change the maximum term from, say, twenty-five years to twenty years on certain types of property. That does not change the rate of interest, but it does increase the monthly payment. When funds are borrowed to finance a real estate investment, the income from which is used to repay the loan, the size of the monthly payment can make a difference. A shorter repayment period may, in the eyes of the lender, reduce the risk, so if the interest rate is held steady, but the term cut, the lender in effect is earning a better return.

Lenders prefer not to have fluctuations in the interest rate. They would rather alter the other terms of the borrowing contract to reflect conditions of supply and demand. One such adjustable condition is the point charge or loan fee. A point, or loan fee, is one percentage point of the amount of the loan. If the borrowing is at, say 7½ percent and 3 points, and the loan amount is $30,000, the borrower will be charged at the time the loan is made with $900 in points. This fee really is interest in advance, and it is charged because the lender feels that the basic rate of 7½ percent is too low. Instead of increasing the rate—lenders do not like to change rates—points are charged, thus increasing the yield or return. In this example, the borrower would receive $29,100 in loan proceeds but would be obligated to repay $30,000; and interest would be calculated at the outset on $30,000. In this situation, the annual percentage rate will be more than the mortgage interest rate of 7½ percent. The difference is due to the point charge. The only

advantage the borrower gets is being permitted by the Internal
Revenue Service to charge points or loan fees as deductible interest expense against income.

Conventional financial institutions such as banks and savings or
building and loan associations ordinarily grant *only* first mortgages.
Individuals and organizations that deal in second mortgages charge
higher interest rates and offer shorter repayment terms to offset
the risk factor in such financing.

And there is a risk factor. If the borrower finds he cannot make
the monthly payments on the mortgage, he may attempt to sell
the property and have someone else take over the loan or abandon
it to the lender. Lenders do not like to acquire real estate in the
latter way, and they try at the time they make the loan to avoid
such adverse consequences by checking credit ratings carefully.

Only a person with a good credit record, employment stability,
and other indications of reliability will receive favorable consideration, especially if, in addition, the overall financial position
of the borrower and the financial plan for the project are healthy
—particularly in terms of estimated income, expense, and con-
tingency margin.

Borrowing proportions

Don't be misled by advertising of 100 percent loans. The qualified
purchaser of a single-family home, with Veteran's Administration
benefits, may be able to buy without a down payment, but the
investor-borrower in residential income property will *not* be able
to. The starting point·is always the appraised value of the property,
and the loan available will be some percentage of that figure.

Conservative lenders have conservative appraisers and will
start by suggesting a 60 to 65 percent loan. At the other end of the
spectrum, a hungry lender may almost automatically agree to the
proposed purchase price as the value and grant a loan of 80 percent
of that figure. There may or may not be restrictions by the first
mortgagee (lender) on the use of secondary financing such as a
second mortgage.

The lender *wants* the borrower to have something to lose so that
if the going gets tough there will be no incentive to walk away,
leaving the lender holding the property. Further, the market value
of the property may go down. As a consequence, the lender wants
to start out with a loan balance that is well below the market price,
established on a conservative basis, and for the borrower to have a
significant stake in the project. The amount of the loan and its

terms may vary from one lender to another. You should shop around for the best arrangement.

Lenders are fussy about whom they lend money to, the kind of property used as security, and the terms on which the mortgage is made. Having made a good loan, the lender prefers that the borrower simply make payments until the loan is paid off. That rarely happens. In fact, although real estate loans are made for anywhere from fifteen to thirty years, the average length of a real estate loan is under five years. In recognition of this kind of turnover, lenders usually include a prepayment penalty in the loan agreement. As described earlier, these penalties may vary from a straight percentage — 1 percent, 2 percent — of the original loan amount to less strenuous penalties. If the original loan is paid off, such as would be the case if the property was sold and a new loan obtained or full cash paid by the purchaser, the penalty would be assessed against the seller. There are two alternatives: to persuade the buyer to do his refinancing with the original lender, in which case the prepayment penalty may not be assessed, or for the purchaser to assume the loan. The latter course is possible if the purchaser can pay off the seller's equity without involving the mortgage. Equity here is defined as the difference between the purchase price and the total of the outstanding loan balances. If the new purchaser is to assume the loan, the lender has to agree to take him on; there is no obligation on the part of the lender to consent to an assumption. The lender will probably go through the loan qualification procedure for the new borrower before agreeing to the assumption. If the loan is assumed, the original borrower may still have some contingent responsibility in the event of default. The seller may prefer to have the buyer "substitute" on the loan. In this case, the lender, in effect, makes a new loan to the purchaser; and instead of assumption documents, the purchaser signs a new mortgage or note and deed of trust.

Sources of real estate finance

If you are a first-time borrower, a good place to start is the bank where you now have your checking account and the savings institution where you keep your nest egg. You will want to discuss mortgage financing with every real estate broker you meet. Your goal is to gain a feel for the current money market and obtain a recommendation. Keeping a notebook is a good idea.

The money market is constantly changing. The more you learn about how lenders operate, the less you should be discouraged about the chances of lining up financing when you need it. By knowing what you are doing you can put together a loan application package that no lender will be able to resist even when he is refusing others. Until a financial institution closes its doors it must make loans to stay in business. Lending policies clearly change with the ebb and flow in the supply of money, and you will want to time your requirements accordingly, but that does not mean that you will not be able to obtain financing for a sound project.

Seller financing

It may develop that the seller wishes to provide the financing, particularly if the property is free and clear of indebtedness and the owner wants to get out from under the management and operational risk and assume the role of mortgagee. The terms offered must be carefully looked at and compared with alternatives. For example, a seller-lender may be more flexible when it comes to the term of the mortgage and the required down payment than an institutional lender. If banks are limiting mortgages to twenty years, the seller may be agreeable to twenty-five years. For older properties, say those at least thirty years old, the majority of lenders would limit their loans to fifteen or twenty years. On new properties the regular lenders will not go over thirty years and will more likely limit loans to twenty-five years. The seller-lender may be persuaded to agree to a term longer than is available from other lenders, depending on how badly he wanted to sell. It is practical for buyer and seller to arrange the financing themselves; there is no requirement that you restrict your borrowing to a financial institution.

An alternative to the procedure whereby a seller takes back a mortgage is the sales contract, referred to earlier. In this case, the seller retains title but signs an agreement with the buyer under which, after all the payments have been made, title will be passed. Buying "on contract" means that the seller is financing the sale, though there may be an underlying mortgage, in which case the seller will be obligated to continue making those payments and the purchaser will want to assure himself that such is the case. From the buyer's point of view the best arrangement is to make his payments to a third party who first makes the payment on the mortgage out of the buyer's remittance and then sends the balance to the seller. With or without an underlying mortgage, the buyer's payments are applied to his total purchase obligation. It is customary for the sales contract to include a rate of interest and other terms, just like a mortgage. The periodic payment serves to pay the interest and a partial payment on the principal. In fact, except for some technical matters, the only practical difference between a mortgage and a sales contract is the way in which the title to the real estate is handled.

In this context, a related device has recently been introduced, particularly in the financing of larger properties. It is called the *wrap-around mortgage*. Assume the following situation:

You have found an apartment complex for sale at a price that is satisfactory. The seller's equity is greater than the cash you have available, so some special arrangement must be made if the deal is to go through. The mortgage already on the property can be assumed. The seller could take your cash and a second mortgage and have you assume the first mortgage. On the other hand, he might prefer to sell on a sales contract, retaining title and control. You would prefer the first plan because it gives you title and freedom from any control of the seller. Under the second plan you might be exposed to a problem if the seller did not keep the mortgage current even though you made your payments. The seller's preference and your preference are not the same. Under the wrap-around mortgage you agree to buy the property for the total price with a specified cash down payment. The seller takes back a mortgage for the entire balance, including the amount of the existing first mortgage. This new mortgage, between the buyer and seller, is actually a second mortgage because the first still applies. The payments on the wrap-around mortgage are applied to the total indebtedness, and the seller must keep the first mortgage payments current, as under a sales contract. The main advantage to the wrap-around is the flexibility provided to the seller. He then will more readily be able to sell the mortgage if he wants to cash out than he would with a sales contract.

There may be a provision in the first mortgage that serves to accelerate it if there is a further encumbrance such as a second or wrap-around mortgage. If accelerated, the unpaid balance becomes due immediately when the second mortgaging occurs. That would defeat the whole idea of the financing plan, which calls for the continuation of the existing loan.

In addition to the three methods of seller-organized financing discussed above, there is one more method, involving the straight assumption of the existing loan.

In an era of rising interest rates, buyers look for chances to assume loans with lower than current interest rates. When the rate is low enough, in fact, a larger than customary cash down payment may well be justified. A careful check should be made to determine whether the loan can be properly assumed by the buyer and what fee, if any, is to be charged by the lender. The cost involved in assuming existing financing ordinarily will be substantially less than the cost of obtaining a new first loan. It will be no bargain, however, if the interest rate is too high, the term is too short (high monthly payments), or there is an unfavorable prepayment penalty.

A word of caution against doing what many do when they find that assumption is not permitted. To get around this, a seller may suggest that, even though a deed is executed and recorded, thus passing title, the buyer make the payments on the loan in a fashion such that the lender is not aware of the sale. Once the deed is recorded — if it is not, the buyer has no protection against the seller's selling the property again to someone else — the property tax records will be changed and the chances are good the lender will learn of the transaction.

Assume now that the first loan can be properly taken over but that the seller's equity is larger than the cash you wish to invest. To make the sale, the seller may be agreeable to taking back a second mortgage (assume that the first lender is not opposed to this — as is likely if the lender is agreeable to the assumption in the first place).

The seller gets enough cash to meet his requirements, gets out from under the first loan even though under an assumption that he may have a contingent liability, and has interest income from the second mortgage. By recording the second mortgage the seller preserves his legal interest in the property so that any future transfer of title is subject to those rights. The financing of the purchase has been provided essentially through the seller and without a need to go elsewhere to borrow funds. (In addition, the seller-provided second mortgage can also be used in conjunction with obtaining a new loan.)

Astute real estate buyer-investors look first for opportunities to finance their acquisitions along the lines discussed in the preceding sections. Failing that, they go outside for finance.

Commercial banks

Commercial banks lend money on residential income property, though banks often are more interested in making business loans than property loans. Find out what the conditions are where you live. On the other hand, a bank that does mortgage financing often offers lower interest rates. To justify a lower rate, the bank probably will require the purchaser to have a larger equity than some other lenders.

In the case of *dwelling* mortgages, the lender may be willing to lend as much as 80 percent of the appraised value, sometimes 90 percent if there is mortgage insurance available. Under some FHA and VA programs the amount may be even higher. However, when it comes to residential *income* property, the practice differs. Generally, for individuals investing in relatively small apartment projects, no FHA insured financing is available (for developers and large-scale projects, there is).

That brings us back to conventional mortgage loans. Institutions making conventional loans have no reason to share the ownership risk and require, therefore, that the investor-buyer's equity be sufficient to justify the risk to the lender. This is reflected in the practice followed by the majority of banks, savings institutions, and life insurance companies; these rarely lend more than 75 percent of appraised value and, more typically, about 70 percent.

Investors seeking to minimize taxable current income and maximize long-term capital appreciation usually wish to maximize leverage and therefore want to borrow the maximum possible. In arranging for financing, then, the investor should negotiate for a relaxing of the usual rules and try to obtain a higher percent of the value to be borrowed. Different lenders will have different ideas, and it will pay you to shop for your loan.

If you need the maximum possible amount of funds, it is not likely you will get it through a bank. A bank, even if it will match a competing lender as far as amount is concerned, may not be willing to make the loan for as long a time period. This will mean that payments on a bank loan will be higher but that, in the long run, the total interest cost will be smaller. The cash flow from a project is very important, and there may be a problem for you if your cash expenses are larger than they would be under alternative financing. Further, if you are seeking a tax shelter, the lower interest expense will increase the taxable income and lower the shelter benefit. Of course, no matter what tax bracket you are in, the tax man pays only a part of any dollar spent for expenses. It still costs you *something* when you pay interest or for repairs and so on.

Some commercial banks prefer certain types of loans to others. At a point in time, some banks have more funds to lend than others. Not only should you explore borrowing from a commercial bank as well as other types of financial institutions; you should talk to several banks.

Savings banks

The comments concerning commercial banks generally do not apply to savings banks. The latter are more like, for our purpose, savings and loan and building and loan associations. These all are financial institutions established for the purpose of giving those with money to save a place to deposit it and earn interest and to channel funds into real estate loans, particularly single-family residences. In relating your needs for mortgage money to these sources, we will refer to them simply as *savings institutions.*

Although savings institutions lend money primarily for single-family residences, they also are an important source for mortgages to finance apartment houses. Their emphasis is on long-term lending, and they are particularly interested in new construction. As before, these lenders look for adequate equity, particularly in residential income projects not occupied by the borrower. Except for some unusual situation, you should not expect to be able to borrow more than 80 percent of the appraised value and more likely only 70 to 75 percent. Remember, conditions change, sometimes rapidly, and you will need to keep yourself informed.

If you are seeking maximum proportion and maximum term, a savings institution may be your best bet. Their interest rates, however, may be somewhat higher than those charged by banks. You will need to balance each of the factors in your financial plan; compromise will be in order.

Insurance companies

Life insurance companies make a large number of mortgage loans. Most operate through loan correspondents; you will not deal directly with the mortgage loan department of a life insurer. Many correspondents represent several different life companies and also other sources of loan money such as pension plans. Be sure to check out this source, project by project and company by company. Generalizations work only to the extent of saying that long-term real estate mortgages are important to life insurance companies and such companies always are interested in making good loans.

Mortgage loan brokers and private investors

As suggested earlier, many people with funds to invest prefer to be involved in real estate by way of lending rather than owning. As a prospective buyer-investor, you need to know where some of these people are. You may prefer to deal with an individual (learning how to do it yourself in the process). More importantly, you may want to locate a private investor because he may be a better lender for your project than any of the others. Realize that the private lender will want all the advantages any other lender wants: maximum rates, minimum terms, lowest proportion of loan to value, highest prepayment penalty, highest quality credit risk, and new property as security. So why bother with him? He may be more flexible.

Individuals wishing to make mortgage loans often advertise in the newspaper. They also spread the word to real estate brokers. The prospective borrower may also use the same media. A real estate broker usually will know a great deal about the local money market, and if you are making the purchase through him, you may be able to reach a private lender in that way.

Some private investors prefer to rely on the expertise of others in making a loan decision, so they contract with a mortgage loan broker to obtain prospective borrowers, appraise properties, and handle the paper work. You should be acquainted with mortgage loan brokers in your area. The fee for their services is normally paid by the borrower; it may range from 2 percent to 5 percent or more of the amount borrowed.

Private investors and mortgage loan brokers are not just sources for first mortgage money; additionally, second or junior mortgages can be obtained from these sources.

We have discussed the risk involved in second mortgages. If there is a default on the first and the property value has dropped, the interest of the second mortgagee may well be wiped out. The person making second mortgages is, or should be, aware of this risk, but as a prospective borrower you should also recognize what is involved. When the second mortgage is used to supplement maximum first mortgage financing, obviously the risk for the second mortgagee is potentially serious. In a declining market, the total of the first and second mortgages can easily exceed the possible sale price. You can therefore expect to pay the highest allowable interest rate on a second mortgage in this category. It will also have a fairly short term. That is, even though the payments on the second mortgage are calculated on the basis of an extended period of time, the balance of the loan may be payable on a due date in the fairly near future. This feature is often described in the following way: Second mortgage for $10,000 at 10 percent interest on unpaid balance, with monthly amortization over fifteen years, due date in five years, no prepayment penalty.

If the loan is to be repaid in monthly payments for the full fifteen years, no principal would remain outstanding at the end of that time. With a five-year due date, however, the balance of the principal is due and payable at that time.

When you borrow with this type of due-date situation, you must plan on refinancing the project by the time the due date arrives. This is a feasible and widely used financing technique.

Amortization

If you borrow a sum of money, agree to pay interest, and repay the loan in a lump sum at some date in the future, you are *not* involved in amortization. The interest charge is computed by multiplying the rate times the term times the amount, and the repayment amount will be the same as the amount borrowed, the principal.

Example: Borrow $5,000 at 6 percent and repay in lump sum two years hence.

Interest $5,000 × .06 × 2	$ 600
Principal	5,000
Principal & interest combined	$5,600

The interest of $300 each year may be paid separately. That is an example of a nonamortization situation. The principal amount remains constant during the time the loan is outstanding.

But what about paying off the principal in monthly installments? As said before, this is the way most real estate mortgages are handled. The key difference to note here is that out of each monthly payment a portion is assigned to repayment of principal and the interest portion is based on the balance of the unpaid principal.

Example: Borrow $10,000 at 7½ percent to be repaid monthly over twenty years. You are looking for a way to calculate the amount that, paid monthly, is exactly enough to pay all the interest that is due and all of the principal so that at the end of twenty years, after you have made the last payment, the principal is completely repaid. The monthly payment amount for our problem here is

$$\$8.05639 \times 10 = \$80.56$$

If it takes $8.05639 to repay $1,000, then it takes ten times that for a loan of ten times $1,000.

In each succeeding month the interest portion is less and the principal reduction is more. The monthly payment amount remains constant. As a service to the borrower, most lenders provide a statement at the end of the year showing the total amount of interest paid; this figure will be needed when preparing an income tax return.

Insurance

As long as the market value of the property is equal to or greater than the loan balance, in the event of default it can be sold and the lender's interest restored. What about the possible destruction of the property? Loss or damage by physical perils such as fire, windstorm, explosion and others can be insured against by obtaining a fire or multiple-peril insurance policy. The lender obtains protection by requiring that the policy include a loss-payable clause naming the lender. The policy should always be written in the name of the titleholder. Usually the lender holds the original policy and the borrower-insured has a copy. Under these circumstances the lender is protected against the insured's canceling the policy and leaving the property uninsured. The amount of the insurance should be not less than the amount of the unpaid loan balance.

What if the premium is not paid when it is due? The insurance company will cancel the coverage. Under FHA and VA rules for mortgages, lenders are required to maintain impound, or loan trust fund, accounts and collect each month from borrowers the amounts needed to pay insurance premiums and property taxes when they are due. This money belongs to the borrower but is administered by the lender to guard against nonpayment of taxes and insurance, thus protecting the lender. Some mortgage lenders extend this practice to non-FHA and VA loans as a matter of convenience for both lender and borrower.

As a borrower you will have to have property insurance. If your lender is agreeable, you will be able to keep this reserve yourself. You may wish to set up a savings account for the purpose and thus earn some interest.

One final word about loan trust fund or impound accounts. Earlier we stated that in amortizing a mortgage, the periodic payment remains constant. If the lender requires a loan trust fund, the amounts needed for it to build up reserves for payment of insurance and property taxes will be added to the payment amount for principal and interest. If the cost of taxes or insurance changes, so will the amount to be accumulated in the loan trust fund. When this happens, the lender will send a notice of a change in the monthly payments. This does *not* change the payment on the mortgage, even though you now must send a different amount each month.

We now know that if our investment objective is to maximize current income, we need to minimize expenses and therefore will *not* borrow funds if it can be avoided. On the other hand, if we need to borrow money, which will be the case if we are seeking long-term capital appreciation and minimized current income, there are many different ways in which to do so.

Because the amount of money we can borrow is related to the amount of our own funds we invest in the project, the first step is to establish how much cash we can put into the investment. Assuming we can borrow at least 75 percent of the smaller of the purchase or appraised price, once we know how much cash we have we can estimate closely how big a piece of property we can handle. In our example in this chapter, we accumulated $21,000. That would mean we could seriously consider buying property selling in the neighborhood of $80,000.

Note carefully we have not yet looked for property. Until you know what amount you can invest, you should not get involved in trying to find a piece of property—unless, of course, you are doing so just for the exercise. We now are ready to take the next important step: the search for an investment vehicle.

3

The
Search for an
Investment
Vehicle

Previously we have decided seriously to consider putting our venture capital to work in owning and operating a fourplex, though that does not exclude other forms of property. It goes without saying that the principles employed and procedures suggested relative to a fourplex apply no matter what the size of the property.

Before you begin to search for properties, you must first make basic decisions regarding location and price range.

Location is critical, if only because you are going to manage the investment yourself. This means it has to be practical to journey to the property to show it to prospective tenants, perhaps to collect rents, and generally to keep an eye on it. Decide what is a reasonable distance from where you live. In fact, you should pin down the general area in which it is going to be practical to own income property *before* you start looking.

Once you have decided upon the general location, you should decide on your price range. Your available cash—in our example it was $21,000—must cover the down payment and the closing costs, and it is wise to have a little cushion so that if you find a great opportunity and need a few more dollars to take advantage of it, you will be able to do so.

With $21,000 you can expect to be able to borrow at least three times $21,000, or $60,000 from institutional lenders. To extend further your use of leverage, you might be able to arrange either for a private investor to lend more, for the seller to finance more than 75 percent of the price, or to take back a second mortgage. There are other sources for second mortgage financing too, as described before. At this point, however, you know that, given a satisfactory property, you should have little or no difficulty in financing the purchase of $80,000 worth of real estate.

Now that we know we want to examine in detail properties in a specified area of the community, that the type of greatest interest is a fourplex, and that the offering price should be around $80,000, let's take a closer look at the various sources of information we'll use.

Real estate brokers

When you buy property through a real estate office you are paying for the services rendered by way of a commission. The rates vary and are subject to negotiation and local custom, though the point at which the bargaining begins is around 6 percent of the purchase price. This sum normally is paid by the seller out of the proceeds of the sale, but inasmuch as the purchaser is providing those proceeds he is really paying the commission. Are the services of the real estate licensee worth the cost?

The seller offering property other than through a real estate office expects to save the commission, so the offering price, in theory, is going to be the same as if the property is listed with a broker. However, the prudent buyer will make an offer based at least in part on a price *less* the commission, knowing that the seller would receive that amount if he had used a broker. Any compromise will result in a lower price to the buyer and higher net proceeds to the seller.

Yet many sellers still use brokers. Many owners do not want to be bothered with qualifying prospects, then showing the property and negotiating a deal directly with a prospective buyer. To them the commission is a reasonable fee. If the broker does ferret out a buyer who would not otherwise be available to the seller, that in itself could be worth the commission. The broker usually advertises the property and incurs expense promoting it. It is his time and effort that goes into finding prospects and negotiating the sale. Unless that is the ultimate result, nothing is paid to the broker. Then, many buyers would rather make offers and negotiate with an agent instead of the seller personally — they feel more comfortable.

A qualified real estate person will be familiar with the market and can provide useful advice to both buyer and seller as to the market value of a particular piece of real estate.

Financing is often the most important aspect of the deal. A real estate dealer can be expected to know where the money is and to line up financing on the most favorable terms to the buyer. If you do not have access to the money market, the real estate commission is a small price to pay for overcoming that problem.

Finally, the broker and his staff should be able to handle the paper work. This may mean obtaining the services of an experienced attorney or escrow agent or title abstractor.

Thus both seller and buyer can get good service out of a broker. But how do you know which office to use? Not all real estate firms are expert in handling residential income property. What you want is one that specializes in the field. If you are going to use a real estate office, find one that knows how to handle income property.

Once you have become sophisticated in making investments in income property, you may decide that you will want to use a real estate broker for every investment. The right person can save you time and energy, provide you with information, and generally arrange deals you could never hope to do on your own. Some investors feel just the opposite and prefer to handle everything they can themselves. There is one nagging reality, however, always to be taken into account: some investment opportunities are available *only* to clients of real estate offices.

If the seller is knowledgeable and wants to provide the financing, you will be ahead in dealing with him. In contrast, an owner who has no idea of what market values are and expects the buyer to figure out how to give him all cash needs to be educated; you will have to decide whether you want to be the teacher. Find out as soon as possible how much the seller knows about the business and take appropriate action. The seller's inexperience can cost *you* money. If the seller obviously is smarter than you, you should run, not walk, to the nearest skilled real estate man.

Basic analysis

What you need for the decision-making process is information. You need data from each of several different pieces of property, and you need to have knowledge to use in evaluating and comparing. What is market value? What is reasonable financing? What is a good yield? Set up your criteria, then develop data and do an analysis. Investors who do this on a systematic basis find their results are substantially better than if they operate on a hit-and-miss basis, buying and selling on emotion, whim, and fancy.

As illustrated on the following pages, you should use a fact sheet and a set of analysis worksheets. The fact sheet data are for use in performing the computations required by the worksheets. Then you pull the results together on a summary sheet. With the summary sheet, you can make a decision as to the property you *should* buy.

Let us take an example. Using the initial criteria—location, type of property, and price range—we have located a property at 1234 Wistful Vista in the community of Utopia, California. We located this prospective gem through talking with Mr. I. M. Realtor, who represents the owner and who showed us through one of the units and provided most of the information we needed. We now are going to verify his data. Whenever possible we are going to get answers to questions from at least two reliable and pertinent sources. The fact sheet tells us what questions to ask and gives us a place to record the answers.

Fact sheet

Referring now to the fact sheet reproduced on pages 60 and 61, let's examine each of the major entries that require some comment. The form is designed to be filled in by hand and allows for putting down not only facts such as rents and expenses but also other items you think may be useful in the ultimate decision-making process. You will see more than one piece of property, and you will find it difficult to separate, in your memory, one property from another after you've been looking for a while, so record on the fact sheet everything of importance at the time you think of it and while on the premises.

Gross monthly rents. You want to know the total number of dollars from rent received from all units, assuming they are all occupied (even if they are not at the time), on a monthly basis. The exact rent per unit is not important at this time, just the total. This is the figure you will use later to arrive at the gross annual income (by multiplying by twelve).

Information about rents usually will be given by the real estate broker; he obtains it from the owner. Whenever possible you should verify, by talking with the tenants, the rental figure given. If this

FACT SHEET FOR PROPOSED INVESTMENT IN INCOME PROPERTY

LOCATION: _1234 Wistful Vista_ OWNER OR BROKER _I.M. Realtor_ PHONE _765-432_
Utopia, California
NUMBER OF UNITS: _4_ DESCRIPTION: _2-1BR, 2-2BR_ GROSS MONTHLY RENTS: $ _900_

LOT SIZE: _60 x 125_ BUILDING SIZE IN SQUARE FEET: _4000_
SQUARE-FOOT COST TODAY: $ _1900_

OTHER FEATURES: _Owner's unit – 1500 sq. ft._
Landscaping worth $500

DESCRIBE EQUIPMENT: _Stove/Ref. in each unit_ ITS CASH VALUE $ _2000_

	ASSESSED VALUE	TAXES FOR 197-	BUILDING AGE _10_ YEARS
LAND	$ _3,750_	$ _511_	ESTIMATED USEFUL LIFE REMAINING:
IMPROVEMENTS	$ _15,000_	$ _2,045_	BUILDING _30_
PERSONAL PROPERTY	$ _500_	$ _69_	EQUIPMENT _5_
TOTALS	$ _19,250_	$ _2,625_	OWNER'S PROPERTY TAX EXEMPTION TAKEN? _No_

ANNUAL OPERATING EXPENSES (ACTUAL _XX_ OR ESTIMATED _____)

PAID BY OWNER:

GAS_____ POWER_____ WATER _X – garden only_

GARBAGE _XX_ OTHER_____

CONDITION OF PROPERTY: _Good._
One unit needs paint.
_____

PAST DEPRECIATION RATE _1_ % PER YEAR

PROPERTY TAXES	$ _2,625_
UTILITIES	$ _240_
INSURANCE	$ _100_
MAINTENANCE	$ _250_
GARDENING	$ _185_
MANAGEMENT	$_____
	$_____
TOTAL ANNUAL OPERATING EXPENSE	$ _3,400_

INVESTOR'S DATA:
DESIRED YIELD BEFORE INCOME TAX: _9_ % FEDERAL & STATE TAX RATE: _40_ %

EXPECTED NUMBER OF YEARS BEFORE RESALE: _5_ . ANNUAL APPRECIATION RATE: _2_

EXPECTED RESALE EXPENSE $ _1000_ FOR FIX UP; SALES COMMISSION: _6_

EXPECTED VACANCY ALLOWANCE WHILE OWNED: _2_ % OF ANNUAL INCOME. MAXIMUM GROSS MULTIPLIER _8_

REMARKS: _Good rental record. Adjoining property about_
same value – shopping 2 blocks away.

INANCING:

LOAN	AMOUNT	RATE	TERM	PAYMENT	FEES OR POINTS	DUE DATE
FIRST	$ _54000_	_8%_	_20_	$ _452_	_1%._	_____
SECOND	$ _7000_	_9%_	___	$ _70_	_____	_6/80_

MMENTS ON PREPAYMENT PENALTY

First mtge – 1% on unpaid bal.

_____

ASKING PRICE $ _79,000_

TOTAL BORROWING $ _61,000_

CASH DOWN PAYMENT $ _18,000_

TIMATED CLOSING COSTS:

PRORATIONS $ _50_

MORTGAGE POINTS/FEES $ _540_

TITLE INSURANCE/ESCROW FEE $ _500_

OTHER ONE-TIME FEES $ _60_

TOTAL CLOSING COSTS $ _1,150_

TOTAL CASH REQUIRED: $ _19,150_

LCULATION OF MORTGAGE PAYMENT:

$ _54_   x _8.364758_ = $ _452_
LOAN IN 1000s   FACTOR

MPUTATION OF FUTURE DEPRECIATION:

BUILDING: VALUE TO BE DEPRECIATED IS $ _60,000_ OVER _30_ YEARS

STRAIGHT LINE RATE = 100% ÷ _30_ = _3⅓_ % PER YEAR.
                  NUMBER OF YEARS

METHOD _straight line_

ANNUAL DEPRECIATION CHARGE IS $ _60,000_ x _3⅓%_ = $ _2,000_
                           VALUE   RATE

EQUIPMENT: VALUE TO BE DEPRECIATED IS $ _1,800_ OVER _5_ YEARS.

METHOD AND COMPUTATION: _straight line – $200 salvage_

1800 ÷ 5 = $360 each year

DATE PREPARED _4-20-7–_

is not possible before offering to buy, then put a provision in your offer that your offer is subject to verification that the actual rental income is as stated in the preliminary negotiations. This is only one of several possible qualifications to your offer. There cannot be too much stress placed on the importance of working *only* with accurate data, and accuracy requires checking. You may feel some reluctance in speaking to a tenant. Overcome that reluctance by remembering it is your money that is going on the line.

Lot size, building size. Later you will use this information in estimating the value of the property. Owners and their real estate agents should have this information readily available. You may have to pace off the building and make an estimate of the number of square feet of living area. If the garages are separate, make a note of the size. If they are part of the building, do not include the garage area in the total area figure.

Square-foot cost today. Arriving at this figure may provide a challenge. Best of all, locate the contractor who built the building and ask him what it would cost today, on a square-foot basis, to build the same structure. Note that the lot is not involved here, only the building. If the builder is not available, ask other contractors and obtain building cost data from the local contractors' association, real estate brokers, and mortgage lenders.

Other features. Record the items you have noticed that relate to the property's desirability from the point of view of a prospective tenant. Also, put down items that should be allowed for in estimating costs or values. Be careful not to inject your own personal likes and dislikes into this project. You are not appraising the property in terms of your own occupancy. What appeals to you may not be of interest to a tenant and what is unattractive to you may not concern tenants. Be as objective as possible in viewing the property and recording data about it.

Equipment description. Here you are concerned with the equipment either in the individual rental units or in the building for the use of all or some of the tenants — stoves, refrigerators, laundry appliances, and so on. You need an estimated cash value of those items that are not included in the value of the structure. Generally, whatever rule you apply for separating depreciation between building and equipment should be applied here. Units not built-in are clearly equipment. Built-in stoves, for example, may be considered a part of the building although you can, under some circumstances, treat such a unit, for depreciation and tax purposes, as separate. At this time, make a note of what is there in such detail as will be enough for later computation. Estimating the value will not be easy at first, but with practice you will get better at it. Be conservative. Be certain to check to see if replacements are needed.

Assessed value and taxes. Ask for a copy of the most recent tax bill and copy the information from it. If not available, call the local tax assessor's office and ask for the assessed values and tax amounts. This information is a matter of public record, and you are entitled to it. Be sure to find out if the present owner has obtained any special tax exemptions that have resulted in lowering his taxes but that will not be available to you. Buyers can easily be misled by using tax costs for the seller that will not apply to the new owner —you, the buyer.

A tax assessor is obligated to review periodically the value of each parcel of property and arrive at an updated, assessed value. A reevaluation of assessed value frequently takes place just after a property has changed hands. In some states the buyer is obligated to tell the assessor the purchase price and financing details of the transaction. The prudent investor will adjust his property tax expense figure for possible change in the assessed value.

The property tax amount is obtained by multiplying the assessed value by the tax rate; tax rates usually change every year. If the tax rate has not been established when you are evaluating an investment opportunity, you will have to guess at it.

In some states—California, for example—by law the county tax assessor is expected to determine the market value of the property and use 25 percent of that amount as the assessed value. As long as that is done, you can take a current assessed value and multiply it by four to get an idea of what the assessor thought the property was worth. Be aware, however, that this will be *only* a guide. The assessed value may not be up to date; the assessor may not be following the rule; and there may be other good reasons for the market price to be other than a multiple of the assessed valuation.

Assessed values are separate for land and improvements (building); personal property is valued by itself. The ratio of the value of the land to the total of land and improvements may be useful later in estimating values. Ultimately we will need a value for the building by itself for depreciation purposes. If, for example, in the assessment, the ratio indicated is four-to-one for the land, you may want to say later that the portion of the total purchase price attributable to the lot is 20 percent. This would leave 80 percent of the price as the beginning book value of the building. We have ignored, for this simple example, the relatively small amount of personal property when estimating the book value. To be precise you should calculate the percentages of the total assessed value represented by each component: land, building, personal property. Those percentages could then be applied to a purchase price.

Building age. If you are looking at a new structure, there is no problem. Otherwise, there are several sources of information. The best is the building department at city hall. Ask for the date on which a building permit was issued for the property. You can assume the building was completed within a year of that date in the absence of information to the contrary. If the seller is the original owner, he may recall the date. But if the property is relatively old, don't rely entirely on the owner's memory or the assertion of the real estate agent. You need to get some idea of how old the property is so that you can intelligently estimate the remaining useful life, a figure needed for depreciation computations.

For income tax purposes a new apartment building of the type we are considering will have an estimated total useful life of forty years. Many buildings that are much more than forty years old continue to function quite well. This arbitrary estimated life is only for the purpose of spreading the cost of the building over the future. If you own a building that is ten years old, by applying the forty-year rule, you come up with thirty years remaining.

Equipment does not last as long as the building, so there is a shorter period over which to spread its cost. The actual lifetime is dependent in large part on the kind of treatment and use it is given. The shorter the period, the larger each year will be the amount of depreciation to be charged against income, thus reducing your taxable income. In a situation where there is a special difficulty in arriving at estimates, contact the Internal Revenue Service for guidance. Apartment house equipment such as appliances is often depreciated over five to eight years.

Annual operating expenses. We have already discussed the property tax item. The other expense data will come from the owner directly or through the real estate broker who obtained it from the owner. Some investors ask to see the accounting records to verify the information given. As you gain experience, you will be able to evaluate expense data and recognize unreasonable figures. The total of the operating expenses is going to play an important role in our evaluation. The numbers need to be accurate, and you should make some allowance for the unexpected.

Be certain to find out precisely which *utilities* the owner is responsible for and try to avoid those where there is little or no control over the amount of expense incurred. It is best to have tenants pay for their own power, for example.

The *maintenance* figure will be an estimate because you cannot tell in advance what costs you will have. By looking closely at the property at this stage you should be able to see where there is likely to be some maintenance cost in the near future. Try to guess, based on what you have learned from the seller about his maintenance costs and what you think you will have to do, what a fair expense will be for the first year of ownership. If you underestimate, you will not realize the profit your analysis would suggest. If you overestimate, you may decide against investing in a property that is in fact satisfactory.

For tax purposes you must separate maintenance and repair costs from *capital improvements.* If you install new plumbing fixtures, such as a stall shower, or replace the roof or the water heater, such costs are considered capital improvements. The cost would be added to the cost of your investment. Having a plumber clean out the pipes would ordinarily be viewed as maintenance and treated as operating expense to be charged against current income. Again, if in doubt about a particular item, ask the Internal Revenue Service.

For the cost of *insurance,* ask your insurance agent. You will need not only fire and other physical peril coverage to satisfy the lender, but also public liability insurance. This is readily available in one insurance policy, and your agent can quickly tell you its annual cost. Even though you might take over the policy on the property and thereby pay out less than a full term's premium, you want to know the *annual* cost for insurance.

As to the cost of *management,* we have already decided you are going to run the show yourself. You cannot pay yourself for this work. If you generate a profit and long-term gain, you get paid then, but you cannot charge for things you do. If you pay someone for services in connection with managing the property, it will be a proper expense and you record the expected annual amount. (If the payment is to be in the form of reduced rent, it is good accounting practice to show the gross rent as income and the allowance as an expense.)

Past depreciation rate. Shortly, you are going to calculate a value of the property by taking into consideration the extent to which it has depreciated in the past; the present figure, however, is not affected by what depreciation the seller has taken. It is your *estimate,*

as you look at the property, as to how it has weathered the passage
of time. Even though we have said that for tax purposes an apartment house may have an estimated useful life of forty years (a
depreciation rate of 2.5 percent a year), we know the actual depreciation may not be that great. Further, a building depreciates
at different rates during its lifetime. If a structure has been reasonably well cared for, a rate of 1 percent per year gone by is
probably workable. That would mean, for example, that a ten-year-
old property would have depreciated a total of 10 percent. For
older properties the rate might be higher. If a building has been
renovated and remodeled you may require professional help with
determining an appraised value.

Investor's data. You must decide what you think would be a fair
yield from an investment in residential income property, and that is
not an easy decision to make. What is reasonable? What is par for
the course? And even more important, what do we mean by *yield?*

Shortly, we will calculate several different yields; for the time
being, however, let's take the desired yield to be a before-income-
tax annual rate of return on an investment that has some risk. The
rate, therefore, will be greater than we could get by putting our
funds in an insured savings account, which, as this is written, is at
least 6 percent and can be 7.5 percent. We will also, for the time
being, ignore the long-term capital appreciation return and deal
only with current income return. We will use the rate we decide on
to capitalize the income to arrive at a fair purchase price. If we
require a yield that is unrealistically high, we will miss out on
some good investments. If it is too low, we might be deluded into
paying too much for the property. In our example, we use 9 percent. By experience you will learn whether this is a good rate for
you to use.

Federal and state tax rate. This is for income taxes. By looking
at your last tax return, you can tell what federal and state rates
(and city, in some places) applied to the last increment of taxable
income. Because most income taxes are assessed on a graduated
scale, to know the rate to apply to a particular source of income
you must know to what total the incremental income would come.
For this purpose make a careful estimate of what your situation
would be and use the percentages indicated. Add together the
federal, state, and city taxes, if any, to get a single rate. In our
example, we are using 40 percent.

Expected number of years before resale. This is the holding
period or investment horizon. It is likely to be the same for each

investment you are analyzing, but it does not have to be the same. We will see what differences there are in using different holding periods when we consider the comparison process. The time at which you would resell the property is governed by many factors not ascertainable at this time. If you use accelerated depreciation, that will influence your choice of resale date. A future emergency might govern what you would do. Investing in real estate is a long-term proposition. To obtain the benefits of favorable income tax rates on gain you must hold the property long enough to qualify. For federal taxes that is at least six months; in some states it is a longer period. For our example, and to approximate the typical situation, we use five years.

Annual appreciation rate. If you assume that the market value of this property will increase in the future, reflect that in your analysis. If it is likely to go down, you also want to reflect that. How do we know what to do here? If you look around you, it will be apparent that property values have been increasing steadily in most areas for the past thirty years or more. Will this continue? If the past is an indicator of the future, the answer is yes. By how much? Compare selling prices of similar properties over the past several years. Discuss this subject with real estate brokers, bankers, and builders. The actual rate will vary from one area to another, even within a community. Be conservative when you pick a percentage.

Here we use 2 percent. Remember, this is saying that each year the value goes up 2 percent of the preceding year's value. In five years that will be more than 10 percent. If you think values will go down, then choose a rate but apply it as a negative.

Expected resale expense. The work to be done to make the property presentable when you want to sell it is often referred to as *deferred maintenance.* You will have to decide on your maintenance policy. Either keep the property painted and fixed up all the time or let things go until they have to be done. Even then you may decide to offer the property "as is" rather than pay the cost of a thin coat of paint to make it look good to prospective buyers. You cannot really know what shape the place will be in five years hence. Even though you plan now to keep it painted, if you run into cash flow problems, you may not be able to implement such a policy. Be conservative and put something into your figures for fix up. If you do not have to spend it when the time comes, you will simply be ahead further than you expected. Here we are using $1,000.

Sales commission. You are planning at this point to use a real estate agent to find a buyer. If you manage to do that yourself, you will have saved the commission—usually, though not always, 6 percent.

Expected vacancy. You can have rent loss either from vacant units or from occupied units for which the tenant does not pay. Some investors use as much as 10 percent of gross rental income as an allowance to cover their losses. If demand for housing is strong and is expected to remain strong and you plan to avoid bad debt losses, you may want to use a nominal rate. Here we have 2 percent.

CR   *Maximum gross multiplier.* The computation and use of the gross multiplier are covered later in the chapter. Through experience and analysis of the market place, you will reach a conclusion as to how high you should go. In most areas a multiplier between six and eight will be reasonable. For use in the analysis to be made from the fact sheet data you will enter the maximum multiplier you feel is right for your purposes.

Financing. Either the seller or the real estate broker will indicate the nature of the financing he has lined up. You may want to arrange your own, but for now you should record what others have available. To show some of the options, the example covers a first and second mortgage for a total borrowing of nearly 80 percent. In your efforts to maximize leverage you may be able to raise this to 90 percent.

As discussed previously, a lender will obtain an appraisal and use that figure in determining the amount to lend. Here we assume the first mortgagee will lend just under 70 percent of the offering price. The interest rate is 8 percent and the term of the loan is twenty years. The monthly payments, the first of which is payable about a month after the date the loan is made, cover both principal and interest, with interest computed on the unpaid principal balance. This is an amortization loan. Because the lender feels that 8 percent is not high enough, he is asking for a loan fee of 1 percent. This is, in effect, interest in advance.

When discussing a loan, the lending officer simply looks up a table to give you the amount of the monthly payment. For example, in order to reduce the monthly payment, you may want to try to persuade the lender to make the loan for twenty-five years instead of twenty.

For the second mortgage in our example we are assuming the payment is stipulated to be 1 percent of the amount borrowed, a typical condition for second mortgages. That will mean that the

A Fact Sheet Checklist

Now that you have some idea of what goes into the first page of the fact sheet, look at a checklist of some of the things you need to look for—plan on adding to this list as you learn from experience.

1. A termite inspection report should be obtained and studied before deciding on purchase. Local custom will determine whether buyer or seller pays for this report. It may also be important to get a soil engineer's report or one from a structural engineer. In some areas building inspection services will provide a complete report on the soundness and condition of the property. The cost will vary by area and size. Expect to pay at least $100 for a proper report.

2. Are there problems with sewage, drainage, streets, earth movement?

3. Is property due to be annexed to adjoining city or is there other change in taxing jurisdictions?

4. Are there improvement bonds or other assessments outstanding?

5. Are all apartment units legal? This is a prospective problem particularly for remodeled property. Even though occupied and tenants pay rent, the apartment may not be legal and owner may not be permitted to continue to rent it. Apartment may be deficient with respect to building, health, and safety code requirements.

6. Will you need to make appliance replacements soon? Check water heaters, furnaces, and cooling equipment.

7. How about the roof? It never lasts as long as the building.

8. Why is the owner selling? What's the *real* reason?

9. How does the value of this property compare with others in the neighborhood? A luxury apartment in a depressed area will not command adequate rents.

10. What features are likely to appeal to tenants?

11. What has been the rental or vacancy record?

12. Are present tenants on lease? Provisions for changing rents?

13. Have any tenants given notice of leaving?

14. Are there unresolved disputes or special "understandings" between present tenants and landlord?

15. Will landscaping require attention? Has enough allowance been made for gardening in expense estimates?

16. Have tenants paid a rent deposit to be applied to last month's rent?

17. Which tenants have paid damage deposits and how much?

18. If needed, is TV cable available? How about noncable reception?

monthly payment will not fully pay the loan by the due date and that, therefore, on that due date the borrower will be faced with paying off the unpaid balance in full. In making your plans for this prospective investment, you might expect to sell the property before the due date and thus pay off both mortgages. Otherwise, you must make necessary provision for taking care of this second mortgage. Of course, the lender might be willing to rewrite the note, particularly if you have been making the payments on time.

Also under the heading of advance planning, you will want to make a note of the prepayment penalty, if any. Here, it is 1 percent of the balance due at the time the first mortgage is paid off. That is a very liberal penalty. You should aim for financing without a prepayment penalty, but that may be hard to obtain. When you compute the gain on the resale five years from now, you will want to include the impact of the prepayment penalty.

In this section you calculate the total amount of cash the project requires *for the asking price.* You, of course, are not going to offer to pay the asking price. A lower purchase price will not automatically reduce the amount of cash required. Recall that the amount of the first mortgage is related to the lender's appraisal. It is also related to the purchase price the buyer and seller have agreed to. If it goes down, so may the lender's first mortgage.

Here, we see that we should have around $18,000 in cash. Is there more needed?

Closing cost. More dollars over the cash down payment will be needed to pay the mortgage loan fees or points. Here, $540.

In addition, there will be title insurance or fees to abstractors and attorneys for handling the title search and documents and perhaps appraisal, inspection, and recording fees. Finally, we may have to reimburse the seller for property taxes or insurance he has paid in advance.

In our example we have assumed a purchase as of December 31, with property taxes paid to that date, but we are going to take over an existing fire insurance policy that has been paid in advance to the extent of $50.

The total for closing costs is $1,150. This could have been a great deal more, and you should make liberal allowance in any analysis for closing costs. You will need *cash* for these expenses. You will be able to recover some of these costs almost right away, but they will have to be covered at the time the purchase is made.

On the form is an example of how to compute a mortgage payment. For use in the subsequent financial analysis we also calculate the depreciation charges at this point. The basis for the computation is to be found in the information recorded on the first page of the fact sheet.

Future depreciation. Digressing somewhat from the example, you cover here the essential elements of depreciation for income tax purposes. These elements must be considered when you make decisions as to how you will treat depreciation either in analyzing a prospective investment or in reporting income from property you own. The ultimate authority for information on this subject is the Internal Revenue Service and your tax accountant or attorney.

When you invest in an income-producing asset, such as an apartment house, the taxable income is basically the difference between the income you receive from it and the expenses incurred in generating the income. It is easy to state the income. It is the sum of the dollars paid to you by your tenants during the accounting period. That usually is a calendar year—January 1 to December 31. You may have some other incidental income—such as from coin-operated appliances. From the total you deduct the operating expenses. These include maintenance, insurance, interest expense, property taxes, utilities, gardening, management, travel, postage, telephone, advertising, and so on. Any expense incurred in connection with generating the income can be deducted. What about the cost of the property in the first place? (If you were in the business of selling merchandise, you certainly would include in your deductions from income the cost of the goods.)

How do you properly apportion the cost of this type of capital asset over time? The goal is to match the cost of the building and equipment against the income. The cost of the land does not enter into any of this because it is not "used" the way the building and equipment are. If you knew with certainty exactly how long the building could be used, that it would then become worthless overnight, and that the value of its use was uniform throughout its lifetime, the problem would be easy to handle. In fact, even though the use and value of a structure do not turn out that way, in effect we pretend that they do and allow for making an adjustment at some time in the future.

The portion of an asset used up with use and passage of time is called *depreciation.* By careful calculation after making certain assumptions you arrive at a dollar amount of depreciation for a given time period, usually a year, to serve as the *cost* of the building. This amount then becomes an *expense* to be charged against income.

Two aspects should be apparent at this point. The larger the amount of depreciation, the greater will be the total expenses and the smaller the income or profit. In turn, there will be a smaller amount of income tax to be paid on the income. Second, this expense does not involve the payout of cash in the same manner as for other expenses. In a sense, it was paid out beforehand when the property was purchased. From these two aspects flow the procedures we are concerned with, particularly in the case of real estate investments.

The fact that you can charge as expense the amount of depreciation, yet not disburse funds, means that you may have a surplus of cash from income over expenses that differs from the calculated net income or profit. Later we will look at this "cash flow" more closely. For now, concentrate on the methods we can use to compute the amount of annual depreciation, keeping in mind we are looking for a way to apportion the total cost over the life of the property and thus avoid distorting the results of ownership provided by accounting records and reports.

Until you sell the property and compare the price realized with the original cost, you have no way of knowing what actual depreciation (or appreciation) in value has taken place during the period of ownership. As a consequence, depreciation amounts are estimates. (There can be an appreciation in the value of the property. As a general rule, you assign the appreciation to the land and consider that the building is wearing out with the passing of time.)

From a practical point of view, the primary reason to concern yourself with an accurate estimate is to take advantage of the income tax rules administered by the Internal Revenue Service and state offices. In addition, the prudent investor wants a realistic picture of income and therefore needs a way to apportion costs accurately. The question is: how do you do it?

Straight-line charges the depreciation in equal amounts, spreading the total cost over the lifetime. For example, if you expect to use an asset for twenty years, then you would charge 5 percent a year of its original cost, provided there is no value left. For assets other than buildings it is customary to estimate the salvage or scrap value, deducting that value from the cost and depreciating the difference. For real estate investments, by custom you ignore the salvage. For tax purposes we depreciate the building during the time we own it, but on the resale, we calculate the long-term gain on the basis of the selling price of the whole property—land *and* structure.

If you use straight-line, the term applied to the equal apportion-ment of the cost over the lifetime, all you need is an estimated remaining useful life. That can be expressed as a percentage for each year.

Let's assume you are looking at a newly constructed apartment house. To maximize the amount of depreciation and to minimize the amount of income tax, you want as short a life as possible because that will give you the most depreciation to charge each year. The IRS has decreed that you may use forty years as a maxi-mum useful life for a new building of this type; you would have trouble, on the audit, if you tried using less. For forty years the annual straight-line depreciation rate would be 2.5 percent (40 $\times 2\frac{1}{2} = 100$ percent).

For used property you use another figure. If the building is, say, ten years old, you might consider using thirty years. But this will depend upon the condition of the property. It might not have thirty years left because of abuse or other factors. Whatever num-ber you use, you must be prepared to justify it to the IRS.

Assets do not necessarily depreciate at an even rate, and you may use methods other than straight line. For new construction and to provide incentives to build new housing, the income tax rules include optional depreciation methods called *accelerated.* The *declining balance* and *sum-of-the-years'-digits* formulas are available to increase the amount of depreciation in the early years of the lifetime of a capital asset. Their use will reduce the amount of tax payable in the beginning.

It is sufficient to realize that if you use an accelerated method, you may have to adjust your declaration of taxable income at some future time to offset partially some of the advantage gained earlier.

You and your tax adviser may well decide to make a particular investment because the property is eligible for accelerated depre-ciation, especially if it is newly built. In such cases, you may be able to charge twice the straight-line rate of depreciation. Used property is subject to lower accelerated rates and only under certain condi-tions. Full and current information is readily available from the Internal Revenue Service.

For our purposes we will stick to the straight-line method. You can't go wrong. It will give conservative results. As you progress in your investment activities, you will want to see how you can use accelerated depreciation rates and increase your immediate returns.

If you are considering a property that contains any significant value of equipment, use an accelerated formula.

Assume you have equipment worth $5,000, and that it has an estimated remaining useful life of five years. To calculate the first year's depreciation charge, you need a factor or ratio to apply to the total amount to be depreciated. Assume you can sell the used equipment at the end of five years for $500. You have $4,500 to depreciate.

The formula requires that we add the years' digits: $1 + 2 + 3 + 4 + 5 = 15$. (For eight years, it would be 36.) The factor for the first year is 5/15; second year, 4/15. Note that the numerator is the number of the years of useful life for the first year, and one less for each succeeding year. The denominator remains the same and is the sum of the years of useful life. For the first year's depreciation then: $5/15 \times \$4,500 = \$1,500$. For the second year: $4/15 \times \$4,500 = \$1,200$.

During the last years of the asset's life the accelerated depreciation charge would be *less* than what it would be under straight-line. For example, take the fifth year. Under straight-line we would have taken the $4,500 and divided that sum into five equal parts: $900 would be the annual depreciation charge. Using the sum of the years' digits method: $1/15 \times \$4,500 = \$300$.

In total, under *both* methods, $4,500 would be depreciated, but by differing amounts each year and with different effect on your tax status. The sum-of-the-years'-digits method can be used for any capital asset including buildings, provided it meets the eligibility requirements. In practice, this method is used on new equipment rather than buildings.

The declining balance method is widely used by aggressive investors to maximize early returns from newly constructed apartment projects. Assume that the asset meets the eligibility requirements and we can use the formula producing the maximum amount of depreciation—the *double declining balance* method. Another way of saying the same thing is to state that the depreciation rate is 200 percent of the straight-line rate. But, unlike the straight-line procedure, the declining balance formula requires that the rate be applied to an amount reduced by the depreciation charge of the preceding year. This will produce a much larger depreciation charge in the early life of the asset than does straight-line. Let's look at an example.

Assume we have a new building used for residential purposes and from which at least 80 percent of the income is from such residential use. The first user could elect to use the double declining balance method. The cost is $100,000 for the building (ignore land

and equipment). The estimated remaining useful life is forty years, so the annual straight-line rate would be 2.5 percent. We double this to get 5 percent (200 percent of 2.5 percent equals 5 percent). This rate will be applied to successive ending book values.

First year depreciation charge:
   5 percent of $100,000=$5,000 ending book value $95,000
   Second year depreciation charge:
   5 percent of $95,000=$4,750 ending book value $90,250
If we had used straight-line:
   2.5 percent of $100,000 $2,500 each and every year.

In our example, we have opted for straight-line for both building and equipment. To depreciate the building over thirty years (even though we have no intention of owning it for thirty years), we use an annual straight-line rate of 3.3 percent. That rate times the value of the structure gives us $2,000 as the charge to be made each year we own the property. If we were to remodel or extensively repair the building, we would change the $60,000 base, which would in turn change the depreciation charge. For the equipment, we started with a $2,000 value and estimated $200 salvage. Over the five-year period we want to allocate the difference, $1,800. This gives us $360 to be charged each year. As we replace the equipment with new units, we recalculate, using new costs and perhaps different lifetimes. We could use, say, the sum-of-the-years'-digits method on the equipment even though we use straight-line on the building. We could even use a different method on different pieces of equipment.

Analysis worksheets

The analysis of the property is divided into four parts: indicated economic value, cash flows, yields, and resale results. By using the information gathered and the tables provided you can forecast the financial picture according to the assumptions made. In this manner you can obtain an idea in advance of what the situation would be if you bought the property.

Refer to the example reproduced on pages 77 and 86. For convenience, show clearly the total of the down payment and costs to arrive at the total cash required. You had better know where that sum is coming from, or the analysis will be just an exercise, no matter how good an investment it appears.

Indicated economic value. Since you intend never to pay more for something than it is worth, you must find out what a particular piece of property is worth. There are three different computations to make and when you have made them, the figures can be averaged. The goal is to arrive at values using the customary approaches for valuation and then to be able to compare the offering price.

The offering price is simply a beginning point. Investors generally determine independently what they think a property is worth and prepare an offer accordingly. You must not feel any compulsion to accept the seller's idea of value. Find out for yourself.

Cost approach. The objective is to find out what it would cost today to replace. Start by computing the current cost to build the structure today, using the square-foot area and building cost. Then estimate what percentage of that value has disappeared through usage. Recall you examined the building to see if you could judge a rate of past depreciation. Now use that rate and apply it to the current cost. To the depreciated cost of the building, add values not a part of the structure but a part of the total property. When these are added together, you have a total reproduction cost.

Recall the earlier instructions on how to estimate the value of the lot by using data on the property tax bill. If there is a similar vacant lot on the market, use the sales price as the value of your lot. Because a number of factors have a bearing on the market price, the cost approach value often is not the same as the offering price.

Gross multiplier. This method allows you to compare this property with other similar properties. If you could locate other properties identical to the one being studied and determine what they sold for recently, you would have a good way to compare the offering price. That is not practical, however. Instead, you look for a common denominator and find it in the relationship of gross rental income and sales price. Because property rented to others is being used to generate a return on the investment, it is reasonable to think that the level of rents is related to the value of the property, though the net return will vary according to expenses.

By reading newspaper classified advertising you will be able to find offering prices and gross rental income data. Divide the gross income into the asking price to obtain the gross multiplier. Enough checking will reveal what the going gross multiplier is in your area. It will vary slightly for different types of property, so, if your interest is in fourplexes, try to use only data for fourplexes.

Property offered at, say, five times gross may have some serious

ANALYSIS OF PROPOSED INVESTMENT*

LOCATION: _1234 Wistful Vista, Utopia, California_

PURCHASE AND FINANCING DATA

ASKING PRICE		$ _79,000_
FIRST MORTGAGE	$ _54,000_	
SECOND MORTGAGE	$ _7,000_	
TOTAL BORROWINGS		$ _61,000_
DOWN PAYMENT		$ _18,000_
PRORATIONS	$ _50_	
MORTGAGE POINTS/LOAN FEES	$ _540_	
TITLE INSURANCE/ESCROW FEE	$ _500_	
OTHER ONE-TIME FEES	$ _60_	
TOTAL EXPENSES		$ _1,150_
TOTAL CASH REQUIRED		$ _19,150_

INDICATED ECONOMIC VALUE

A. COST APPROACH: _4,000_ SQUARE FEET @$ _19.00_ EACH = $ _76,000_

LESS DEPRECIATION @ _1_ % YEARLY FOR _10_ YEARS = $ _7,600_

DEPRECIATED COST OF BUILDING $ _68,400_

ADD: EQUIPMENT/LANDSCAPING $ _2,500_
     LAND VALUE $ _15,000_
     TOTAL ADDITIONS $ _17,500_

TOTAL REPRODUCTION COST $ _85,900_

B. GROSS MULTIPLIER

$$\underset{\text{ASKING PRICE}}{\$\ \underline{79,000}} \div \underset{\text{GROSS ANNUAL INCOME}}{\$\ \underline{10,800}} = \underline{7.3} \text{ TIMES}$$

$$\underset{\text{YOUR MULTIPLIER}}{\underline{8}} \times \underset{\text{GROSS ANNUAL INCOME}}{\$\ \underline{10,800}} = \underset{\text{MAXIMUM PRICE}}{\boxed{\$\ 86,400}}$$

C. CAPITALIZATION OF INCOME

GROSS ANNUAL INCOME LESS VACANCY	$ _10,600_
LESS ANNUAL OPERATING EXPENSES	$ _3,400_
NET OPERATING INCOME	$ _7,200_

$$\underset{\text{NET OPERATING INCOME}}{\$\ \underline{7,200}} \div \underset{\text{DESIRED YIELD}}{\underline{.09}} = \underset{\text{MAXIMUM PRICE}}{\boxed{\$\ 80,000}}$$

$$\underset{\text{NET OPERATING INCOME}}{\$\ \underline{7,200}} \div \underset{\text{ASKING PRICE}}{\$\ \underline{79,000}} \times 100\% = \underset{\text{YIELD}}{\underline{9.1}\ \%}$$

ASSUMPTION: PURCHASE MADE AT FIRST OF YEAR; ALL ANNUAL FIGURES deficiency. Very high gross multiples may indicate either a tight rental market or an owner who does not know what his property is worth. Any property having a multiplier of 8 or less will be of interest. Properties with much higher multiples may not be worth investigating. Use the gross multiplier as a means of sorting out properties you hear about, going after the lower multipliers first.

In our example, the subject property has a 7.3 multiplier. Going one step further, we compute the maximum price to pay for the multiplier we have chosen, and, not unexpectedly, it is greater than the offering price. The property offered at $79,000 is favorable when measured against both cost and market as calculated by use of the gross multiplier. How about net income?

Capitalization of income. Many analysts feel that the most useful and important measure is that on net income. They argue that when putting money to work to produce a return, it is the return that counts, relative to dollars invested. So they capitalize that net income.

Assume you have not borrowed any money and have used all cash to buy the property. Out of rents you pay all expenses. Without regard to income taxes — no depreciation charge — what does the property provide in the way of a net income? If you put $10,000 in a savings account and receive $600 at the end of a year, the rate of return is 6 percent. How about the apartment house? Note we are working only with current income and have not allowed for long-term potential capital appreciation. We are assuming either that we will not sell the property or that, if we do, we get back only what we paid.

In the example, we see that the net operating income is $7,200. This is our return on an investment of the purchase price. What should we pay for this asset? That depends on how much we want as a yield. Previously we had decided on a 9 percent yield, and we use that figure here. By dividing the yield into the income, we get a value of $80,000. If you put $80,000 to work at 9 percent per annum, the income would be $7,200. This gives us another bench mark. We compare the $80,000 against the $79,000 asking price. We could go as high as $80,000. The other way of looking at it is to see that the operating income related to the asking price will give a yield of 9.1 percent.

Our goal was to reach indicated economic values. We now have three. If they are averaged the result is $84,100. When this is measured against the asking price of $79,000 plus the closing costs, other than prorations, we can conclude that we would have a satisfactory investment if we bought at the asking price—better if for less. But there is more to check first.

Cash flows. If you owned the property, collected the rents, and paid the expenses, would you have enough cash? Ordinarily you want an investment to be self-sustaining, though it is not automatically bad if the investment is not. If the expenses exceed the income, you will have to put up the difference and that would be viewed as increasing your cash investment. In some situations this would make sense—ordinarily, not so.

In our example, we already have decided on the vacancy allowance so we can calculate the expected rental income after vacancies. The cash-paid operating expenses have been totaled on the fact sheet. Because we have borrowed funds for the project, we will make the mortgage payments out of the rental income. The annual mortgage disbursement is twelve times the actual monthly payments of $452 and $70. If our operating expenses turn out to be what we estimated, we should have a surplus of $936 at the end of the year. We conclude the property will be self-sustaining on a cash basis.

But, as everyone knows, the only useful dollar is the one remaining *after* taxes have been settled.

Annual taxable income. You need to compute, for tax purposes, the return. From the actual income deduct all those expenses deductible under the Internal Revenue Service rules. The first computation is mortgage *interest.*

In our example, what part of the $5,424 paid in first mortgage payments was applied to interest? What part of the $840 was for interest on the second mortgage? We rounded the monthly payment to an even $452 in our example. This would not be necessary when preparing estimates.

The second mortgage in the example came with a stipulated payment. In this case, for a rate of 9 percent, the interest expense factor is 88.72974 to be applied to $7 for total interest expense of $621, as entered on the form.

The depreciation charges were calculated on the fact sheet, so now we can make the necessary entries of $2,000 for the building and $360 for the equipment. After deducting all expenses, both those paid in cash and the depreciation not paid in cash, the net annual taxable income amounts to a loss of $63.

We have assumed you have other income and that this investment was to help you accomplish a goal of minimizing current income and maximizing long-term gain. You can charge a loss

ANNUAL CASH FLOW - BEFORE INCOME TAX

GROSS ANNUAL RENTAL INCOME	$ *10,800*	
LESS VACANCY ALLOWANCE OF *2* %	$ *200*	
NET ANNUAL SCHEDULED INCOME		$ *10,60*
LESS: ANNUAL OPERATING EXPENSES	$ *3,400*	
1ST MORTGAGE (12 X MONTHLY PAYMENTS*)	$ *5,424*	
2ND MORTGAGE (12 X MONTHLY PAYMENTS)	$ *840*	
TOTAL ANNUAL CASH EXPENSES		$ *9,66*
NET ANNUAL BEFORE-TAX CASH FLOW		$ *93*

*PRINCIPAL AND INTEREST ONLY - DO NOT INCLUDE PROPERTY TAXES AND INSURANCE.

ANNUAL TAXABLE INCOME

NET ANNUAL SCHEDULED INCOME		$ *10,60*
LESS: ANNUAL OPERATING EXPENSES	$ *3,400*	
FIRST MORTGAGE INTEREST	$ *4,282*	
SECOND MORTGAGE INTEREST	$ *621*	
DEPRECIATION:		
BUILDING - $ *60,000* OVER *30* YEARS	$ *2,000*	
EQUIPMENT - $ *1,800* OVER *5* YEARS	$ *360*	
TOTAL ANNUAL DEDUCTIBLE EXPENSE		$ *10,66*
ANNUAL TAXABLE INCOME		$ *<63*
TAX LIABILITY** - FEDERAL AND STATE COMBINED RATE OF *40* %		$ *<25*

ADJUSTMENTS FOR FIRST YEAR

MORTGAGE POINTS/FEES	$ *540*	
TITLE INSURANCE AND ESCROW FEES	$ *500*	
OTHER ONE-TIME FEES	$ *60*	
TOTAL ADDITIONAL DEDUCTIBLE EXPENSES		$ *1,100*
INCOME TAX CREDIT -- COMBINED RATE TIMES PRECEDING TOTAL		$ *440*

INCOME TAX PAYABLE ON OTHER INCOME FOR YEAR IN WHICH THESE ADDITIONAL EXPENSES ARE INCURRED WILL BE REDUCED BY THE AMOUNT OF THE INCOME TAX CREDIT SHOWN.

**IF ANNUAL TAXABLE INCOME IS NEGATIVE, THE AMOUNT OF THE TAX LIABILITY IS YOUR TAX SHELTER BENEFIT.

against your other income and thus reduce the number of dollars paid out for income taxes. Here, the loss of $63 is actually worth $25 to you—your total income taxes will be less by that much because of owning this property for the year.

In addition, under current income taxes rules, you can charge against income certain other expenses in the year in which they have been incurred. At the time of purchase you spent money for mortgage loan fees (interest in advance), title insurance, and other costs. The $50 for prorations has already been recovered out of income during the year because it was for prepaid expenses. The total of $1,100 is deductible expense, increasing the first year's operating loss. The value of this is the tax rate (state and federal) times the loss.

Here we reduce income taxes by a further $440. This loss is only to be taken in the first year. Leaving for later the long-term aspects, let's state these returns in a form easier to use in comparison—percentages.

Yields. In this section we deal only with current income yields. The long-term results will be handled later.

On the previous sheet we determined the income would be enough to produce a surplus of $936 after all bills were paid, before income tax. Because we have a loss, there is also a tax shelter benefit of $25. The *net spendable* is an important figure because of its widespread use in real estate investment analysis.

For the first year we have an additional tax saving of $440 (for our tax bracket and one-time expenses). The total first-year spendable cash figure, $1,401, is important if we used some short-term borrowing for the cash needed; this sum is a source for repayment.

You are considering the investment for the long term and want to compare against alternative properties and alternative investments. What will you receive typically each year?

Compute the before-tax yield of cash as to down payment, not to total cash invested. You could do the latter, but the smaller figure generally is used because of the partial recovery of the closing costs in the first year. True, there is some remaining money at risk, but most investors prefer to make comparisons relative to different down payments at risk.

The most important yield is that on an after-tax basis. Here we have a yield of 5.34 percent *after* taxes. That compares favorably with savings accounts at 6 percent or even 7 percent *before* taxes. As pointed out before, the mortgages are being reduced each time a payment is made. As the rental income is the source of the funds

YIELDS

A. **ANNUAL**

NET ANNUAL BEFORE-TAX CASH FLOW $ _936_

INCOME TAX LIABILITY (DEDUCT IF TAXABLE
INCOME IS POSITIVE, OTHERWISE ADD.) _add_ $ _25_

NET SPENDABLE CASH AFTER TAX $ 961

B. **FIRST YEAR**

ADD INCOME TAX CREDIT FROM ADJUSTMENTS $ _440_

TOTAL SPENDABLE CASH FIRST YEAR* $1,401

*PRESUMES PROPERTY OWNED FOR FULL 12 MONTHS.

C. **TYPICAL ANNUAL RETURNS ON CASH INVESTED**

1. BEFORE INCOME TAX:

$ _936_ ÷ $_18,000_ X 100% = 5.2 %
NET ANNUAL BEFORE - CASH DOWN
TAX CASH FLOW PAYMENT

2. AFTER INCOME TAX:

$ _961_ ÷ $_18,000_ X 100% = 5.34%
NET SPENDABLE CASH DOWN
CASH AFTER-TAX PAYMENT

3. INCLUDING MORTGAGE REDUCTION:

NET SPENDABLE CASH AFTER-TAX $ _961_

MORTGAGE REDUCTIONS FIRST YEAR $_1,361_

TOTAL RETURN $2,322

$ _2,322_ ÷ $ _8,000_ X 100% = 12.9%
TOTAL RETURN CASH DOWN
PAYMENT

NOTE: YIELDS FOR SUBSEQUENT YEARS WILL NOT BE THE SAME IF THERE
IS A MORTGAGE NOR IF THE INCOME AND EXPENSES DO NOT
RETAIN THE SAME INITIAL RELATIONSHIP.

to make the mortgage payments, the reduction is a form of yield from the investment.

When we computed the interest expense, we also computed the figures needed for entry here. The sum of $1,142 and $219 is $1,361. We should consider this a return, however, only if we are confident that the property will ultimately sell for *not less* than we paid for it. Otherwise, the loss will cut into the equity provided by this mortgage reduction. Given that assumption, we now have a yield of 12.9 percent from current operations. If there is capital appreciation, the return will be greater.

We now have simulated the results from owning this apartment house. If we have no alternatives that will provide better than a 5.34 percent after-tax return of cash or 12.9 percent return including equity buildup, we will want to consider seriously making the purchase. Before we make up our minds, let's look at the long term.

Estimated results from resale. The investor in real estate expects, as a general rule, that the market value of the property will increase over time. If that gain is realized, it supplements the annual gain. In evaluating the opportunity, you should make some assumption concerning appreciation and reflect it in the statement of overall results.

Here we assumed 2 percent annual appreciation rate and recorded it in the fact sheet. We assume that the market value each year will be 2 percent greater than in the preceding year, so the increase is compounding. Referring now to our example, you can see that we have used a factor applied to the original purchase price to obtain the figure of $87,000 as an expected selling price. You certainly would not be wrong in using a straight 10 percent— 2 percent a year for ten years. The expected selling price at best is a rough estimate, however; many factors determine the ultimate value.

When you sell, there will be expenses to pay. The real estate commission amount is governed by the sales price; we originally felt that the usual 6 percent is the rate that likely will apply. If you can negotiate or make the sale yourself, the difference is a saving. The expected fix-up expense of $1,000 may turn out to be a different amount when the time comes; experience will guide you here. Then there is the prepayment penalty.

When gathering the data for this evaluation, we found that we would be subject to a penalty of 1 percent of the loan balance at payoff time. In this resale forecast we are assuming the purchaser will obtain new financing, thus resulting in a payoff of our loans.

We need to know what the loan balance would be at the end of five years.

Eight percent for twenty years will provide a balance-due factor of 875.2207 for each $1,000 of the original loan at the end of five years. By multiplying this factor by $54 we get $47,262 for the unpaid balance, for a prepayment penalty of $473 — making the total expenses to be deducted from the sales price $6,693. Gross cash proceeds are $80,307.

The mortgages also are to be paid off out of the proceeds. The first mortgage balance is already known — $47,262. For the second mortgage, the payment was stipulated and the amount does not amortize the debt in a specified term. We find a factor of 811.4309. Multiplying it by $7, we obtain a payoff amount of $5,680. If we do not sell the property and pay off the second mortgage prior to the due date, we will have to settle this debt anyway. After paying off the mortgages, we have net cash of $27,365.

Because this is a capital asset held long enough to qualify, the profit or gain will be taxed on a long-term basis. We can apply our regular income tax rate to half the gain *or* half the rate to all the gain. That is a generalization that would apply to the vast majority of taxpayers. Those in a tax bracket greater than 50 percent and with other capital gains and tax preference income may have to calculate their tax on a different basis, coming up with proportionately more tax to pay. In our example we have assumed none of that would apply. The first step is to calculate the taxable gain. This amount will depend on the way in which we have handled depreciation.

In the example, depreciation was figured on a straight-line basis. For the building it was $2,000 each year, for a five-year total of $10,000. For the equipment, depreciation will be complete in five years and will total $1,800. Because these amounts of depreciation have already been charged against income, we must reduce the book value or "basis" accordingly. The ending book value represents, in a sense, the *cost* of the property for use in computing how much we have gained by selling it. The difference between what we sell it for and this adjusted cost will be the gain or loss on the sale. Expenses incurred in connection with the sale are deductible, and we get the benefit of those costs when computing taxable amounts. Here we arrive at a $13,107 gain to be shared with income tax collectors.

If we had used accelerated depreciation, the foregoing computations might have been different. The rules are complex, however.

ESTIMATED RESULTS FROM RESALE

XPECTED SELLING PRICE:

$$\underset{\text{APPRECIATION FACTOR}}{1.104076} \times \underset{\text{PURCHASE PRICE}}{79,000} = \$87,000$$

ESS: SALES EXPENSE @ __6__ % COMMISSION = $ 5,220

FIX-UP EXPENSE $ 1,000

PREPAYMENT PENALTY $ 473

TOTAL EXPENSES $ 6,693

GROSS CASH PROCEEDS $ 80,307

ESS: FIRST MORTGAGE BALANCE $ 47,262

SECOND MORTGAGE BALANCE $ 5,680

TOTAL AMOUNT PAID OFF $ 52,942

NET CASH PROCEEDS FROM SALE $ 27,365

OMPUTATION OF LONG TERM TAXABLE GAIN:

BEGINNING BOOK VALUE (ORIGINAL COST) $ 79,000

LESS ACCRUED DEPRECIATION - BUILDING $ 10,000
                                - EQUIPMENT $ 1,800

TOTAL DEPRECIATION $ 11,800

ENDING BOOK VALUE $ 67,200

TAXABLE GAIN: GROSS CASH PROCEEDS $ 80,307

LESS ENDING BOOK VALUE $ 67,200

GAIN/LOSS ON SALE $ 13,107

NCOME TAX ON GAIN/LOSS:

$$\underset{\text{GAIN/LOSS ON SALE}}{13,107} \div 2 = \$ 6,554 \text{ TAXABLE AMOUNT.}$$

NCOME TAX LIABILITY = $ \underset{\text{TAXABLE}}{6,554} \times \underset{\text{RATE}}{40}$ % = $2,622

NET CASH PROCEEDS FROM SALE $ _27,36⁹_

LESS: INCOME TAX LIABILITY $ _2,622_

        CASH DOWN PAYMENT $ _18,000_

        MORTGAGE FEES AND TITLE INSURANCE
        LESS TAX CREDIT TAKEN PREVIOUSLY $ __660__

        TOTAL DEDUCTIONS $ _21,282_

NET GAIN AFTER TAX AND RETURN OF FUNDS INVESTED $ _6,083_

ADD ADJUSTED ANNUAL NET SPENDABLE CASH GAIN:

        $ _900_   X   _5_   = $ _4,500_
        ADJUSTED   YEARS HELD
        CASH GAIN

TOTAL AFTER-TAX GAIN FROM THIS INVESTMENT $ _10,583_

                            TOTAL YIELD

AVERAGE ANNUAL YIELD:

        $ _10,583_   ÷   _5_   = $ _2,117_
        TOTAL AFTER-TAX GAIN   YEARS   ANNUAL GAIN

        $ _2,117_   ÷ $ _19,100_ X 100% =   _11.1_%
        ANNUAL GAIN   CASH INVESTED   YIELD AFTE
                                                                          TAXES

COMPARISON WITH SAVINGS ACCOUNT:

        TOTAL AFTER-TAX GAIN FROM INVESTMENT $ _10,583_

        IF YOU DEPOSITED ORIGINAL CASH INVESTED
        TO EARN _6_ %, COMPOUNDED DAILY FOR
        _5_ YEARS IT WOULD HAVE GROWN TO

        $ _19,100_   X _1.349618_   = $ _25,778_
        CASH INVESTED   FACTOR

                              LESS DEPOSIT $ _19,100_

                              TOTAL EARNINGS $ _6,678_

        LESS INCOME TAX @ _40_%   = $ _2,671_

                NET AFTER-TAX EARNINGS $ _4,007_

                DIFFERENCE BETWEEN GAINS $ _6,576_

Recall, simply, that accelerated depreciation gives you larger amounts to be charged in the early years. On the other hand, if you sell the property before you have owned it—under current rules—at least 100 months, some of the accelerated depreciation may have to be charged back as current income, thus reducing the benefit. In given cases it will be worthwhile to use accelerated depreciation, but careful study is required to know just when. We have kept our example simple by using straight-line depreciation. In most cases this will produce the most satisfactory investment return.

How much of the gain must we share? In the example we have divided the gain by two. To this we apply the full, ordinary income tax rate to reach a tax amount of $2,622. This would take care of both state and federal taxes if our 40 percent rate is the correct total of the two rates. There is another consideration. If in the year we make the sale we have a substantial change in our other income, the estimated rate we chose when gathering data may not be usable. Tax rates apply to marginal income. The actual tax to be paid on the long-term gain from the sale of a capital asset will depend on rates applicable at the time the sale is made, your other income, and the way in which you computed depreciation. Notwithstanding these complexities, you can prepare forecasts along the lines illustrated. As long as you use the same assumptions as to income tax rates for each property analyzed, you will have a proper basis for comparison.

The next item to compute is the net gain *after* paying income taxes and recovering the investment.

Referring to the example, note the $660 for mortgage fees and other costs. Certain one-time expenses were deducted for tax purposes the first year. By way of the tax credit we recovered part of that money—$440, to be exact. The original amount was $1,100; we have recovered the "missing" $660. The original total closing or settlement costs were $1,150. What about the $50? We had to pay it at the time of purchase to reimburse the seller for fire insurance paid in advance; we recovered it out of income during the first year.

After getting our money back and paying income taxes on the gain, we have $6,083 in hand. This is only part of the gain, however. Because the interest expense will be less each year as the mortgage principal is reduced, even though income and expense remain in proportion, the dollars of gain in subsequent years, after income taxes, will be fewer. The tax shelter benefit might even be eliminated. When we add the annual income to the gain or resale, we must make an adjustment — we cannot just multiply the annual return by five. An arbitrary procedure is to take 90 percent of the annual amount and then multiply that figure by the number of years the property is owned. We have adjusted the $961 to an even $900 for simplicity. When this total of the expected annual return is added, we have a grand total after-tax gain of $10,583.

Total yield. We started out to determine what kind of overall return we could achieve by investing in this property. The best measure is the number of dollars you have after all obligations are settled. Here we have $10,583 in hand as well as all of the money we invested: the dollar return. All taxes are paid. To compare this gain with investments that employ different amounts of money, we need a percentage, obtained by dividing the cash invested into the net gain, expressed in annual terms, even though most of the gain was realized at the sale of the property.

We received, on the average, $2,117 each year ($10,583 here divided by five), on a total initial investment of $19,100. The return represents a yield of 11.1 percent per annum *after* taxes. We can use that figure to compare against other properties and even other types of investment for which an annual return has been computed allowing for the same considerations.

For example, if we had put $19,100 in a savings account that pays 6 percent compounded daily for the five-year holding period, it would have grown to $25,778. Of course, the interest earnings are subject to income tax as current income, hence at the full rate. When we deduct income tax and the deposit, the net gain is $4,007. The real estate investment, given the assumptions used in our computations, would provide $6,576 more.

So we are dollars ahead. What did we give up or contribute to earn this difference? We took a risk. The results could be quite different. There could be vacancies and unexpected expenses that would eliminate or reduce seriously the annual gain. At resale time we might have found that the market value had dropped substantially or that we could not find a buyer at any price. Finally, when we add up the number of hours devoted to the project and divide it into the dollars of gain, we may find that we worked for a ridiculously low hourly rate.

Analysis summary

The third step is to analyze carefully the results obtained for each property evaluated and reach a conclusion as to which one you

Date __4-25-7-__

PROPERTY ADDRESS	PRICE	CASH REQUIRED	AVERAGE INDICATED ECONOMIC VALUE	YIELD REQUIRED	NET ANNUAL SPENDABLE CASH	TAX SHELTER VALUE	ANNUAL YIELDS AFTER TAX	ANNUAL YIELDS INCLUDING MORTGAGE	HOLDING PERIOD	TOTAL AFTER TAX GAIN	AVERAGE ANNUAL YIELD
1234 Wistful Vista	79,000	19,150	84,100	9%	961	25	5.34	12.9	5	19,583	11.1%
1111 Gold St.	40,000	5,080	43,850	8%	392	176	9.8	23.4	5	5,916	24.74%
536 Mission St.	84,000	16,400	85,000	9%	765	200	5.1	8.2	5	7,455	9.09%

want to buy. Repeat the fact sheet and analysis worksheet procedures for each of several similar properties. From this work you
can take appropriate data to complete an investment analysis
summary. This summary will enable you more clearly to see which
property offers the best returns. After reaching your conclusion,
you can obtain the property. A word of caution: numbers can fail
to disclose pertinent factors. You would not want to decide on a
particular property solely on the basis of the yields or dollar calcula-
tions. Be certain your assumptions are reasonable and that you are
comparing comparable opportunities—apartment houses with
apartment houses and so on. You can use different size projects and
even different holding periods; you can vary the financing. This
type of investment is a long-term proposition offering very good
but *not* fantastic returns.

CHAPTER 4

Making
the
Offer

After considerable searching and extensive analysis we have decided to buy the property at 1234 Wistful Vista. We must prepare a formal offer, in writing, and be prepared to "sell" the seller on our proposal. There are several points to be kept in mind in this important phase, and they will be reviewed along with an illustration of a typical purchase contract.

Formulating the offer

The price we will offer is a good starting point. Going back to our analysis of each of the properties we have been considering, we find that we prefer 1234 Wistful Vista because it offers the greatest return on the funds we have available to invest. From the calculation of indicated economic values we know the offering price of $79,000 is below what we can pay. The cash flow analysis and computation of long-term gain were made on the basis of a purchase price of $79,000. Is that the amount we should offer?

Obviously the seller wants the highest price possible. If you offer $79,000 you will never know whether he would have taken less. One way to find out is to offer less. For our part, we want to obtain the best deal possible and certainly do not wish to pay more than we have to. If the prospective returns are good at $79,000 they will be even better at a lower purchase price. All of this points to an offer of something less than the asking price.

Possibly even more important than getting a reduced price is obtaining maximum financing. Perhaps we would prefer to borrow even more than the amounts we used in the analysis. If so, we want to redo the analysis on the new basis of financing.

In formulating the offer we want to ask for the best terms possible while leaving ourselves open if we don't succeed on all points. That is accomplished by making the offer "subject to" specified conditions.

Before setting into motion an action designed to result in purchase, you should have clearly in mind exactly how you want the offer to be framed. If you are using the services of a real estate broker you will be able to ask his advice on various terms. If he also represents the seller, he should be able to judge the acceptability of your ideas. If you use an attorney he will know how to frame the offer in legal terms to protect you, but he is not likely to be familiar with the market situation or the seller's position. How feasible is it for a lay investor to formulate an offer, write it up, and present it on his own?

The most conservative approach is to use a real estate broker and employ an attorney to draw up all the papers. Assuming both are competent, the job will be done in the best possible fashion. It will also cost the most as far as fees are concerned. As a general rule, the real estate broker does not charge a fee for drafting the offer, but the attorney does.

You might feel that an attorney's fee would be a small price to pay to save yourself grief. If you are dealing with an owner directly and not through a real estate broker, you might save the real estate commission; but, then again, you might not, and you will not have had the benefit of his financing contacts, market knowledge, advice, and expertise.

It is possible for you—on your own—to prepare an offer, present it to a seller yourself, have it accepted, and complete the purchase. Regardless of who is involved, you must make certain basic decisions with respect to the details of the offer. We will concentrate on those, leaving unresolved the question of using brokers and attorneys.

We need to formulate the offer and communicate it to the owner and/or his agent. This should be done in writing. It is probable that an oral contract either would be unenforceable because a written contract is required by law, or would be unsatisfactory because of misunderstandings due to the absense of written terms. The written offer may be called a "purchase contract," "contract of sale," or "deposit receipt." The terms will vary according to local custom and practice. We will use the term "purchase contract."

Purchase contract

The form reproduced on pages 96-97 has been created by the California Real Estate Association for use by its members. The blanks have been filled in to illustrate possible terms to be offered in purchasing the property we have been considering. In California it is customary to prepare four copies of the contract. When signed by all parties, the copies are distributed to buyer, seller, real estate broker, and, usually, the title insurance company or escrow agent. A reproduction may be used for a lender.

In this example, we have made certain assumptions concerning your use of the services of others. When a real estate broker takes a listing, he may also obtain a preliminary title report from the title insurance or abstract company. He may also obtain a pest control report, or the owner may already have done so. These reports will be of considerable use to all parties. If they are not obtained before the execution of a purchase contract, they will be afterwards. In our example, we are assuming, for instance, that the pest control report shows only minor damage and that the inspector will issue a report that the property meets the standard of state law after work costing less than $500 is performed. Further, we know from the preliminary title report that there are no special features of the record title to be handled in advance of the transfer of title when the deal is closed. As a general practice, the real estate broker will prepare the purchase contract after discussion with the parties. The buyer must know what he wants and communicate it to the person preparing the contract. The seller must be certain he understands the terms of the contract before he accepts the offer by signing the documents.

Read the form through carefully, then come back to the following description.

Deposit amount

This is sometimes called the "earnest" money. The buyer should make this amount as small as possible, because it will be tied up either until the offer is rejected and the deposit returned, or until the deal is closed and the money is applied to the purchase. The seller wants as large a deposit as possible. If he accepts, he does not want to find that the buyer has subsequently reneged and that he has no way of recovering whatever loss that has caused. The deposit is subject to forfeiture if the buyer does not proceed once the offer is accepted. The real estate broker may receive some part of a forfeited deposit. He has earned his commission when he brings buyer and seller together. He will want the deposit to be large enough so if there is a default it will be relatively easy to collect something for his efforts. This is covered in the form we are using. If you are dealing directly with the owner-seller he will want a deposit large enough to provide you with an incentive, faced with forfeiture, to complete the transaction.

Recall that you will need enough cash to cover the down payment and the closing or settlement costs. Many buyers consider the deposit made at the time the offer is drawn up to be simply an advance payment on the closing costs, and some real estate brokers make it a practice to ask for a deposit equal to the estimated amount required for such costs. As you can see, the actual amount for a given case is a negotiable one. Here we decided $1,000 was a good amount, one that would tell the seller we were serious. This is important, especially when we are asking the seller to reduce his price. The assumption is that we want the property on our terms and will do what we can to persuade the seller to accept.

Who should get the deposit? Ideally an escrow has been opened so that the deposit is placed in neutral hands. A real estate broker serves quite well as a holder of deposit funds when he is involved in the transaction. You may even find yourself making the deposit check payable to the seller. Unless you have reason not to trust the seller — in which case you shouldn't be trying to buy from him — there is nothing wrong with giving him the deposit. The risk you take, of course, is that it might be difficult to get your money back if he does not do his part in the transaction. You can ask a bank or an attorney to serve as a third party if none of the other alternatives appeals to you.

If you either postdate your check or ask the person who is to take care of the deposit not to cash it, then you probably have not given a valid deposit, and a seller might have grounds later for rescinding. On the other hand, two parties can agree on a course of action, and if the seller accepts a postdated check, knowing and acknowledging the conditions, there may be no problem.

We are going to try $77,000. There is no special reason for think-
ing the seller will take $2,000 less, but we know for sure that if he
will, we have saved $2,000. At worst, he can reject the offer; at
best, he can accept it.

It is customary to use both the legal and common description to
avoid a controversy later over which piece of property was intended.
The legal discription, exactly as it appears in the public record, will
be stated in the title company report. It may be copied from the
deed produced by the seller. If you use the latter source you should
take some action to confirm that the deed actually relates to the
physical premises you have been looking at. If the seller happens
to own more than one property and has several deeds lying around,
you will have to make sure you have the right one. Deeds do not
include street addresses.

You are cautioned against not using an escrow. Both buyer and
seller need the protection afforded by a competent escrow agent.

Balance of purchase price

The essence of our offer is this: we expect to be able to borrow
at least $54,000 on a first mortgage or trust deed basis from a
financial institution. This might be financing the seller has arranged
in advance, a source the real estate man has, or arrangments we
have made ourselves, preliminarily.

Before formulating the offer you should have some idea of how
the financing can be done. Even though the deal is subject to obtaining the loans stated, you do not want to include wild terms that
have little hope of being realized. We want the seller to take back a
second mortgage of $7,000. It is likely we were told the seller
would entertain such an idea. If the seller is not a candidate for a
second mortgage, we should have another source lined up. By
borrowing a total of $61,000 we will then have to put up in cash a
down payment of $16,000 plus the closing costs. It is presumed that
we know where this cash is coming from—at least in time to meet
the closing date. If the proposed purchaser fails to keep his part of
the bargain, most likely he will lose his deposit. Don't make offers
lightly unless you don't mind forfeiting money.

Although we believe at the time of making the offer we can
obtain the financing as stated, we want the seller to share the risk
that we might not. We do that by using the expression "subject to."
When the seller signs the purchase contract, he is agreeing, for
example, that he cannot hold us to the offer if it turns out that the
only first loan we can get is at 8.5 percent (or any other adverse

CALIFORNIA REAL ESTATE ASSOCIATION STANDARD FORM

Real Estate Purchase Contract and Receipt for Deposit

THIS IS MORE THAN A RECEIPT FOR MONEY. IT MAY BE A LEGALLY BINDING CONTRACT. READ IT CAREFULLY.

................Utopia.............................California,.........May.1.................. 19..7....

Received from.......John.A..and.Mary.B..Investor..
....herein called Buyer,

the sum of......--ONE.THOUSAND.DOLLARS.ONLY--..Dollars ($..1,000.00.....)

evidenced by cash ☐, personal check ☑, cashier's check ☐, or

as deposit on account of purchase price of ......--SEVENTY-SEVEN.THOUSAND.DOLLARS.ONLY--.......Dollars ($..77,000.00....)

for the purchase of property, situated in..........Utopia..............County of......Glory..........California, described as follows:

.....1234.Wistful.Vista,.Utopia,.legally.described.as.................................
.....Lot.4.in.Block.20,.as.designated.on.the.map.entitled..............................
....."Happy.Haven,.City.of.Utopia,.County.of.Glory,.State.of...........................
.....California,".filed.in.the.office.of.the.Recorder.of.the.County......................
.....of.Glory.on.August.10,.1960,.in.Volume.3.of.Maps,.at.page.9........................

Buyer will deposit in escrow with.......ABCDE.Insurance.and.Trust.Company..

the balance of purchase price as follows:.....Subject.to:.(1).Buyer.obtaining.a.first.loan.secured.by.this...
..property.of.not.less.than.$54,000.at.interest.not.more.than.8%.plus.loan.fees.....
..of.not.more.than.1%.of.loan.with.a.prepayment.penalty.not.greater.than.1%.of.......
..unpaid.balance.for.a.term.of.not.less.than.20.years;...(2).Second.deed.of.trust...
..to.seller.for.not.less.than.$7,000.with.interest.at.9%,.payable.$70.per.month,......
..principal.and.interest,.combined.purchase,.right.and.unpaid.balance.due.on.June.30,.1980...

.....covenants,.easements.and.restrictions.shown.in...................................
.....ABCDE.Insurance.and.Trust.Company.preliminary.report.#48756.......................

Seller shall furnish to Buyer at.........Buyer's............expense a standard California Land Title Association policy insuring title in Buyer subject only
to liens, encumbrances, easements, restrictions, rights and conditions of record as set forth above. If Seller fails to deliver title as herein provided, Buyer at his option may terminate this agreement and any deposit shall thereupon be returned to him.......................XXX..................................

2. Property taxes, premiums on insurance acceptable to Buyer, rents, interest, and..............................(Insert in blank any other items of income or expense to be prorated) shall be

provided as of (date and acknowledgement) (2).....Close.of.escrow.............................(Strike (1) if (2) is used).The amount of any

bond or assessment which is a lien shall be ☒paid☒ (Strike one) by...seller.................Seller shall pay cost of revenue stamps on deed.

3. Possession shall be delivered to Buyer (Strike inapplicable alternatives) (a) on close of escrow, or ☒☒☒☒☒☒☒☒☒☒☒☒☒☒☒☒☒☒☒☒☒☒☒☒☒☒☒☒☒☒☒☒

(c)...XXX...

4. Escrow instructions signed by Buyer and Seller shall be delivered to the escrow holder within.......14.......days from the Seller's acceptance hereof and shall

provide for closing within.......30.......days from the opening of escrow, subject to written extensions signed by Buyer and Seller.

5. Unless otherwise designated in the escrow instructions of Buyer, title shall vest as follows:

.....John.A..Investor.and.Mary.B..Investor,.his.wife,.as.joint.tenants................

(THE MANNER OF TAKING TITLE MAY HAVE SIGNIFICANT LEGAL AND TAX CONSEQUENCES. THEREFORE, GIVE THIS MATTER SERIOUS CONSIDERATION.)

6. If the improvements on the property are destroyed or materially damaged prior to close of escrow, then, on demand by Buyer, any deposit made by Buyer shall be returned to him and this contract thereupon shall terminate.

7. If Buyer fails to complete said purchase as herein provided by reason of any default of Buyer, Seller shall be released from his obligation to sell and may proceed against Buyer upon any claim or remedy which he may have in law or equity; provided, however, that by placing their initials here _____ Buyer and Seller agree that it would be impractical or extremely difficult to fix actual damages in case of Buyer's default, that the amount of the deposit is a reasonable estimate of the damages, and that Seller shall retain the deposit as his sole right to damages.

8. Buyer's signature hereon constitutes an offer to Seller to purchase the real estate described above. Unless acceptance hereof is signed by Seller and the signed copy delivered to Buyer, either in person or by mail to the address shown below, within ___three___ days hereof, this offer shall be deemed revoked and the deposit shall be returned to Buyer.

9. Other terms and conditions: (Set forth any terms and conditions of a factual nature applicable to this sale, such as financing, prior sale of other property, the matter of structural pest control inspection, repairs and personal property to be included in sale.)

___This offer is subject to Seller paying the costs of repairs indicated by a___
___structural pest control inspection report but not to exceed $500. Seller___
___to provide a bill of sale for all items of personal property of his ownership___
___currently at the premises, the consideration for which is included in the___
___purchase price___

10. Time is of the essence of this contract.

Real Estate Broker ___I.M. Realtor, Inc.___ By ___I.M. Realtor___

Address ___321 Main St., Utopia, CA___ Telephone ___765-4321___

The undersigned Buyer offers and agrees to buy the above described property on the terms and conditions above stated acknowledges receipt of a copy hereof.

Dated ___May 1, 197-___

Address ___220 Angus Crescent, Utopia, CA___ ___John H. Investor___

Telephone ___123-4567___ ___Mary B. Investor___

Buyer ___

ACCEPTANCE

The undersigned Seller accepts the foregoing offer and agrees to sell the property described thereon on the terms and conditions therein set forth.
The undersigned Seller has employed the Broker above named and for Broker's services agrees to pay Broker, as a commission, the sum of ___
___Forty-Five Hundred --- ___ Dollars ($ ___4500.00___) payable as follows: (a) On recordation of the deed or other evidence of title, or (b) if completion of sale is prevented by default of Seller, upon Seller's default, or (c) if completion of sale is prevented by default of Buyer, only if and when Seller collects the damages from Buyer, by suit or otherwise, and then in an amount not to exceed one half that portion of the damages collected after first deducting title and escrow expenses and the expenses of collection, if any.

The undersigned acknowledges receipt of a copy hereof and authorizes Broker to deliver a signed copy of it to Buyer.

Dated ___

Address ___

Telephone ___ Seller ___

Broker consents to the foregoing.

Dated ___ Broker ___

A REAL ESTATE BROKER IS THE PERSON QUALIFIED TO ADVISE ON REAL ESTATE. IF YOU DESIRE LEGAL ADVICE CONSULT YOUR ATTORNEY.

THIS STANDARDIZED DOCUMENT FOR USE IN SIMPLE TRANSACTIONS HAS BEEN APPROVED BY THE CALIFORNIA REAL ESTATE ASSOCIATION AND THE STATE BAR OF CALIFORNIA IN FORM ONLY. NO REPRESENTATION IS MADE AS TO THE LEGAL VALIDITY OF ANY PROVISION OR THE ADEQUACY OF ANY PROVISION IN ANY SPECIFIC TRANSACTION. IT SHOULD NOT BE USED IN COMPLEX TRANSACTIONS OR WITH EXTENSIVE RIDERS OR ADDITIONS.

Copyright 1967 by California Real Estate Association

FORM NCR-D

variation from the terms stated in the offer). You might wonder if this provides a loophole for the buyer to use to back out if he changes his mind. It probably does. Some sellers might ask that the offer include a provision such as: "buyer to use all diligence in arranging financing." Then, if the buyer backs down and it can be shown he really could have obtained financing on the terms stated, presumably the seller would be sustained in keeping the deposit.

Title

No title is entirely clear. At a minimum, the property is subject to current taxes, which until paid are a lien against the property. Frequently there are easements for utility companies. There may have been covenants and restrictions with respect to the use of the land recorded when the ground was originally subdivided. This is another reason for obtaining a preliminary title report whenever possible. The buyer, however, is protected by providing in the purchase contract that he is agreeable only to certain "clouds" on the title. To the extent there are other liens, such as mortgages or trust deeds, the seller will have to satisfy them as a part of completing his side of the transaction. Otherwise he cannot pass "clear" title. In our example, we don't know what loans are on the property before the sale and we don't care. The seller is going to pay them off, probably out of the proceeds of the sale.

Title insurance

The cost of title insurance is negotiable between the buyer and seller. By custom — in California, for example — for property located in the southern half of the state, the seller pays; in the northern half, the buyer; and in the middle of the state, they share this expense. Then again we find — in new residential subdivisions, for example — the developer-seller pays the cost.

The owner of property must pay certain items in advance, such as property taxes, insurance premiums, and perhaps interest. Adjustments will be needed between the buyer and seller as of the date the deal is closed. We refer to that as the "close of escrow," which will ordinarily be the date on which the deed, transferring title, is recorded. Rents are invariably payable in advance so the seller should have some funds to be applied in the future, and these should be passed to the new owner. The customary basis for these adjustments is proration. For example, the property taxes are proportioned at so much a month, or day; the time period between closing and the date the taxes have been paid is used to determine how much is owing to the other party. In some cases money is due the seller because he paid items in advance. In others, where payment has been deferred and the new owner will have to pay the bill, a charge is made against the seller for his proportionate share. The details of these computations are set forth in the statement of the transaction prepared by the escrow agent.

The total amount of credit or charge will be governed largely by the time of the year the sale is made. If we assume a December 31 date and payment of property taxes by the seller for only the first half year, no adjustment would be needed. If all tenants had paid one month's rent in advance, the total would be credited to the buyer. As a consequence, the cash required by the buyer may be less than otherwise expected.

In order to finance the cost of improvements a municipality may float a bond issue and charge the repayment to the property owners whose property has been improved. This may be for street lighting, water or sewer systems, or street paving. You may insist that a seller pay off this obligation and base your offering price accordingly. On the other hand, you may reduce the price and agree to assume the indebtedness. Your decision is reflected here.

A levy is made now by some states on transactions involving transfer of title. Until 1968, the federal government required that documentary stamps be applied to all deeds on the basis of $0.55 per $500 of value of equity transferred. Many states have continued on the same basis from the time the federal government relinquished this taxation. By custom the cost is borne by the seller in most localities.

The normal arrangement is for the buyer to obtain possession of the property as of the date the escrow is closed.

The escrow or closing agent cannot proceed until instructions from the parties have been received; some time thereafter must be allowed for the work to be performed. If necessary, this time provision (and others) is subject to extension by agreement of the parties or on the authority of the real estate agent. The most important time provision, however, is that for the close of the escrow relative to the acceptance of the offer. This should be stated clearly in the purchase contract. Enough time must be allowed for the financing and so on to be arranged. The seller, of course, will want this money as soon as he can get it. Thirty days is often not too long a time in which to do whatever has to be done.

The buyer should give careful thought to vesting of title and obtain legal counsel if necessary. In our example, we have shown "joint tenants" as a typical way in which a buyer takes title where it is possible to do so.

Until title passes, the seller retains the insurable interest. No action should be taken with respect to changing fire insurance until the escrow is closed. Meanwhile, a buyer may choose to obtain insurance, but it is unlikely that he will be able to show an insurable interest prior to the date when title passes, and therefore he would not be able to collect if a loss occurs. Unless you suffer the loss you do not have an insurable interest. Of course, if the property is substantially damaged or destroyed, the buyer may rescind the contract and get his deposit back, at his option.

You will recall that the purpose of the deposit is primarily to protect the seller against loss due to nonperformance of the prospective buyer. When the seller signs a purchase contract, he cannot realistically continue trying to sell the property to someone else. So, during the time it takes the buyer to come up with the funds, the seller has to wait. If the deal falls through because of inaction on the part of the buyer, the buyer should have to pay damages to the seller. The measure of damages is difficult to make. If in fact the seller could not have obtained another buyer in the meantime, it could be argued that the seller had not suffered any damages at all. The parties can agree—and this is customary—that the amount of the deposit is a fair measure of damages and will be forfeit if default by the buyer occurs. If the seller defaults, the buyer would have ordinary legal remedies for damages by bringing a law suit.

Time for acceptance

From a practical point of view, as well as the legal requirement, there must be a time limit on the offer. It is automaticaly void or revoked if not accepted by the time stated in the contract. There are many legal niceties to refer to if there is an argument over whether the offer was accepted within the time, or in the manner prescribed by the contract or law. For our purposes, the seller either signs within the time limit or rejects. As a practical matter, if the seller doesn't care much for your proposal he will let you know, directly or through the intermediary, what he would like instead. In effect, the seller now makes a counter offer. In these circumstances, either the original offer is modified on its face, with the parties intialing appropriately, or you start all over with a new contract document. It is common practice to give the seller only a short time in which to make up his mind. In our example, we use the customary three days.

Other terms

In areas where termite infestation is common, it is customery to have property inspected by a licensed pest-control inspector who prepares a report showing how the building measures up to the standard set forth in the applicable state law. The parties are free to agree on who will pay for the work to be done if the report specifies corrective action. Lenders often make loans subject to the completion of such work. Buyers and sellers not subject to outside lenders' requirements are free to buy and sell on an "as is" basis. It is still a good idea to obtain a termite report and if there is a significant problem, it can be reflected in the price. If the buyer suspects an earth movement or other structural problem, he should ask for an appropriate inspection and make the offer subject to resolving whatever problems are identified. In addition to regular soil inspection services there are structural inspection services available. Particularly for older properties, it would be prudent for the investor to spend a few dollars (perhaps $100) to obtain an expert's opinion. This, of course, either would be done before the offer is prepared, or the offer would allow for the prospective consequences of such an inspection.

As a general rule, it is customary for the buyer to pay for inspections and for the seller to pay for the work to be done.

For applicances and other equipment not considered a part of the structure, there should be a bill of sale to establish transfer of title and value or cost. In practice, this step is often ignored. The bill of sale can be set forth as a straight statement on a piece of paper; blank printed forms can be purchased at stationery stores.

At this point in the purchase contract, the name and address of the broker are recorded simply as information. Technically, the broker is not a party to the contract; he has been serving as an agent for one or both of the principals. He may be a party to a contract between the seller and himself.

The buyer's signature is important. The date here starts the time running for the seller's acceptance and should be clearly stated. Sometimes even the time of day is included. To avoid possible legal entanglements, it is best that all buyers sign and the signatures be in the same form as identified at the top of the contract. The same form should also be used for vesting title.

Acceptance

As a general rule, the commission payable to the broker will be spelled out (as in our example), disclosing the amount. If the seller and broker wish to keep that information confidential, they can do so by preparing a separate contract. If that is the case, the seller would simply accept the offer and cross out any reference to the payment to the broker.

By signing the contract the seller acknowledges receipt of the deposit and agrees to the terms and conditions stated. When this is handled by the real estate agent, a signed copy will be returned to the seller and a copy given to the buyer. Now the process of completing the transaction begins.

It is probably a rare event when the original offer is accepted exactly as made and without changes. For simplicity, we will assume in our example that the seller does agree, and will conclude the transaction accordingly. You should be prepared, however, for much bargaining and negotiation. If you are not a good face-to-face negotiator, you should use the services of an agent, whether a real estate person or an attorney.

We have prepared our offer to provide for the most advantageous terms from our point of view. It should be no surprise, however, that the seller may have other ideas. When we learn what terms are acceptable to the seller, we may need to reevaluate the deal.

If the change in terms will not affect basically the financial returns, we will not need to do any refiguring. On the other hand, for a different price and/or financing arrangements, we should go back to the analysis and work out the results using the new figures. Then, and only then, can we determine whether we should accept the counter offer. It may be better to consider one of the other properties we analyzed before but did not consider to be the number-one opportunity. We can maximize our return from the effort expended on the evaluation only by using the analyses and comparing against a new set of figures for the seller's offer. Avoid making any decision solely on the basis of emotion.

After analyzing several pieces of property, we have narrowed our interest to the one we think is best. We have obtained as much advance information as possible, perhaps even an inspection report and preliminary title report. We have been working with a realtor who has done a professional job in getting information, lining up financing, and persuading the seller to accept the offer we put together. We now have a signed and accepted purchase contract.

CHAPTER 5

Closing the Deal

You and the seller have agreed on the terms and signed the purchase contract; you have put up your earnest money or deposit.
You both now need an independent third party to do all the things
necessary to complete the transaction on the terms agreed upon
and to protect the rights of all parties involved. As the buyer, you
will need to come up with the balance of the money; the seller will
have to execute a deed that will be satisfactory. Once documents
are prepared and recorded, money is available, and keys are turned
over, the buyer takes possession, makes contact with the tenants,
and is then a landlord.

We have assumed the real estate broker opened an escrow with a
title insurance company and obtained the preliminary title report.
This is not always done in advance and in fact is more frequently
done following the signing of the purchase agreement by buyer and
seller. The buyer's deposit is normally placed in escrow.

In sections of the country where title insurance companies do not also provide escrow service, this service is provided by attorneys. It is commonplace for the buyer to retain an attorney who will prepare all the papers, obtain an abstract of title, handle the money, deal with the seller's attorney, and see that the deed is recorded. Although, in theory, a buyer can do all of these things himself, he is much wiser to use the services of professionals; the cost is minor indeed, especially when compared to the cost when things go wrong.

There will be one or two things for the buyer to do, aided by his real estate broker, but most of the activity will involve the escrow agent's following the buyer's and seller's instructions.

Opening the escrow

As indicated, the practice in most areas is to have the title to the property searched or abstracted to determine not only who has title but what liens, encumbrances, easements, or other "clouds" may be on the title. For simplicity, we will use the procedure followed by title insurance companies, including escrow services; but in doing so we do not mean to slight abstractors and abstract companies. For all practical purposes the process is the same. When an escrow is opened a preliminary title report is ordered. This report will show the manner in which the title stands, a brief comment on encumbrances, and a sketch of the parcel of land showing survey indicators. But there may be a problem. You have looked at the property and are certainly aware of its address—1234 Wistful Vista. You recall we said that the legal description does not include the street address. How can you be sure that the legal description used on the purchase contract, and later to be used on the deed, actually represents the property you think you are buying?

As you look at the sketch on a copy of the title company's preliminary report, and then compare it with the property as you stand on the street in front of it, you ordinarily will not be able to confirm that they are one and the same. If you look for the surveyor's monuments, don't expect them to be easy to find. You have a nagging feeling that although the documents suggest lot four in block twenty Happy Haven, and 1234 Wistful Vista are one and the same, perhaps they are not. Are you about to obtain title to some other property? When the documents are recorded, you will have title to the property represented by the legal description on the documents, and no other, regardless of the agreement between the parties. Correcting this kind of mistake will cost money.

Even if the legal description is in order and you are in fact getting the' property you think you are getting, there is another question. Where are the lot lines and property boundaries? There are fences, perhaps, but what does that prove? It may prove that the guy who put up the fence didn't know what he was doing. To find a way to solve these problems, you hire a land surveyor.

The surveyor will take the legal description, obtain official survey data for the area, and go to 1234 Wistful Vista. His job is to mark off on the ground the boundaries of the property in such a way that these boundaries can be compared with the legal description to be used on the deed. If he finds an inconsistency between the two descriptions, he will soon let you know. He will also determine where the lot line is and confirm whether the fencing is in order. Depending on how complex the survey is, the cost will range from $100 on up—well worth it if you avoid more costly trouble later. When you buy a car, do you not verify by visual inspection that the serial number on the vehicle matches the title document you receive from the seller? This is the equivalent of confirming the physical location of the property against the legal description, except it will ordinarily take a land surveyor to do the job for you.

car serial no.

Clouds on the title

A primary reason for obtaining a preliminary report is to determine whether the seller can in fact produce a marketable title. This may be the time the seller learns he has a problem. Perhaps there is some unsatisfied debt still standing against the property. It might be his, or it may have been the previous owner's. If the current owner did not obtain a title search at the time be bought the property, he may have taken over an unsatisfied obligation. That will have to be taken care of by the seller before he can pass clear title and get his hands on your money.

If there are title defects, ordinarily the real estate broker or escrow agent will contact the seller and let him know about them. Of course, if it will take a lot of time to clear the title and if the time is important, the purchaser can decide against going ahead with the deal.

The underlying law and practice is that interests in property are established by "recording"—making a part of the public record—a document such as a mortgage, deed, judgment, or contract. In the case of a mortgage, for example, the original lien or encumbrance will be recorded at the time it is originally executed and the money lent. When the debt is paid off, a satisfaction or release should then be recorded to show that the property is no longer subject to the debt because the debt has been settled. All of these documents are recorded in chronological order in the public records office.

An abstractor or title searcher literally searches the public records for any and all filings pertinent to the legal description you started with. He then prepares a copy or note of what he finds. When this is all put together it is called an "abstract" or "title search." Some title insurance companies obtain copies of all filings each day and sort them out, first rejecting any that have nothing to do with property. The remainder then are noted in records by property description. This makes it much easier to prepare a title report when the time comes.

But even with microfilm and other automated processes, title searchers are human, and humans can make mistakes. Assume you have gone through the process of buying the property and a title search was made and a deed recorded transferring title to you. Everyone assumes all is in order. Later you decide to sell and another title search is made that uncovers an unsatisfied mortgage in addition to the ones you know about. Who is responsible? If you had the foresight to purchase title insurance, the title insurance company would be faced with paying the cost of whatever was necessary to clear the title. That could even involve paying off the amount of the debt.

When you buy title insurance you transfer the risk or uncertainty of loss to the insurance company. There is one difference, however: the premium is paid only once and the protection stands for as long as you own the property.

There also may be some legal encumbrances that are not required to be recorded in the public record. Unless the title insurance policy provides otherwise, these would not be covered. This is not a problem in the vast majority of transactions. Further, the title insurance may protect only the lender, or may be written to cover both lender and owner. As a general rule, financial institutions require title insurance; private lenders may not, but they certainly should have it. In some areas a title insurance company automatically provides both escrow service and title insurance; in others, the services are separate and are charged for separately. You will not have any trouble finding out the local practice. Ask a real estate broker, banker, or attorney who specializes in real estate, or a title company.

Completing the financing

The seller has agreed to take part of his price in the form of a second mortgage. A second mortgage is easily handled. Those documents will be prepared by the real estate broker, the title company or escrow agent, or the attorney handling the paper work. We know how much the first mortgage is to be, so now we go to the lender.

As a part of the negotiations leading up to the signing of the purchase agreement, either we as prospective buyers, or the real estate broker, had discussed the loan with a financial institution. Sometimes a real estate broker will obtain a commitment from a lender that it will make a loan on a specific property if the buyer qualifies. These are all preliminary steps.

If we have not already done so, now is the time to prepare a financial statement and submit it to the lender. We would show as part of our assets the deposit of $1,000 made on the property. The lender would obtain a credit report on us and do what is necessary to confirm the information we provided, including verifying the bank balances and other assets and liabilities shown on the financial statement. We probably also ought to show the lender our analysis of the property and therefore show clearly why the lender can expect to get his money back.

The lender will now obtain an appraisal of the property, if he has not done so already. Lenders employ professional appraisers either on contract or as employees. As a general rule, you will not be told what the appraised value is. If the lender agrees to make the loan for the amount requested, you can assume that the property was appraised for enough. Although the ratio of loan to appraised value used by lenders will fluctuate from time to time, the loan officer will probably give you some indication of the ratio he is working with at the time. Assume for the kind of property we are expecting to buy, the lender we are dealing with uses a figure of 75 percent. This will mean that for each $100 of appraised value—appraised by the *lender,* not the buyer or seller—he will lend $75. We need $54,000. We would not have made the offer without obtaining at least some tentative indication from a lender that we can raise the necessary amount. Lenders generally will not obtain an appraisal and firm up the loan amount before an offer has been made and accepted. The loan ratio is also applied to the purchase price; regardless of the price agreed to by the parties, the lender's loan will not exceed 75 percent of the appraised value or the purchase price, whichever is smaller.

If, after getting an appraisal and evaluating our loan application, the loan officer says he will grant the $54,000, we are all set— except for the terms. Those will be checked shortly. What if he says he will lend only $50,000? This would probably mean that the appraised value was less than $72,000. (75 percent of $72,000 equals $54,000.) But we have some protection. We offered to buy *subject to* certain conditions including obtaining a first loan for $54,000. It was also subject to interest rate, term, and loan fee conditions. If one or more conditions cannot be met, we do not have to go ahead with the purchase. Or course, we are free to go ahead anyway, but those purchase contract provisos give us a chance to take another look and back away if we want to.

We have assumed the lender was agreeable to our use of secondary financing by way of a second mortgage from the seller. It is customary to provide the banker with a copy of the purchase contract at the time of applying for the loan so that he is aware of the terms of the purchase agreement. He will also need a copy of the title report.

We can always go to another lender if we fail to get what we need from the first one. Not all lenders take the same position, and it is quite possible to get a loan from another lender if we are turned down initially. However, this takes time, and we agreed to take care of our part of the bargain within a time limit stipulated in the contract. To avoid forfeiting the deposit we will have to show that we tried, in good faith, to obtain the financing stated. It is important to make all possible preliminary arrangements for financing before making an offer to buy contingent upon loans.

We will assume that the loan for $54,000 has been approved. The lender will prepare the mortgage loan agreement and promissory note and either have us sign them at the lender's office or forward them to the escrow agent's office, where we will sign them. Prior to this time, we have an important decision to make, however. In what form do we want to take title?

Form of title

You will want to consult with your attorney before making a final decision on this point. The following comments are offered to assist you in gaining an understanding of what is involved so you can consider the matter more intelligently. The entity to which title is to be passed will also be the same entity borrowing the money. Your lender will have something to say about the form of the entity. What are the possibilities?

In the majority of cases relevant to this book, the purchase is made by a husband and wife. In most states the purchase would be made either as community property or in joint tenancy. The law is quite specific on this point in every state and you may not have this choice. The legal standing of the title is governed in large part by the wording on the deed and other documents. If you choose to take title in joint tenancy, the deed in particular would read: John A. Investor and Mary B. Investor, as joint tenants. In some areas the expression "with right of survivorship" is added; it is probably unnecessary.

The alternative: John A. Investor and Mary B. Investor, his wife, as community property.

What is the difference? As joint tenants, the survivor automatically acquires 100 percent interest in the property. As community property, the interest of the surviving spouse is subject to the laws of the jurisdiction and the last will and testament of the decedent. Some say that under joint tenancy, probating the estate can be avoided, but as community property, probate may be necessary. There may be other reasons, in both situations, for probating to be required.

Remember, consultation with your attorney in advance is a good idea before deciding this important matter. There are also some important income tax considerations as well as estate and inheritance tax angles.

While both parties are living, both must sign a deed if title is to be transferred. Under both forms, each has an undivided half interest in the property. This presumes that the property was purchased with community-property funds. Property acquired before marriage would have title vested in one party. Subsequent to marriage the property may continue to be held as separate property, but that status might be affected by community-property laws and the manner in which earnings from the property were handled.

For property held in joint tenancy by other than husband and wife, the extent of the individual interests would also be equal in the absence of an agreement to the contrary. Upon the death of a joint tenant, the survivors automatically acquire the interest of the decedent. On the death of a spouse, the simple filing of a "termination of joint tenancy" supported by a death certificate is frequently all that is required to clear title for transfer. In our example, we are taking title as joint tenants.

It is imperative that all documents relating to the title be uniform in the manner in which the parties are designated. The escrow agency checks for this and a lender will be very specific. This uniformity includes insurance.

Insurance

We will have an asset to protect, and even if the lender were not standing at our elbow, we would want to have, as a minimum, fire insurance on the building and some liability coverage against loss arising from accidents connected with the property.

Fire. The lender will require that the amount of fire insurance be at least equal to the unpaid balance of the loan. The second mortgagee will also want protection. Both will want their names to appear on the policy.

Basic property insurance policies cover the actual cash value of the property. This value, arrived at when the loss occurs, is the current replacement cost, less depreciation. This is the maximum amount payable. The cost to repair will always be greater than the actual cash value unless the damaged property is new. The value of the land is not included; land cannot be damaged by the perils we insure the building for, so we have to have a separate structure value. All of this means, for example, if the roof is damaged, we will have to add our own funds to the insurance settlement to pay for the repairs. Insurance is not designed to afford a profit. If written properly, it is to put us back in the position we were in the moment before the loss — no better, no worse.

The insurance industry has found a way around this problem by offering *replacement-cost* coverage, sometimes called *depreciation* insurance. By agreeing to buy an amount of insurance that is related to the entire replacement-cost value of the building, we can have the benefit of replacement-cost coverage for our apartment house. That will mean that in the event of a loss, if our coverage amount is in accord with our agreement, depreciation will not be deducted and the insurance settlement will be equal to the repair bill.

As the value of the structure changes with time we will want to make sure we adjust the amount of the policy. This is obviously much more important if replacement costs are increasing rather than decreasing. Going on our own figures for the property we want to buy, we would consider buying a policy based on a replacement cost of $72,000. In some areas this coverage is available if the insured buys not less than 80 percent of the replacement cost; in others, 100 percent is required. You will be discussing all of this with your insurance agent or broker and he can tell you what the situation is. In our example, if we bought a policy for $72,000 we would have enough to satisfy both lenders, but even more important, for any losses up to complete destruction, the insurance settlement would take care of the entire cost of repairs. We could even get a new building out of it.

Perils. The minimum coverage is fire and extended coverage endorsement; the latter is a group of perils, such as windstorm, explosion, and riot. Most lenders will settle for the minimum — "Fire and ECE," as it is called. You should seriously consider buying a policy containing additional perils, such as water damage and vandalism. You also should have coverage on whatever personal property you own, such as equipment. But the most important coverage of all is liability insurance.

Liability. If someone other than your employee is hurt on the premises, you may be sued for damages. Initially, the liability coverage will provide the cost of legal services to defend you. In fact, if the claim alleges that you were negligent and were the person responsible for the injury or damage, the insurance company will hire the attorney and undertake your defense at no cost to you. If there is a settlement, in or out of court, the company will pay the amount, up to the amount of insurance. How much liability insurance should you buy? You can never have too much, because you cannot know in advance how big the claim will be. The more the claimant thinks you have in assets—or the more serious his injuries—the greater will be his claim. The amount of coverage is somewhat dependent on the extent of the assets you have to protect. But don't be misled into thinking that if your net worth is modest you do not need much insurance. Without enough insurance you could spend the rest of your life working to pay the person you injured. And bankruptcy is not likely to get you out from under. Liability limits of, say, $300,000 are considered modest and limits of $1 million are not unusual. Talk to your insurance man.

Perhaps you are not enthusiastic about buying all these policies. Would it be more palatable if all you needed came in one policy and at a reduced cost? Most property and casualty (to distinguish them from life) insurance companies offer a package policy for apartments. You can get one for your home, too. It covers the building, equipment, rents and liability exposures. If there is a fire or explosion and some of the tenants cannot continue to occupy the property, during the time the repairs are being made your loss of rents is covered by the rental income coverage of the policy. There is a choice of perils. A package like this is the best way to insure your investment.

If you are concerned about earthquake or landslide or flood

damage, you may also be able to insure against those kinds of losses. They are not covered by the standard policy, but coverage is available. If you have a resident manager and want to cover the burglary or robbery exposure, policies are available. If you employ someone, you may need workmen's compensation coverage to take care of injuries incurred on the job. If you need to protect against the dishonesty of your employees, you can buy a fidelity bond.

The lender will require the escrow agent to see that proper insurance is in force before the escrow can be closed and the loan proceeds given to the seller. You will want to arrange for the original policy and a copy for the second mortgagee to be delivered to the escrow company in time. The policy, regardless of the type of coverage, is to be endorsed to show that the first and second mortgages have an interest in the subject insured. They are called *loss payees*.

When the insurance company prepares a loss draft or check, it will make it payable first to the named insured and also to those entities included in the policy as loss payees. The check or draft will be sent to the insured. He will not be able to negotiate it without the endorsement of the loss payees. This is the way in which lenders can protect themselves. If repairs are to be made the lender can wait until they are completed before endorsing it. If the property is not going to be repaired, the lenders can insist that the proceeds of the loss be applied first to the outstanding loan balances. To avoid problems, the lender will insist, and the escrow agent will check, that the insured's name on the policy be exactly the same as on the mortgage or trust deed documents and that the loss payee's name be exactly as designated by the lender.

The final step for the buyer to take is that of signing the escrow instructions. A copy of this document is reproduced on pages 114-15.

Escrow instructions

The escrow company is acting as the agent of all the parties. As the agent of you, the buyer, the escrow company will require written instructions; forms are provided for this purpose. They may be prepared either by the real estate broker, by the escrow agent, or by you. The original is filed with the escrow company. You will receive in return a copy signed by the escrow agent. The seller also is required to specify his instructions to the escrow agent. The form reproduced in this book can serve both buyers and sellers, but we have illustrated only the buyer's instructions.

The objective of the instructions is to give the escrow agent the terms of the agreement between buyer and seller and set forth the conditions under which the escrow agent can release the funds to the seller and other parties. Once the funds are placed in escrow, the person handling the transaction must be sure that all the documents required are in order and all parties have performed all acts required by the escrow instructions before making payments from the escrow account. Probably the most important step is to have the deed and loan documents properly recorded, protecting both buyer and lender. When that is done, the funds can be released safely to the seller.

Buyer's instructions. Refer now to the buyer's instructions (page 118). Note that the source of the borrowed funds is stated. When the loan is approved the lender will send the proceeds, together with the note and deed of trust (or mortgage papers), to the escrow agent. The lender will stipulate that the money is to be used only after the title to the property is vested in the name of the borrower and the loan security document is recorded as a first lien against the property. Further, the title insurance policy ordinarily will apply to the lender as well as to the borrower, and the protection must be effective with the disbursement of the loan moneys.

The timing of the acts is very important. Several things must take place simultaneously and all parties must be protected. It is apparent that an independent entity, rather than one of the parties involved, can handle these matters best.

In our example, the seller is providing part of the financing. The second trust deed may be prepared by the escrow agent or by the seller or his attorney. The escrow agent has the obligation of seeing that all the documents requiring execution by the buyers be properly signed and ultimately recorded. No particular action will be needed by the seller beyond seeing that the appropriate documents are delivered to the escrow agent.

Although deposits or earnest money may be held by the seller or the real estate agent, the preferable practice is to place those funds in the escrow. As suggested earlier, the buyer usually will arrange for the amount of the total purchase price to be transferred to the escrow, leaving the deposit to be used for the closing costs. In our example, it is implicit in the instructions that the buyer will deposit an additional $16,000 with the escrow agent before the date given. It is not necessary to specify the precise amount of the balance. As the time approaches to close the escrow, the escrow officer will make up a preliminary accounting and determine whether all funds

ESCROW INSTRUCTIONS

SELLERS ☐   BUYERS ☒   BORROWERS ☐

From: John A. and Mary B. Investor   Order No. 48756

To: ABCDE INSURANCE AND TRUST COMPANY: Date: May 10, 197-

On or before May 31, 197-, we will hand you the sum of $77,000 of which
~~we hand you herewith~~ $54,000 will be the proceeds of the first trust deed
described below, and of which $7,000 will be the proceeds of the second
trust deed described below. The sum of $1,000 has already been
deposited with you.

Which you will deliver when you obtain for ~~my~~/our account a grant deed in favor of the
vestees herein

and when you can issue your Standard   form of CLTA Owner's   policy of title
insurance with liability not exceeding $77,000   on the real property described as Lot 4 in
Block 20, as designated on the map entitled "Happy Haven, City of
Utopia, County of Glory, State of California," recorded in Volume 3 of
showing title vested in   Maps, at page 9 in the office of the County Recorder.
John A. Investor and Mary B. Investor,
 husband and wife as joint tenants

SUBJECT ONLY TO: (1) property   taxes for the fiscal year 197-,
(2) A trust deed to record, executed by above vestees in favor of the
    Last Savings and Loan Association to secure a note for $54,000, 20
    years, 8%; (3) A trust deed to record, executed by above vestees
    in favor of David M. Seller and Janet R. Seller to secure a note
    for $7,000 payable at $70 per month including principal and interest
    at 9% per annum, due June 30, 1980.

Upon close of escrow, you are authorized to deduct from ~~my~~/our account the following:
1. Adjust property taxes and fire insurance, as of close of escrow.
2. Credit prorations of rents, and security deposits.
3. Fee for termite inspection report.
4. Cost of title insurance and escrow services.
5. Loan fee payable to Last Savings and Loan Association in the amount
    of $540.

Any amendment of, or supplement to, these instructions must be in writing.
The GENERAL PROVISIONS printed on the reverse side of this page of these instructions are by reference
thereto incorporated herein and made a part hereof.
All documents, balances and statements are to be mailed to the undersigned at the address shown below.

Receipt Acknowledged.

ABCDE INSURANCE AND TRUST COMPANY   Address:

By _*John A. Investor*_

Date _May 10, 197-_

John A. Investor
John A. Investor
Mary B. Investor
Mary B. Investor
c/o I.M. Realtor, Inc.,

321 Main St., Utopia, CA

Telephone: ___765-4321___

GENERAL PROVISIONS

All funds received in this escrow shall be deposited with other escrow funds in a general escrow account or accounts of ...e Insurance and Trust Company, with any State or National Bank, and may be transferred to any other such general ...ount or accounts. All disbursements shall be made by check of Title Insurance and Trust Company.

Any commitment made in writing to Title Insurance and Trust Company by a bank, trust company, insurance company, ...building and loan or savings and loan association, to deliver its check or funds into this escrow may, in the sole discretion ...Title Insurance and Trust Company, be treated as the equivalent of a deposit herein of the amount thereof.

All adjustments to be made on a basis of 30-day months, based on the latest available tax bills.

Recordation of any instruments delivered through this escrow, if necessary or proper in the issuance of the policy of ...e insurance called for, is authorized.

No examination or insurance as to the amount or payment of real or personal property taxes is required unless the real ...perty tax is payable on or before the date of the policy of title insurance.

If any party to these instructions obtains a loan on the land involved, and during the pendency of this escrow, you are ...horized to furnish the lender, or anyone operating on its behalf, any information concerning this escrow, including, but ...limited to, a certified copy of the escrow instructions and any amendments thereto.

Execute on behalf of the parties hereto, form assignments of interest in any insurance policies (other than title insurance) ...ed for herein and forward them upon close of escrow to the agent with the request, first, that insurer consent to such ...sfer or attach loss-payable clause or make such other additions or corrections as may have been specifically required ...ein, and second, that the agent thereafter forward such policies to the parties entitled to them. In all acts in this escrow ...ting to fire insurance, including adjustments, if any, you shall be fully protected in assuming that each such policy is in ...e and that the necessary premium therefor has been paid.

Unless you are otherwise specifically requested by written instructions so to do, no examination nor insurance as to the ...licability, amount or payment of any transfer tax, imposed by any local, city or county ordinance or otherwise, is required ...ugh this escrow, as the same will be taken care of by the parties hereto outside of escrow and you are not to be con...ed with the payment of any such tax.

required are on hand; if they are not, he will advise the buyer. The escrow cannot be closed until all parties have performed. Buyer, seller, and lender will be given a closing statement showing exactly how the funds were handled. The expression "closing the escrow" refers to the process of recording documents, disbursing funds, and issuing the escrow closing statement.

The order number—48756 in our example—is the escrow number, a vital identification when communicating with the escrow agent.

When title to land is transferred, it is said that "title is *vested* in. . . ." The entity to which the transfer is made becomes known as the *vestee*; the transferor of the title is the *vestor*. In our example, the escrow agent knows the deed is to be used to vest title in the names and manner indicated in the instructions.

The form of title insurance is governed in part by custom in the area where the property is located and in part by the stipulations of lenders. You may wish to discuss this matter with the title insurance or escrow officer handling the transaction.

The reference to the legal description helps to make sure that all concerned are dealing with the same piece of property. The inclusion of the names of the current vestees provides a further assurance that the proposed sellers are the owners.

The buyers are stating they are agreeable to the release of their funds only if the title they are receiving is clear except for the items listed. Property taxes are always a prospective lien. Here, as is customary, the taxes are to be prorated. Obviously the property is being used as security for the first and second trust deeds, so those obligations will be encumbrances on the title. If there are any other liens or encumbrances, the seller is obligated to clear them because the buyer is specifying that his money is not to be paid out until the title is clear except for the items just discussed.

An escrow agent can act only on the instructions of the parties. The expenses to be paid from the buyer's funds are to be specified, thus authorizing disbursement.

Lenders may deduct the loan fee from the loan proceeds. In our example, we are assuming that the entire loan amount is sent to the escrow agent and that the fee will be paid to the lender at the time the escrow is closed. This serves to emphasize that this is an expense to be met by the borrower-buyer and that funds over and above the total purchase price will be required.

The escrow agent, when all the money has been paid in, will be able to close the escrow, assuming the seller has delivered the deed and second trust deed documents. After recording, the documents will be returned to the appropriate parties with notations as to the date and recording reference.

Seller's instructions. The procedure is basically the same as that described for the buyer, so no example is needed. Out of the funds available, the escrow agent will pay off existing loans, other expenses that are the responsibility of the seller, and in particular, the commission to the real estate broker. The seller may also deliver to the escrow agent such items as keys, bills of sale, and so on, for turnover to the buyer.

The closing statement

You, the buyer, will have less interest in this document than the seller. When he receives his, it will usually have a big check attached to it.

Refer to the illustrations on pages 135 and 137. We have shown the other side of the transaction, the seller's statement, as well as your own.

The buyer's statement. We agreed to buy at $77,000. By borrowing a total of $61,000, our cash down payment would amount to $16,000. We knew, of course, there would be certain costs to pay in addition. The initial $1,000 deposit at the time of signing the purchase agreement was available to apply to the costs. In the original analysis we estimated the actual costs to be $1,150. We did not allow, however, for the fact the seller would be holding rents paid in advance as well as damage or security deposits. In the escrow we are credited with these items, and that will reduce the amount of cash actually required to complete the transaction.

Once the escrow officer has a copy of the purchase agreement and escrow instructions, he can estimate how much money the buyer will have to come up with to meet his obligations. From the illustration of the buyer's closing statement you can see that $15,500 in additional cash was requested, and even so, there was a refund of $232.

The purchase was effective as of May 31. The escrow is closed coincident with the recording of the documents and passing of title. In areas where property taxes are paid in semiannual installments and the tax year ends June 30, there would be one month's taxes to be charged to the buyer; the seller had previously paid the installment for the second half of the year. In our example the prorata tax expense is $218. This is credited to the seller, as can be seen in the next illustration.

ABCDE Insurance and Trust Company

DATE May 31, 197-   ORDER NO. 48756   ESCROW OFFICER J.H. Fee

ESCROW CLOSING STATEMENT   (For Buyer)

⌐   ⌐
. John A. and Mary B. Investor,
. 220 Angus Crescent,
. UTOPIA, CA 99999
.
L   ⌐

I T E M S	DEBITS	CREDITS
SALE/PURCHASE PRICE	$ 77,000	
DEPOSITS		$ 15,500
DEPOSIT RETAINED Earnest money		1,000
EXISTING LOAN		
NEW LOAN First Trust Deed		54,000
Second Trust Deed		7,000
PRO-RATA — TAXES	218	
— INSURANCE	50	
— INTEREST		
— RENTS paid in advance		900
Security deposits from tenants		200
TITLE INSURANCE POLICY FOR $77,000	449	
ESCROW FEE		
RECONVEYANCE FEE		
PREPARING DOCUMENTS	10	
NOTARY FEE	6	
TRANSFER TAX		
RECORDING:	8	
TAX COLLECTOR		
COMMISSION		
INSURANCE		
Termite Inspection Report	50	
Loan Fees--Last Savings and Loan Association	540	
Inspection and Credit Reports	37	
CHECK HEREWITH	232	
BALANCE DUE		
TOTALS	$ 78,600	$ 78,600

SAVE FOR INCOME TAX PURPOSES

By custom, certain expenses are charged to the buyer, others to the seller. Here the buyer is charged with the cost of title insurance. He had agreed to pay the termite inspection report fee and, of course, must pay the loan fee.

When it comes time to establish the accounting records the buyer will be able to find some of the figures he will need by examining this closing statement.

The seller's statement. The seller owed $38,800 on an existing mortgage and because the buyer is obtaining a new loan the existing loan is paid off in the escrow. Giving the escrow officer the details of this loan, he will notify the lender that there will be a payoff and ask for a demand and reconveyance. Quite simply, this is a request for the amount of the unpaid balance as of a certain point in time, plus a basis for charging interest from that time to the closing, and a document, a *reconveyance,* which will be recorded to show that the original loan had been satisfied. The lender is protected by the escrow process.

The seller does not have to contribute the advance rents and security deposits because those amounts will be subtracted from what is otherwise coming to him. He has agreed to pay the cost of the termite repair work and the commission to the real estate broker.

In our example, the transfer tax is shown as $84.70; it is payable by the seller. The rate is $0.55 per $500 of equity transferred. If the buyer had assumed the existing mortgage, the transfer tax would have been levied on the difference between the purchase price and the outstanding loan balance. Here, because of the refinancing, the tax applies to the entire $77,000.

The seller receives a check from the escrow agent in the amount of $25,464.30 plus a note and second deed of trust for $7,000. Actually the documents sent for recording will be returned to the seller by the county recorder. The promissory note may not be recorded and therefore will be sent directly to the seller.

The escrow agent has completed his function when the escrow is closed, statements are sent to the parties, and all funds are properly accounted for. If mistakes have been made, there is recourse to the escrow organization. If this service has been rendered as a part of providing title insurance, the escrow agent will also distribute the title policies. Otherwise, the escrow agent will work with the title insurer by providing information and copies of documents, and the title insurance company will issue the policy separately from the escrow handling.

ABCDE Insurance and Trust Company

DATE May 31, 197-   ORDER NO. 48756   ESCROW OFFICER J.H. Fee

ESCROW CLOSING STATEMENT   (For Seller)

```
┌                                              ┐
   . David M. and Janet R. Seller,
   . 879 Regal Road,
   . UTOPIA, CA  99999
   .
└                                              ┘
```

ITEMS	DEBITS	CREDITS
SALE/PURCHASE PRICE		$77,000.00
DEPOSITS		
DEPOSIT RETAINED		
EXISTING LOAN	$38,800.00	
NEW LOAN Second Trust Deed to Seller	7,000.00	
PRO-RATA — TAXES		218.00
— INSURANCE		50.00
— INTEREST		
— RENTS paid in advance	900.00	
Security Deposits from Tenants	200.00	
TITLE INSURANCE POLICY FOR $		
ESCROW FEE		
RECONVEYANCE FEE	10.00	
PREPARING DOCUMENTS	6.00	
NOTARY FEE	1.00	
TRANSFER TAX	84.70	
RECORDING: Reconveyance	2.00	
TAX COLLECTOR		
COMMISSION Paid to I.M. Realtor, Inc.	4,500.00	
INSURANCE		
Termite Repair Work--paid to Hungry Termite Co.	300.00	
CHECK HEREWITH	25,464.30	
BALANCE DUE		
TOTALS	**$77,268.00**	**$77,268.00**

SAVE FOR INCOME TAX PURPOSES

Your tenants

A notice of change of ownership should be given to the tenants. The seller can do this either orally or in writing. It is best if done in writing and signed by the seller. If there are leases, they should formally be assigned to the buyer and processed through the escrow. In one way or another, tenants should know that after a specified date they are to make rental payments to the new owner.

It is important to establish contact with your tenants. They will have a chance either to confirm or allay whatever suspicions they have about the new owner. You can confirm to them you now have their rent and security deposits — if that is the case. You may wish to stress how you feel about people who pay their rent on time and about those who don't. If you have in mind making some adjustments in the rents, you can lay the groundwork for that.

Closing the deal means exchanging your money (including the borrowed amounts) for a good title and the right to collect rents and earn a return from the investment. Because several things must take place at one time, it is best to employ an escrow agent. It is also wise to obtain title insurance even if a lender has not insisted on it. Both you and the seller employ the escrow organization to protect your interests. Documents are recorded to establish your legal interest in the property, and the seller is assured of receiving his money in exchange for the deed. You have done what you think necessary to be sure that you ended up with the property you thought you were buying, including having a land surveyor mark the boundaries. Now all you have to do is learn how to manage your property.

6

Managing the Money Machine

Now you are a landlord. This chapter covers what is involved in taking care of your property and the present tenants, how to get new tenants, the difference between leasing and renting, and in general, what to do to maximize your overall return.

In one way or another the tenants have been notified there is a new owner. You should make contact and, among other things, confirm with each tenant the amount of rent and when it is payable, and whether there is an advance rent payment in hand. You should also cover the matter of a damage or security deposit if there is one. If a lease has been transferred you should confirm that to the tenant. Probably the best practice is for the new owner to send a letter to each tenant in which these items are recited and ask the tenant to sign and return a copy, thus acknowledging agreement.

If you acquired personal property in the purchase, you took inventory at the time the deal was closed. In turn, if tenants are renting furnished units you should take inventory in their presence and reconcile any differences. The furniture should be listed and its description be made a part of the rental agreement or lease.

You may find a tenant has changed a lock. The owner generally has a right to enter the property in order to safeguard it. To avoid an argument in this connection it is good practice to include that provision in the rent or lease agreement.

In some localities a business license is required. A phone call to the city hall will produce the information you need.

You should resolve to take an interest in civic affairs. You might even want to attend a city council meeting. For all you know, there may be a proposed ordinance that, if passed, will affect your operation. You may want to exercise your rights as a citizen to influence such legislation. Keep in touch by carefully reading the local newspaper. Read the classified advertising for real estate rentals and income property. You are in business now and the more information you can acquire the better off you will be. You may wish to join a property owners' association or the local taxpayers' group.

Particularly if you anticipate expanding your property ownership activities, you should consider becoming affiliated with a national association such as the Institute of Real Estate Management of the National Association of Real Estate Boards. This will require association with a local real estate board. Full details can be obtained by writing to the Institute at 155 East Superior Street, Chicago, Illinois 60611.

For assistance with local matters relating to building ownership, you may want to inquire into membership in the local chapter of the Building Owners' and Managers' Association, (BOMA). You may find this group listed in your telephone book. You can write to BOMA International, 224 South Michigan Avenue, Chicago, Illinois 60604.

Your objective is to do what is necessary to maximize your ultimate return from this investment. By properly maintaining the property, you should obtain the maximum price on resale. By learning how to handle tenants and maintenance matters, you will minimize operating expenses. By getting the best possible tenants and learning how to keep them, you will maximize rental income.

You should open a new checking account. You will find it desirable always to pay bills by check and to deposit all rental income in a bank account. Your first deposit to the account should be the rent advances and damage deposits credited to you in the escrow. Recall those credits reduced the amount of cash you had to produce in order to complete the transaction. You need the money now and you should resist the temptation not to put this money in your property-operating account.

You may think it feasible to use your family checking account. With a small apartment building you will have only a limited number of banking transactions each month and you may be able to avoid a bank charge by using only one account for both business and personal activity. We recommend you have a savings account into which you transfer the surplus of income over expenses each month from the checking account. Once again, you may not wish to have another savings account if you already have one. But in one way or another, you should have the use of a checking account for processing income and expenditures associated with the investment, and a savings account into which you deposit surplus funds so they will earn interest. Some of the so-called surplus will be surplus only for a time and will be needed to pay property taxes, for example. You can earn interest on the money while it is accumulating. Like it or not, you will require good records of the financial transactions and you should start off your ownership on the right foot by recording everything that takes place in terms of money.

We will assume your apartment is fully occupied and, for the time being, you will not be faced with obtaining new tenants.

Minimizing operating expenses

As you become thoroughly familiar with your new asset, you may notice things that should be repaired. If you are able to make minor repairs yourself, you should take care of as many as you can now. Because emergencies may arise concerning the plumbing or wiring or the roof, you should decide, before the emergency arises, which plumber or electrician or roofing company you will call when needed. Write down the results of your research and put the information in your property-operating file folder.

As soon as you become aware of a repair problem, take care of it. Nothing frustrates a tenant more than a landlord who procrastinates. If the complaint or request for repair, concession, or amenity is not justified, don't stall. Give the tenant your decision as soon as possible. That will give the tenant longer to get used to the idea. Developing your judgment for this kind of problem takes practice. It is also helpful to compare notes with other property owners to learn what is the common practice in the area.

Who should paint the apartment and how often should it be done? In relatively tight rental markets you may be able to say to tenants that you will provide the paint if they will put it on. First, of course, be aware of the problems. If you don't control colors you may be faced with a serious problem in finding a new tenant. Not everyone prefers a black living room and a chartreuse bathroom. The quality of the paint is also to be considered—not to mention the quality of the painting. You will have to decide whether the tenant is skillful with a paintbrush; if the conclusion is negative you had better do the job yourself.

Paint stores are known to offer discounts to property owners. Visit some and see how good a deal you can get. Get the color charts and decide on the brand and quality, hence the cost. Tell the paint store they can honor requests for paint and charge them to your account if the tenant presents a written authorization from you. You, in turn, after discussing the matter with the tenant, can write out the appropriate authorization. The tenant then picks up the paint and paints his own apartment. You can offer the tenant a choice; stick to neutral colors. What about the exterior?

Work to be done by independent contractors should be subject to bid. Ask two or three presumably qualified firms to give you a bid on the work. You may choose the lowest, but it may not always be the best. Getting references from previous customers is often worth the effort. Watch for ads in the classified section of the newspaper placed by people who solicit work you need to be performed. For fairly small jobs there often are a number of moonlighters who, because of limited overhead, are willing to charge less for their work. You may not be able to get them to stand behind their work, of course, as you could with an established business firm. You will have to weigh the risk.

It will be important for tenants to let you know about plumbing problems. A leaky pipe can cause serious problems and expense apart from loss of water. Washers should be replaced promptly in dripping taps. Once again, if a tenant complains, and if the complaint is justified, fix whatever needs fixing! You are going to have to do it anyway, so do it now and be a hero. Once in a while you may want to drive by to see if the building is still there; but be sure you respect your tenants' right to privacy. This is not a social relationship. The tenant is paying for sound and safe living accommodation; he is not buying an opportunity to socialize or be pestered.

You will be faced with spending some money no matter what the age or condition of the property. If you handle these matters correctly your tenants will be inclined to stay and the property will sell for the maximum in the future.

Expense for utilities

There are two basic types of expense for the landlord: fixed and variable. If you are obligated by law or local custom to pay for some of the utilities, try to pay for those that are fixed. Water, gas, and power are usually variable; the cost varies with the quantity used. The same usually holds for electricity and gas. You should try to avoid renting on the basis of including the cost of variable expense utilities.

In some communities garbage service is provided by the municipality and the property owner has a legal obligation to pay for it. This is common practice. Keep this in mind when you are doing your evaluation and preparing the cash flow analysis.

If you find you have no choice but to be responsible for the expense of variable utilities you may be able to include a provision in the rent or lease to pass some part on to the tenant. Competition from other apartment owners may limit this opportunity.

What should your costs for utilities, repairs, and maintenance be? When you did your analysis you included certain figures. These were probably based on information received from the seller. He may have been optimistic about what expenses you would have. By keeping complete records you will be able to build up, over time, some information on your actual experience to use for comparison purposes. If you owned one or more large apartment buildings you would soon know what was a reasonable and typical cost for the usual maintenance items, but for a fourplex or other smaller building the range of costs can be great. You could go for a whole year without spending any money on painting, for instance. It will be important to keep track of what you are spending, preferably by each rental unit separately, and by type of repair. The national organizations referred to previously offer cost data to their members and you may be able to compare your experience with that of others. Again, this is not as meaningful for the small apartment owner as it is for the large.

Under income tax laws, expenses incurred in the production of taxable income may be deductible. You have already resolved to pay all bills by check and to obtain receipts. If you have some small items paid for in cash, lump them together and write a check for the total to reimburse yourself.

In managing an apartment house you will have postage and telephone expense. You may need stationery and record-keeping supplies. You may use your car and travel in the course of a year a significant distance. Keep a record of these expenses and be able to show them as expenses when it comes time to prepare an income tax return. Don't wait until the end of the year to try to recall what these expenses were. Not only are you unlikely to recall correctly, but you won't have records considered adequate by the Internal Revenue Service to support the deduction. Many investors keep a diary of the activities associated with the property and an envelope in which to place receipts.

Persons new to operating a business, realizing that expenses associated with the business are deductible, often fall into the trap of thinking that they should maximize such expenditures. This is fallacious, of course. No matter how large your tax bracket, the tax collector is paying only part of every dollar paid out and the taxpayer is paying the balance.

Assume you are subject to a 40-percent income-tax rate. If you spend $100 on deductible expenses, it is true you reduce your taxable income by $100. You reduce the number of tax dollars, however, by only 40 percent. *You* are paying the other 60 percent, or $60. It is all right to say that Uncle Sam is paying 40 cents out of every dollar of your expenses, but don't forget who is paying the remaining 60 cents.

Another item for expense control is property taxes. By now, as an expert in real estate matters, you know that the amount of your property tax bill is governed by both the assessed value and the tax rate. While you may not individually be able to do much about lowering the tax rate, you can do something about the assessed value if you think it is too high.

Early in the year you should receive a notice from the tax assessor's office advising you of the assessed value for the upcoming year. You have a legal right to the information the assessor used in arriving at your assessment. You can challenge his computation. When it is based on the market value of similar properties you may be able to develop information on other similar properties that would support your contention that yours is too high. Be aware, of course, that a reassessment could result in a higher value. Visit your assessor's office and find out the procedure for appealing an assessment. Do that before you need it. That information will be useful to you in knowing what steps you might take to keep your assessment at a minimum.

Maximizing rental income

We are still working on the assumption that your apartments are all filled with rent-paying tenants. If you treat the tenants right they will probably stay longer than otherwise. Turnover is to be avoided unless a tenant is undesirable.

Rents are payable in advance. Most apartments are rented on a monthly basis and a month's notice of intention to leave is expected. One way to protect yourself against loss because a tenant leaves without notice is to require the payment of two months' rent at the time of initial occupancy (the first and last month's rent). This should be stated clearly in the receipt for the funds so the tenant understands how the money is to be applied. Then, if the tenant does not make the usual rental payment of the last month, the landlord has the month's notice he should have. Responsible tenants, not motivated by a last month's rental payment, will give adequate notice anyway. You have to protect yourself against the other type of tenant who has other things on his mind besides your welfare. Unless you collect two months' rent in advance you cannot be certain of avoiding a loss. Even at that, you might not be able to get a new tenant; but that is the regular risk you have as a property owner.

From an operating point of view, it is best to have rents from all apartments due and payable on the same date. Under those conditions you can quickly become aware of any delinquency. If tenants are paying rent at odd times during the month, unless you are particularly careful, you can lose track of a nonpaying tenant. Once time has gone by it becomes difficult to collect from a tenant who decides he doesn't want to pay you. You should be firm, but fair, in dealing with tenants who do not pay on time. If the delinquency is because pay day comes after rent day, you may want to adjust the rental period.

Some landlords prefer to call in person to collect the rents. In some situations this may be necessary. A better arrangement is for tenants to assume the responsibility of delivering the rents to you or your designate on or before a stipulated time. Tenants who pay by mail and on time, with checks that don't bounce, and who stay without making unreasonable demands, are to be desired.

When you have notice of a prospective vacancy, make appropriate arrangements with the departing tenant to show the premises to prospective replacements. Most people will be reasonable about this if the landlord is reasonable. Your goal is to line up a new tenant to move in exactly at the time the present tenant leaves, with no gap.

Usually, if you start your tenant-seeking activity two weeks before the occupancy date, you will be all right. This depends, of course, on the current rental market. You may have to compromise and be prepared for it. Assume, for example, a prospect says he will take the apartment, but the rent on his present apartment is paid until the tenth. Your unit is available as of the first. What do you do? If the market is strongly in your favor, and the prospective tenant is anxious to have your apartment, he'll take it as of the first. Otherwise, you may have to suggest that you will split the difference—rent it as of the fifth, say. You may be able to make other concessions, such as offering to provide the paint if the prospective tenant would like to choose the color (within your range), and apply it himself. In turn, the tenant would have to take the apartment from the first to have this opportunity. Develop your imagination and bargaining skills. The motivation is the realization that there is no way to recover rent for lost time.

If the departing tenant has to vacate before the time rent has been paid, he wants a refund. You may be inclined to say you will make a refund provided you can find a tenant to take up from the date of vacancy. Under those conditions you will not lose rental income and you may gain some valuable goodwill.

Eviction

If you have to evict someone from your property, it is going to be nasty. Timeliness of action is vital if you are to minimize your loss. Not only will you lose rent but you will have the expense of the eviction. The longer you put it off, the greater will be your loss. The law is on the side of the landlord, under appropriate conditions. It is also on the side of the tenant—to an extent you will learn about only after you have been involved.

Basically, if a tenant refuses to pay rent or otherwise breaches his rental agreement or lease, you may have a right to evict. The precise procedure varies from one community to another. In general, the following considerations apply, regardless of the way in which it may be carried out in a given jurisdiction. You should consult your local municipal court for exact details.

There are several reasons why eviction action may be taken. If rent is unpaid, that may be sufficient grounds. Tenants who damage the property, invade the privacy of others, or consistently create disturbances are subject to eviction. The tenant may have some defenses. Rent may be withheld because the landlord has refused to make repairs. The extent to which others are being disturbed will be a matter of opinion. To protect both parties to the dispute, there is a court procedure.

Probably the initial step, once the landlord has checked with the local authorities, is to deliver to the tenants a three-day notice to vacate the premises. If that does not succeed, application should be made to the municipal court. The technical name of the action is *complaint in unlawful detainer.* A summons and complaint will be served on the tenant. Local custom governs whether the local authority or the landlord (employing a process server) arranges for this. If the tenant does not respond to this summons and complaint by filing his answer, a default judgment will be awarded to the landlord. The court will issue a *writ of possession* and instructions to the sheriff to remove the tenants and their possessions from the property. The landlord will have to post a bond and pay the expenses.

If the tenant wishes to argue his case, he will be able to present his side to a judge. Meanwhile he will remain in possession of the property and the landlord will undoubtedly not be receiving rent in the interim.

How does a landlord recover the financial loss? To attempt to recover the costs of the eviction and lost rent, the landlord may ask the court to attach the tenants' possessions. In the complaint you would allege damages for lost rent and expenses and ask for the money judgment as well as eviction. The sheriff will seize the personal property and it may subsequently be sold to satisfy the judgment if the court awards it to you. An alternative is to proceed in small claims court.

If a tenant owes for unpaid rent you may wish to sue him in small claims court, where the cost is limited to filing fees; attorneys are not employed in this situation. You tell your story to the judge; and if the tenant responds to the summons, he will tell his. If the judge awards you a judgment your next problem is converting the judgment to cash. You will need to locate some property belonging to the tenant and obtain a legal attachment. Again, it will have to be seized by the sheriff and sold to satisfy the judgment. You may be able to use the small claims court when eviction is not involved. Some defaulting tenants don't wait to be evicted; they just leave. The key to avoiding eviction and rent loss is good tenants.

New tenants

We assumed the apartments were all occupied when you bought the building, but now one of the tenants is moving out and your job is to get a replacement. If you are adequately prepared for this important activity you should have no difficulty. The assumption here is that you are handling all of the property management yourself. Before we explore what you will have to do, let's look at some of the alternatives.

You may decide to employ a property manager; perhaps one of the tenants would like to rent the units, collect the rents, and generally take care of things. You have to decide whether the cost is worth it to you. Even if the payment is in the form of reduced rent, be sure to keep your records as though it were paid-out expense. Real estate offices often provide the service of getting tenants. In some areas the cost for this is paid by the tenants; in others, by the landlord. Before you decide to use someone else, find out what it will cost and be sure you want to reduce your return. Call real estate offices and ask what their charge is for collecting rents and getting tenants. Call more than one so you can compare. This will be a basis to use also if you are thinking of having a tenant take care of the property.

Rent collection involves two points: safeguarding and promptly remitting the funds, and collecting on time and avoiding rent losses. In some cases all a real estate office might agree to do, for example, is collect the rent if it is sent to them. They may not be prepared to pursue delinquents. This is not hard to understand, because the fees for collection service cannot be great enough to support the expenditure of effort.

Only you, as the owner, have the incentive to work day and night to get a new tenant. Even if a real estate office can earn a rental commission amounting to a large proportion of the first month's rent, that may not be enough to prompt superhuman effort. Never forget while you own rental property, rental income for time gone by can never be recouped. Keep this from happening by always renting the property effective with the departure of the previous tenant.

If you decide to do all the work yourself, what is involved? You have to decide on leasing versus renting; you have to have a supply of rental applications and contracts on hand; and you have to have a pricing policy. You have to know how to advertise the property and how to handle prospective tenants when they respond to your advertising.

Renting versus leasing

When a tenant agrees to pay for the use of premises and the landlord is in accord, a rental agreement is thereby created. This agreement should be in writing, regardless of the length of time involved. If the agreement extends beyond one year, the courts will not enforce it unless the agreement is in writing. This is the effect of the "statute of frauds." For apartment property, the unit of time for a rental agreement generally is one month. This is established by the amount of the payment and the length of time for which the payment is applied. In our discussion we assume a monthly basis.

The landlord may decide that he prefers to rent on a month-to-month basis. Good property management calls for collecting, prior to occupancy, a sum of money equal to two months' rent. Local custom may prevent you from doing this, however. But you should always collect rent in advance. A receipt, if given, should clearly show the time period for which the rent payment applies. By renting on the month-to-month basis, the tenant is obligated to give a month's notice of departure. For example, when the tenant makes a rental payment on the due date he then can say, "This will be my last month." That would provide a notice in compliance with the usual law governing such matters. Typically, the amount of notice is to be equal to the time period for which each rental payment applies. There may be a local ordinance that provides otherwise, so check to see what your specific situation is.

The month-to-month basis also allows for rent increases to be made, but advance notice of a change is also required on the same terms as notice. When you want to raise the rent, give notice in writing and allow more than enough time for the change to become effective. The same time terms apply to a notice to vacate, other than when the notice is for nonpayment, preceding potential eviction proceedings.

Thus the advantage to the landlord of renting on a month-to-month basis is that rents can be changed, and tenants can be asked to leave, with no more notice than the length of time for which rent is paid. This also means, of course, that the tenant can decide to move on and be obligated for no more than a month's rent. If he wants to leave right away, the landlord could theoretically hold him for rent for the notice period. If you already have the money in hand your position is substantially stronger.

If the basis is month-to-month, there should be a written rental agreement. This is *not* a lease. An example of a typical rental agreement is illustrated on page 134 and can be used by you as a sample in preparing your own contracts.

Either the tenant or the landlord may prefer an agreement that provides for more protection—that is, an agreement that obligates the landlord to maintain the rental terms for more than a month at a time, or for the premises to be retained by the tenant for longer than a month at a time. This means we want a lease.

A lease is the name customarily applied to a rental agreement having a rental period of some multiple of payment periods as its term. Assume a one-year contract, with a monthly rental of $200. The lease contract (see pages 136-139) would be written to provide that the tenant agrees to pay a total rent of $2,400. It will acknowledge receipt of the initial payment, which should be $400. This should be stated to apply as follows: $200 to the first month and $200 to the last month of the twelve-month term of the lease. Note carefully that the tenant, by signing the lease agreement, becomes obligated for the total of $2,400 less the amounts paid in advance. If he moves out early and breaches the contract, he still owes the balance of the money and can be sued accordingly.

The landlord, under such a lease, cannot change the rental terms *during the term* other than by agreement with the tenant. Provision is usually made for a renewal of the lease, with the amount of the rent for the ensuing period left open to negotiation. The parties can, of course, agree in advance on a specific amount.

The basic idea of a lease is that the tenant is protected against rent increases but is obligated to stay or at least pay for the term of the agreement. The landlord, in theory, can forget about looking for a new tenant as long as the lease is in force. If his expenses increase he has no way — in the absence of a provision in the lease — to increase the rent to offset such an increase. It is not usual in residential property leases to provide for increases in rents to cover increases in operating expenses. It has been said that a lease protects only the tenant, because if the tenant wants to leave, the landlord probably cannot collect for lost rent, whereas the tenant is guaranteed that his rent will not be increased. You will have to consider the pros and cons and decide. Some landlords offer either a rental or lease basis and let the tenant decide. If the prospective tenant is concerned about increasing rents, he may choose your apartment over a competitor's because you are willing to lease it to him. On the other hand, you may find it more difficult to get an undesirable tenant out of your premises if he has a lease rather than a month-to-month rental agreement.

Rental application form

When you offer an apartment for rent you are providing an opportunity for someone you know nothing about to occupy your

RENTAL AGREEMENT

This Agreement, executed on _____between

_____

hereinafter called the landlord, and _____

_____ hereinafter called the tenant,

provides that

1. The landlord rents, to the tenant, the following property:

   _____

2. At a monthly rental of _____

3. Beginning on_____

4. Receipt is hereby acknowledged of the sum of $_____
   to be applied: $_____ to the first month of occupancy
   and $_____to the last month of occupancy.

5. Receipt is hereby acknowledged of the sum of $_____
   as a damage and cleaning deposit. This deposit will be returned at the time the tenant surrenders the apartment in a
   condition judged satisfactory by the landlord.

6. The landlord agrees to pay the cost of _____
   _____, said services to
   be included in the rental payment.

7. Tenant agrees to _____

8. Tenant agrees to make rental payments not later than
   _____of each month to the landlord at

   _____

   _____   _____
          Landlord   Tenant

   _____   _____
          Landlord   Tenant

property. Your risks include potential damage to the property, nonpayment of rent, and the possibility the new tenant will drive the other tenants away. How do you protect yourself against these risks?

When a prospect says, "Yes, we'll take the apartment," you should respond by explaining you would like them to complete the rental application and give you a deposit to hold the apartment. In addition, you will let them know whether they can have it no later than by a specified time. You should not ask for more than forty-eight hours in which to check out their application. It should be made quite clear that the deposit will be refunded in full if they do not qualify. If they do qualify, they should know that a rental agreement or lease will be prepared and signed by both parties.

A sample rental application form is reproduced on pages 140-141. Your form should be as brief as possible and ask for only essential information. Some people may resent what they feel to be an intrusion of their privacy. You may have to point out diplomatically that they are going to have possession of your property and it only makes good sense for you to. learn something about them. You can assure them the information will be kept confidential and is for your use only.

There are two major items: employment and previous landlords. You should plan to verify the information on both. By checking with a previous landlord, you can find out whether he paid his rent and left in good standing. Ask what amount of rent was paid—that will help to determine whether he can afford yours. In checking employment, you can verify that he does in fact have a job. You should also ask if the job is expected to continue. It is unlikely you can obtain income data and probably should not ask. Other references may be useful in determining how responsible the party is.

After you have had some practice in handling tenants, you may be able to make up your mind about someone on the basis of a conversation. It is still good practice to obtain the information asked for on this form. You never know when you might need it later.

Pricing policy

At what rent are you going to offer the apartment? If you found the rents were under the market you may have decided to raise them. Unless rents are out of line, the best time to change them is between tenants. Many successful investors deliberately set their rents just under the current market in order to provide present

LEASE

CALIFORNIA REAL ESTATE ASSOCIATION STANDARD FORM

THIS INDENTURE, made the......Twenty-fifth.......day of....August............, A. D. 19.7.-.

between......John A. Investor and Mary B. Investor...

...., hereinafter called the lessor,

and....Margaret A. Tenant...

...., hereinafter called the lessee.

WITNESSETH, that the lessor does by these presents, lease and demise unto the lessee all of the property

situated in the......City of Utopia...,

County of......Glory..........................., State of California, described as follows, to wit:

Apartment 3, 1234 Wistful Vista, Utopia, CA,
including stove and refrigerator.

for the term of......Twelve Months***..

beginning......September 1...............19.7.-.... and ending.August 31........., 19.7.-...

for the total rent or sum of.**Twenty-Four Hundred Dollars***

....Dollars, in lawful money of the United States of America, payable as follows, to wit:

Four Hundred Dollars ($400) upon execution of this lease,
$200 of which to be applied to rent for the month of
September, 197- and $200 for the month of August, 197-;
and $200 on the first day of each month, beginning
October 1, 197-.

All of said rent shall be paid at the office xk..... 220 Angus Crescent, Utopia, CA 99999.........

XX XXXXX XXXXX XXXXX XXXXXXXXXXXXXXXXXXXXXXXXXXXXXXXXXXXXXXXXXXXXXX
XXXXXX, or at such other place as may be designated by the lessor.

mailed to

IN ADDITION THERETO IT IS HEREBY AGREED AS FOLLOWS, TO WIT.

First: That the lessee shall pay the lessor said rent in the manner hereinbefore specified, and shall not let or underlet the whole or any part of said premises, nor sell or assign this lease, either voluntarily or by operation of law, nor allow said property to be occupied by anyone contrary to the terms hereof, without the written consent of the lessor;

Second: That should said rent be not paid when due or should the lessee default in any of the covenants or conditions contained herein, the lessor, or his representative or agent, may re-enter said premises and remove all persons therefrom;

Third: That the lessee shall occupy said demised premises and shall keep the same in good condition, including such improvements as may be made thereon hereafter, the usual wear and tear and damage by the elements excepted, and shall not make any alterations thereon without the written consent of the lessor and shall not commit or suffer to be committed any waste upon said premises;

Fourth: That said premises shall not be used by the lessee, nor anyone else, during the term hereof or any extension thereof, for the sale of any intoxicating liquors, nor for any illegal or immoral purpose, and that possession of said premises by the lessee or his successors or assigns shall not be construed as conveying any title thereto or ownership thereof;

Fifth: That all Governmental laws and ordinances shall be complied with by the lessee;

Sixth: That the lessee waives all rights under Section 1942 of the Civil Code of California and releases the lessor from any and all damages which may be sustained by the lessee or any other party during the time he may be in possession of said premises;

Seventh: That should the occupancy of said premises, by the lessee, cause the present fire and liability insurance rates applicable thereto to be increased, the lessee shall pay the difference upon the amount of fire and liability insurance now being carried by the lessor and said difference shall be in addition to the amount of rental specified herein and shall be paid to the lessor upon demand;

Eighth: That should the lessor be compelled to commence or sustain an action at law to collect said rent or parts thereof or to dispossess the lessee or to recover possession of said premises, the lessee shall pay all costs in connection therewith including a reasonable fee for the attorney of the lessor;

Ninth: That the waiver, by the lessor, of any covenant or condition herein contained shall not vitiate the same or any other covenant or condition contained herein and that the terms and conditions contained herein shall apply to and bind the heirs, successors and assigns of the respective parties hereto;

Tenth: That should the lessee occupy said premises after the expiration date of this lease, with the consent of the lessor, expressed or implied, such possession shall be construed to be a tenancy from month to month and said lessee shall pay said lessor for said premises the sum of $200.00.................per month for such period as said lessee may remain in possession thereof;

Eleventh: That said premises shall not be used by the lessee during the term of this lease for other than ....residential purposes occupied by..not more than..2 residents..ꞩꞩꞩꞩ except with the written consent of the lessor;

Twelfth: That at the expiration of said term or the sooner determination thereof, the lessee shall peacefully quit and surrender possession of said premises in as good condition as reasonable use and wear thereof will permit;

Thirteenth: That all words used herein in the singular number shall include the plural and the present tense shall include the future and the masculine gender shall include the feminine and neuter.

Fourteenth: That the tenant shall maintain the garden associated with Apartment #3 at her own expense, in a manner in keeping with the surroundings.

Fifteenth: Receipt is hereby acknowledged of the sum of Fifty Dollars ($50) as a cleaning deposit, to be returned at the end of tenancy and on surrendering the premises in proper order in the judgment of the landlord.

IN WITNESS WHEREOF, the lessor and the lessee have executed this indenture as of the day and year first above written.

Margareth Tenant
Margaret A. Tenant (Tenant)
....
Mary B. Investor (Landlord)
Mary B. Investor (Landlord)

For these forms address California Real Estate Association,
520 So. Grand Ave., Los Angeles 90017
(Copyright, 1928, by California Real Estate Association)

FORM # L-14

LEASE

TO

Dated

RENTAL APPLICATION

Desired Possession Date:_____

Property Address:_____Apt. No._____

Name of Applicant(s):_____Married_____Age:_____

Name of Spouse:_____Other Occupants:_____

Pets (Number and Type)_____

Present Address:_____

   How Long:_____Reason for Leaving:_____

Name of Present Landlord:_____

   His Address and Phone No._____

Employment: Social Security #_____Driver's License #_____

   Present Employer:_____How Long:_____

   Address:_____Phone #_____

   Employed as:_____Salary:_____Per:_____

Employment: (Spouse) Social Security #_____Driver's License #_____

   Present Employer:_____How Long:_____

   Address:_____Phone #_____

   Employed as:_____Salary:_____Per:_____

Bank Accounts (Branch)_____Checking_____Saving_____

Credit References (Please list three)

Name	Address	Phone #

Auto License #_____State of Registry:_____

Make and Model_____Year_____Color_____

Name of Closest Relative:_____Relationship:_____

Address:_____Phone #_____

I hereby sign this application on the basis of the following:
I declare the foregoing information to be true, under the penalty
of perjury, and I understand that the owner of the property, or
his agent, will rely on this information in entering into a rental
agreement with me.

It is further understood that the deposit of $_____
is for the purpose of reserving the apartment for me until this
application is acted upon. In the event this application is not
accepted I am to receive a full refund of said deposit; otherwise
the deposit will be applied to the rental agreement obligation.
The decision concerning this application is to be made on or before
_____ failing which I am entitled to a full
refund of deposit and will have no further obligation.

_____   _____
(Applicant)   (Date)

_____   _____
(Applicant)   (Present Phone #)

tenants with an incentive to stay. Of course, if your expenses increase, you have a legitimate reason for passing the increase on to the tenants. Be sure you explain carefully the basis on which the increase is charged. On the other hand, if you raise the rent when a unit becomes vacant, you may find it hard to get a new tenant. You should keep in touch with what your competitors are doing. See rental units being offered and compare them with your own. Be sure to compare on a proper basis and allow for the cost of utilities or slight differences in facilities. Then decide what monthly rent you should charge. If you overprice your unit you may have trouble getting a rent-paying tenant. Prospective tenants will ordinarily have a very good idea of what the rent should be.

Also related to pricing is your policy concerning advance payments and damage deposits. Get the first month's rent before the tenant moves in; get the last month's rent, too. You may have to compromise slightly and agree to accept some of this total shortly after the move-in. Be careful, however. An indication of softness or lack of desire to enforce agreements can cost you money.

The amount of damage deposit will be governed not only by local custom but also by the prospects of needing it. Your objective is to have some money in hand so that if, at the time the tenant moves out, damage is to be repaired, it can be paid for with the tenant's funds. True, if there is a shortage, you can always sue, but collecting on a judgment can be a tough proposition. When renting to adults who appear to be the kind who will treat the property properly, you may wish to take a modest $25 or $50 deposit. You may stipulate it is for cleaning rather than damage. In either case, the conditions for refund should be stated clearly in the rental or lease agreement. If it is your policy to rent to families with children, you must recognize the possibility of an above-average amount of wear and tear on your property. Obtain a deposit large enough to take care of what you expect will be needed. The same holds true for tenants with pets.

From a marketing point of view, you want to be able to offer an apartment that will be more attractive than anything else on the market at the same time. If people with children and/or pets have great difficulty in locating accommodations, you may decide against a restriction, thus tapping that demand.

Marketing
Decide whether you will advertise the unit to the world at large, or list it with one or more commercial rental agencies. If you want

your applicants to be screened before you show them the apartment, you might find it well to use a rental agency. Have a clear understanding of the cost beforehand. You may cut yourself off from prospective tenants who either do not know about rental agencies or who do not wish to pay the fee, if it is the tenant who pays the fee. Assuming you are going to handle everything yourself, how do you advertise?

The customary place is the classified advertising section of a newspaper circulated in the area where the property is located. Check the "apartment wanted" classification. Perhaps you can find a tenant without having to advertise at all. Some prospective tenants want landlords to come to them.

It is also a good idea to contact the personnel departments of large companies, because many assist their employees in finding housing. If there is a college or university nearby, it will have a housing office glad to hear of your vacancy. You may want to put a notice on the supermarket bulletin board.

Study the advertisements placed by other landlords to see how they word their advertising. The newspaper advertising staff will help you with the wording. The following information should be included in any ad, as a minimum: the size of the apartment (number of bedrooms), whether it is furnished, monthly rent, whether a lease is available, utilities included, amount of advance rent and security deposit required, an indication of the area (preferably not the address), and your phone number. If there are some attractions that will help to rent the apartment, they should be mentioned. For instance: near shopping or transportation; in a particular school district; garage; garden; and so on. If you were a prospective tenant, what would you see that would prompt you to call to make an appointment to see the property?

If you want to restrict renting to certain groups, say so and save yourself some time and effort. For example: "one br studio ideal for retired person." This should eliminate calls from a mother of six or a teenager with a set of drums.

You should not place an ad for only one insertion in a daily newspaper. Go for the extended run at a discount price. You can always cancel the ad or take the phone off the hook if you rent quickly. Don't be discouraged if the first fifty prospects turn you down. Be alert to why the property is not renting and make changes in policy as indicated. Be patient. Be prepared to show the property at a time convenient for the prospect even if it is not the best time for you. If you have to travel a distance to meet people at the property, line up appointments in sequence to eliminate going back and forth. Some property owners hold an open house and advertise the apartment as being open from, say, 10 A.M. to 5 P.M.

Handling prospects

Finally someone says he would like to see what you are offering. You set a time to meet him and go to the apartment early. If the departing tenant has not left yet, you make appropriate arrangements to be sure you are expected. A disgruntled, departing tenant can sabotage you more effectively than a Russian spy.

Never let a tenant show the property to a prospect. Always show the property yourself, unless you have an agent to handle the whole transaction. Whenever possible, show the property only when the current tenant is not around. You will have to take precautions with respect to the personal property lying around. Demonstrate you are familiar with the apartment; if you aren't, become so. This is a business proposition. You have an apartment that affords good accommodation and is fairly priced. The prospect is either attracted to it or not. If the prospect indicates that it will not do, don't harass him in your eagerness to rent the unit.

Avoid showing the property to two different prospects at the same time. (If you hold an open house, that is different.) When making appointments to show it, space them to allow prospects to have your undivided attention. If two happen to arrive at the same time, suggest that one be patient until you get back to him.

Suppose you have two prospects and they both seem interested. Be careful to deal fairly. Take a deposit from the first one who says he wants to do business, but be sure to get a name and address or phone number from the second in case the first one falls through. Don't rely on the second one to check back with you to see whether the first deal went through.

Discrimination in housing is illegal. If you, as a landlord, discriminate on the basis of race, color, or creed, you are violating the law.

Assume now you are about to make a contract with a prospective tenant. During the negotiations you may have made certain commitments. Certainly you will ask the prospect to give you a deposit and complete an application form. If everything checks out, promptly notify him and prepare the rental agreement or lease for signature. Ask the party to bring the balance of the money and set a time for signing the documents. Be sure to include in the agreement whatever commitments you made during the negotiation. Put in writing what you have agreed to.

The time for occupancy will ordinarily coincide with the date from which rent is being charged. Make a date to meet the new tenant at the apartment.

Turning over the keys

Inform the present tenant that the apartment is rented. Confirm his departure date and make arrangements to inspect the property and return the cleaning or damage deposit. If personal property is included you will want to check it over against the inventory and make certain all is accounted for. Check the keys to make sure they have been returned and that they operate the locks. Get a forwarding address from the departing tenant. Turning utilities on and off is normally the responsibility of the incoming and outgoing tenants.

When the new tenant arrives, go through the apartment carefully. When applicable, check off the personal property inventory. Make a note of any damaged areas so they can be repaired, or so you will not blame the new tenant later for the damage. Introduce the new tenant to the neighbors if the opportunity presents itself. Review again with the tenant any special features. For example, perhaps you have included in the agreement that the tenant is responsible for taking care of the garden. Discuss this again at this time. Stress how important it is to make the rent payments on time and confirm that the tenant knows where to send the payments. Accomplish your business and leave.

When you return home, check your property file to see that you have all the documents for the new tenants in the right place. Make any notes you think useful. Be sure the money is properly recorded and deposited.

Some miscellaneous matters

You are now running a business and will want to pay more attention to income tax matters. You will incur expenses in connection with your investment that are tax deductible—provided you have records to support them. Make it a practice *always* to ask for a receipt or invoice. Pay all bills by check; deposit all income to a bank account. Keep detailed records.

If you use a portion of your residence regularly and exclusively for the conduct of a business activity you can charge against income the value of that space. The easiest way to compute the charge is to determine the fair rental value of the entire home and the proportion of the space devoted to the office. That fraction multiplied by the rental value will give you the expense.

If you need a safe-deposit box to safeguard the documents and records associated witn your investment, you can deduct the annual charge.

Travel expenses are deductible. Keep a log of the date and mileage of the trips you take in connection with the apartment. The total tax deductible allowance can be substantial.

Do you need to make any change in your last will and testament? If you do not have a will, prepare one. Sometimes it is important to refer specifically to property and how you wish it to be treated in the event of your death. Now is the time to make whatever adjustment may be needed.

Take another look at your property and casualty insurance program. As a property owner you not only have a greater exposure to loss, but you will be more of a target, and for larger amounts, in the event someone is injured. The potential loss from liability claims is unlimited. Check with your insurance adviser and make sure your liability coverage applies to all the property you own and is written for limits large enough to protect you. The charge for increasing liability coverage amounts is very nominal.

Do you have enough property (fire) insurance to completely cover losses that may occur? Have you done what is necessary to have the benefit of replacement-cost coverage? If the property is damaged badly enough that the tenants have to move out, will your policy pay the amount of the lost rents during the time it takes to repair the damage?

Be conscious of the need to avoid and prevent losses even if you have insurance. Money can never make up for the injury or damage.

CHAPTER 7

Accounting Records

You have put your money to work in a money-making machine. How can you tell if the machine is functioning properly? Good records provide the answer. Bank records will be useful, but you need more. It is best to have a running record of income and expense and to prepare it in a conventional accounting-statement format, such as an earnings or profit-and-loss statement.

Accurate records not only tell you where you are going, but also support your income tax return. To make it easy to achieve these goals we have some specially designed forms; all you have to do is fill in the blanks.

Throughout this discussion, we will assume you will process all income and expenditures through a checking account while maintaining a savings account to which you transfer surplus funds each month. The surplus will be the difference between income and outgo for the month. From time to time you may have to withdraw funds from the savings account to pay certain expenses—taxes, for instance. You may decide to use your regular personal checking account rather than open a separate one for the investment. The assumption is that you have invested cash to generate current income and long-term gain. You do not intend to spend any of the return from the investment; instead, you will let it accumulate. This will allow you to know — when you have ultimately disposed of the property — exactly how much the investment has produced. You will have every cent in the savings account — plus the proceeds of the sale.

The suggested accounting procedure will work just as well if you do not follow the banking suggestion. The system is flexible.

As we review how to handle your records, think in terms of depositing all income to your checking account and paying all bills associated with the property from that same account. The records you keep will tell you how much in that account belongs to the investment. The forms will also show you how much should be in the savings account, assuming you have been transferring as you go along.

Accounting forms

A complete example is reproduced on the following pages. Look at these forms now and then come back to the description of the entries. Recall that the example of the analysis and purchase assumed a midyear transaction date. In order to provide a maximum amount of detail in the accounting forms, we have switched the date to the first of the year. This will serve as a guide no matter when the record keeping is begun. If you already own property, you can set up your accounting records according to the procedure discussed.

Your complete records consist of the following forms: a *monthly record of income expense, depreciation schedules,* an *annual operating statement,* and a *summary of investment results.*

For a complete record on a piece of property, all you need is a monthly record form for each year you own it and the same number of annual operating statements, but only one depreciation schedule and one investment summary. It is assumed you keep a faithful record in your checkbook of checks written and deposits made and that you reconcile your bank statement each time you receive it.

Monthly record of income/expense

You can make the entries on this form at the end of each month, posted the figures from your checkbook and receipt book or other record of rental income. You would have a separate sheet for each property. It is assumed you are operating on a cash basis for accounting and therefore will make the entries according to the month in which the transaction occurred. For example, the mortgage payments are payable on the first of the month. Even though you might write the check a few days beforehand, record the expenditure as of the date used on the check. Further, you will charge as expense the cost of goods or services at the time they are paid for; do not spread it out over the time to be used. You may want to do otherwise if, for example, you bought insurance for a three-year term and paid the premium in advance.

The other accounting basis is *accrual.* It is used by corporations and other business entities but rarely by individuals. The accrual basis calls for recording income as of the date it is receivable, regardless of when you actually get your hands on it, and expenses as of the date the obligation is incurred, regardless of when you actually pay it. Further, the expense is charged against income for the period during which the expenditure applies. For example, if you bought insurance for one year you would charge one-twelfth of the amount against income each month. The objective of accrual accounting is to reflect income and expense more accurately. That accuracy is unnecessary for an individual operating a small apartment building.

You will also be guided by the rules and regulations of the Internal Revenue Service. For example, when you collect rent in advance (such as the first and last month's), all of it is to be recorded as income for the month in which you receive it.

Notice that the monthly record form is divided into two parts, with columns for each month in the year.

Income. Recall in the escrow the buyer received credit for the advance rents held by the seller. This is treated as income for the first month of ownership. The tenants, duly notified of the change of ownership and anxious to impress their new landlord, have all paid their rents on time, so now we have $900 from current rents and $900 credit from the seller as rental income for the first month.

The damage or cleaning deposits of $200 were also credited in the escrow and the amount is to be entered. In the future, as changes take place in the deposits, they will be recorded on this line. Later, when looking at the bank balance, it will be important to remember how much is included for tenant deposits so that you are not misled by what appears to be affluence.

The total income for the month is $2,000, but you received only

Location: 1234 Wistful Vista, Utopia Year Ending 12-31-7_

INCOME	JAN	FEB	MAR	APR	MAY	JUN	JUL	AUG	SEP	OCT	NOV	DEC	TOTAL
Rents	1800-	900-	700-	1100-	900-	910-	910-	910-	910-	710-	710-	1110-	11,570
Deposits	200-		⟨50⟩	50-						⟨50⟩		50-	200
INTEREST			18-			20-			32-		40-		110
TOTAL	2000-	900-	668-	1150-	900-	930-	910-	910-	942-	660-	710-	1200-	11,880
EXPENSES													
Property taxes				1313-								1350-	2663
Utilities	22-	17-	20-	20-	21-	22-	25-	26-	25-	24-	16-	20-	258
Insurance	50-		100-				50-						100
Maintenance	45-	15-	100-		10-	5-	10-			40-		120	345
1st Mortgage Payment	452-	452-	452-	452-	452-	452-	452-	452-	452-	452-	452-	452-	4972
2nd Mortgage Payment	70	70	70	70	70	70	70	70	70	70	70	70	770
Interest													
ADVERTISING			15-						10-	20-	15-		60
TOTAL	117-	554-	657-	1855-	553-	549-	607-	548-	557-	606-	553-	2012-	9168
To Bank	1883-	346-	11-	⟨705⟩	347-	381-	303-	362-	385-	54-	157-	⟨812⟩	2712
Beginning Balance	0	1883-	2229-	2240-	1535-	1882-	2263-	2566-	2928-	3313-	3367-	3524-	
Ending Balance	1883-	2229-	2240-	1535-	1882-	2263-	2566-	2928-	3313-	3367-	3524-	2712-	2712

© Copyright by Douglas M. Temple

$900 in cash. Recall the admonition in the chapter on closing that, although you did not have to put up as much money as you might have because of these credits, you would need the funds later. The time is now. Be prepared to deposit the $1,100 along with the current rental income.

Expenses. Your first month may be a light one. As a general rule, mortgage payments start a full month, or even more, after the papers are signed and the loan, disbursed. In our example, we have assumed that no mortgage payments are to be made in January. The lender may specify the first loan payment to be made on, say, the first of each month; but with an escrow closing more than a month before that first payment, there will be interest charged. For example: the loan is disbursed May 20, first mortgage payment, due July 1. In the escrow the borrower will be charged interest from May 20 to May 31; the July 1 payment will take care of the interest for the period June 1 to July 1. In this case you would enter, as an expense item, "interest" on a blank line, and show the amount in the column for May.

Another item from the closing statement to be entered on the monthly record is insurance. Recall we were charged a proration in the escrow. We treat this as an operating expense in the first month. The other expense items handled in the escrow are not operational so we do not show them here. They will be recorded later, however.

By the end of the first month we will have paid a utility bill. Here we are paying the cost of water and gas used for the building in general; the tenants have their own meters for their individual consumption. We also found we had to take care of a small plumbing problem and incurred a $45 maintenance expense.

All of these entries can be made at the end of the month. Go to your checking account checkbook and post the items as indicated. You will also refer to the escrow closing statement. By subtracting the expenses from the income, we find there is a total of $1,883. Write a check for this amount and open a savings account. The monthly record shows clearly the changes in the savings account as you consistently each month transfer funds to or from the savings account. Each month during the ownership period, you repeat the process. No other monthly accounting record is needed.

Once you have kept your records in this manner, you will have no trouble seeing how to handle any transaction that may arise. There are, however, some unusual items that will come up; here are some examples:

Refer back to the income section for the month of March. Here we lost a tenant. During February we were told the tenant was leaving at the end of March. No rent was received because the advance was to apply; here it was $200. The apartment was in satisfactory condition so the damage deposit of $50 was refunded in full. Note we recorded a withdrawal of the deposit. We also found that the savings account earned $18 interest on the funds on deposit since the beginning of the quarter. This is income attributable to the investment and has been added to the account balance, hence the amount is entered. Write in "interest" in the column on the left. In the example you will see how this interest income has been entered at the end of each calendar quarter, the time most savings institutions credit interest, even though compounding is more frequent.

We found a new tenant at the beginning of April and collected two months' rent and a $50 deposit. Note the entries. A similar in-and-out transaction is shown for October and December. There we had more trouble locating a tenant and had a month's vacancy.

Effective in June, we raised the rent on one of the apartments by $10. No adjustment in the advance rent was made, but that would have been a good idea. If you have a tenant for a while, and raise the rent, remember to obtain an increase in the advance. You may find, when the last month of occupancy has come and gone, you shortchanged yourself for that last month by applying only the original advance, which of course was less than the current rent.

In our previous discussion of tax shelters we pointed out that when there was an operating loss you would have a reduction in the total amount of income tax to be paid. By computing your income tax twice—once including the investment and once without it—you can quickly determine the credit earned by the investment. Take that amount of money and deposit it to your property investment account. In the left-hand column in the income section of the monthly record form, write "tax shelter benefit" and enter the dollar amount under the month in which you make the deposit. This will then be a part of the income from the investment. At the end of the year, of course, you will be taking only the rental income and interest income for tax purposes from the monthly record form.

Property taxes are usually payable in two installments—in the example we have used, April and December. By the due date in April we have accumulated more than enough to pay the taxes, but the funds are in the savings account, earning interest. We want to withdraw the minimum amount required, so, after collecting the rents and making the other disbursements for the month, we can calculate how much cash we need to pay the tax bill. It comes to $705, the difference between the income for the month and the outgo, including the taxes. This difference is the amount to be withdrawn from the savings account and deposited to the checking account. Now we can cover all the checks to be written. Note the use of brackets to indicate subtraction or withdrawal. If our record keeping is accurate and up-to-date, the monthly record bottom line will show the exact balance of the savings account. Here we reconcile the savings passbook balance to $1,535.

For expenses not specified in the left-hand column, simply write the appropriate designation. Notice how we handled the advertising item.

You may have some expenses for which you do not issue a check. For example, you use stamps, or the telephone, or drive your car on business associated with the property. Be certain to keep track of these items and at the end of the year compute the amounts involved. You can reimburse yourself for these deductible amounts by showing them on the monthly record of income/expense and thereby deduct them from the rental income, assuming you are using your family checking account to handle apartment funds. If you have a separate checking account for the property, prepare a tabulation of the expenses like a bill or invoice, write a check payable to yourself for the total, and enter the appropriate amounts on the monthly record form. Check with the Internal Revenue Service for the current allowance per mile for car expense.

If the lender insisted upon collecting for taxes and insurance and maintaining a loan trust fund or impounds account, you will not pay those bills directly. The expense, however, will be included in the monthly payment made to the lender. In this situation, enter on the "mortgage payment" line the part of the payment attributable to principal and interest and apportion the balance to taxes and insurance. That will call for entries every month on those lines. At the end of the year the lender will give you the exact amounts paid out for those items; use them in preparing the income statement. If a surplus has built up in the loan trust fund you can ask the lender to return it to you.

There is no limitation on the different kinds of entries that can be made on these forms. At the end of the year, after all entries have been made, we total the form horizontally and vertically and hope for a balance. From this sheet we will get our income and expense totals. The savings account balance should also check out. This will be the amount to enter on the new sheet for the next year. All funds remaining in the checking account should be transferred if you are to achieve the objectives stated. We have $2,712 in the savings account. You should keep in mind, of course, that $200 of it belongs to tenants in the form of damage or cleaning deposits. Also, although we have treated it as income, there is $900 of advance rent—and rental income will be reduced in future months when tenants move. On the other hand, ordinarily the incoming tenant will also be paying an advance, so it all evens out in the long run.

Perhaps you are saying at this point it looks as though we have made a profit of $2,512 for the first year. Be careful. $2,512 is the cash in hand. Profit is computed in another way.

The only worthwhile profit figure to look at is the one *after* income tax, so let's see what has to be done to calculate it.

Depreciation schedules

As real estate investor, you will be quick to point out that there is an expense for which we do not write a check—depreciation. Each year you will need amounts to show for depreciation. To have those numbers readily available, you will want to prepare the depreciation schedule at the time you set up your initial records.

The information needed for this form will come both from the analysis we made before we decided to buy and from the closing statement. We concluded the building had a remaining useful life of thirty years, so that means the annual depreciation would be 3.3 percent on a straight-line basis. To be conservative and to avoid complications involved in using accelerated depreciation, we selected the straight-line basis. Always remember it is only the structure that is subject to depreciation. We have a $60,000 value, so the first year depreciation will be 3.3 percent of that amount, or $2,000. If you bought the property during the year, you would take only a proportion of the annual amount.

The example assumes we have lumped all the equipment together. If you choose to depreciate pieces of equipment separately you can see from the form what to do. The choice of estimated remaining useful lifetimes is critical. The shorter the period, the larger the amount of depreciation expense, hence a lower income tax liability. A prudent investor will seek guidance from the Internal Revenue Service and his tax adviser.

From the sample depreciation schedule you can see how much

DEPRECIATION SCHEDULES

Enter here the figures to be used in preparing Income Tax Returns

BUILDING: Date acquired _1-1-7-_   Total Purchase Price $ _77,000_

Remaining useful life _30 years_ Costs not expensed $ _0_

Total $ _77,000_

Depreciation method-

Straight Line ~ 3 1/3% per yr   Less land value $ _17,000_

Basis for Depreciation $ _60,000_

End of Year	Beginning Book Value	Depreciation	Ending Book Value	Total Depreciation
7-	$60,000	$2,000	$58,000	$2,000

EQUIPMENT: Description _Stoves & Refrigerators_   Date acquired _1-1-7-_

Cost $ _2,000_

Salvage $ _200_

Amount to be depreciated $ _1,800_   Method _Straight Line_

Estimated useful life _5_

End of Year	Beginning Book value	Depreciation	Ending Book Value	Total Depreciation
7-	$2,000	$360	$1,640	$360

total depreciation you have taken and can avoid going beyond the expected salvage value, something you must do to keep out of trouble with income tax examiners.

With depreciation amounts available, we now are prepared to make up the first annual operating statement in a form customarily used by accountants and easily understood by all.

Annual operating statement

The address is entered because you will have a separate statement for each property. Unless you have chosen otherwise, you prepare your tax return and other records on a calendar-year basis.

Now would be a good time to check the amounts you see in the example with those shown on the monthly record of income/expense. This will confirm where the numbers come from for the first section, "cash flow before income tax." For section B, "income tax computation," there is some figuring to do. The first item is mortgage interest expense. The $4,512 is the total for both first and second mortgages; these must be computed separately.

Recall that each mortgage payment of $452 for the first and $70 for the second is divided between interest and repayment of principal. At the end of the year the coupon payment book or lender's statement will show the totals needed. It is important to confirm such figures to see that they are correct. For income tax purposes we can deduct only the interest portion. Note that in section A, the total payment was used, but that was because we were dealing with cash income and outgo.

Compute unpaid mortgage balances and interest expense. Be sure to note that the second mortgage carries a stipulated payment.

Because our first mortgage payment comes in February, there are only eleven payments made in the year. As a consequence, the total mortgage interest expense of $4,512 is for eleven months, not a full year. On next year's annual operating statement, a full year's expense will be used. Ordinarily you will be working from data provided by the lender and you have reason to assume it will be correct.

For the special first-year deductions, we have elected to treat as expense the title insurance, mortgage loan fees and one-time costs; charges for prorations are not included. They are recovered in effect out of income. From the title or escrow company closing statement we find that these special expenses total $1,100. When totaled we have $11,398 as the sum of deductible expenses. With a gross income of $11,680, the net taxable income is $282. If the

ANNUAL OPERATING STATEMENT

property at _1234 Wistful Vista, Utopia, Calif._ For year ended _12-31-7-_

CASH FLOW BEFORE INCOME TAX

Total Rental Income received	$ 11,570	
Other Income	110	$ 11,680
Less: Property Taxes	$ 2,663	
Utilities	258	
Insurance	100	
Maintenance	345	
ADVERTISING	60	
Total Operating Expenses	$ 3,426	
Mortgage Payments - First	4,972	
- Second	770	
- Third		
Total Cash Outlay		$ 9,168
NET CASH INCOME		**$ 2,512**

INCOME TAX COMPUTATION

Total Income		$ 11,680
Less: Total Operating Expenses	$ 3,426	
Total Mortgage Interest Expenses	4,512	
Depreciation - Building	2,000	
- Equipment	360	
First year special deductions	1,100	
Total Deductible Expense		$ 11,398
NET TAXABLE INCOME		**$ 282**
INCOME TAX LIABILITY: __.40__ x Net Taxable Income		**$ 113**
(rate)		

(If Net Taxable Income is negative, the Tax Liability is your Tax Shelter Benefit.)

MORTGAGE REDUCTION

Total of Mortgage Balances at beginning of year		$ 61,000
Less ending balances, all mortgages, end of year		59,770
TOTAL MORTGAGE REDUCTION		**$ 1,230**

RECONCILIATION OF CASH GAIN

Net Cash Income		$ 2,512
Less Income Tax Liability or Plus Tax Shelter Benefit		113
TOTAL SPENDABLE CASH AFTER INCOME TAX		**$ 2,399**

combined federal and state taxes amount to $113, obtained by applying the correct tax rates, you can calculate the total spendable cash after tax as shown in section D. Here it is $2,399 — on a cash investment of just over $17,000.

We passed over section C, "mortgage reduction." Here we see how much of the mortgage is being paid off by the tenants. To the extent that we can sell the property for at least what we paid for it, the amount of mortgage reduction will be part of our gain. Previously when we calculated the mortgage interest for income tax purposes we had the figures needed to compute the unpaid mortgage balances used in this section in determining the total mortgage reduction for the period. From time to time you will make use of the formula:

total of the mortgage payments = *interest expense* + *mortgage reduction.*

Now we have a picture of our first full year's operation in a conventional business format. Our bottom line is a good healthy figure. And we have that money in a savings account. In April we will be able to prepare our income tax returns quickly because all the calculating has been done.

Each year we do the same thing, using current figures. But we are anxious to know, on a cumulative basis, how the investment is coming out. For that we turn to the final accounting record, the summary of investment results.

Summary of investment results

The entries in the top section should be made at the time we are setting up our records. The figures come from the escrow closing statement. Your decision whether to treat costs as expense or capitalize the closing costs will affect your book value or basis for use in calculating long-term capital gain on resale. As a result of deciding to treat costs as expense, we deducted the $1,100 from first-year income. These amounts would still show on the summary sheet because they are a part of the cash invested. In our example the beginning book value or basis is $77,000. If we had chosen, instead, to capitalize all or part of these costs, we would still make the entries as in the example, to arrive at the amount of cash invested, but we would make a memorandum note of the beginning book value or basis by adding the capitalized amount to the purchase price.

Property at 1234 Wistful Vista, Utopia, California Purchased on 1-1-7-   for $77,000

Costs: Mortgage Points/Fees $ 540   Cash Down Payment $ 16,000
        Title Insurance/Escrow fees   449   Total Costs   1,100
        Other one-time fees   111
        TOTAL COSTS $ 1,100   TOTAL CASH INVESTED $ 17,100

Year	Rental Income	Net Cash Income	Tax or Shelter Benefit	Total Cash Gain	Percent of Cash Invested	Cumulative Cash Recovery	Mortgage Reduction	Total Gain	Percent of Cash Invested	Additional Capital Invested
19	$11,570	2,512	T 113	$2,399	14.02%	$2,399	$ 1,230	$3,629	21.2%	—
19										
19										
19										
19										
19										
19										
19										

Notes: Enter data from the Annual Operating Statement. Prepare a Summary form for each separate
        property. This provides a year-by-year summary of investment returns and performance. The
        Cumulative Cash Recovery column enables you to see when your total cash investment has been
        recovered.

        Total Gain includes the reduction in the mortgages. This will be realized only if the property
        is ultimately sold for at least its original cost plus resale expense. Gain on resale may be
        subject to income tax.

        Do not include the prorations part of the closing costs when computing the amount of cash
        invested.

The primary purpose of this summary is to provide a running record of investment results. With a sheet for each piece of property, one investment can readily be compared with others.

The "cumulative cash recovery" column will show how much actual cash, after taxes, the property has returned, and you can compare it with the total money at risk, In particular, note that the figures for entering on this form already appear on the other sheets, except for the percentages.

The form calls for both rental income and net cash income. The figure in the first column does not include income other than from rents, whereas the second includes earned interest plus any other income you might have—from coin-operated equipment, for example. Identify income tax charge or tax shelter benefit by an appropriate letter in the narrow column. The total cash gain is the last figure on the annual operating statement. Mortgage reduction similarly comes from the statement. With respect to the total gain, notice the qualification stated on the form. The amount is the sum of total cash gain and mortgage reduction. If you purchase additional equipment or make capital improvements on the property, you can show the increase in the investment by using the right-hand column. Under those conditions the total cash invested will change and a new value will be used in calculating entries for the two percentage columns.

All business activity requires adequate accounting records. There is no need to employ someone else to do your record keeping. By bringing together each month a record of the money coming in and the money going out, you will, at the end of the year, be able to obtain totals that can be used in preparing an annual operating statement.

With a very few additional computations you can obtain figures needed to calculate income tax information. By taking the totals for each year and entering them on a summary sheet you can have a complete history of the financial results obtained from the ownership and operation of the property. Perhaps for the first time in your investment experience, you know where you stand: how much is invested, how much has been returned after taxes, and what kind of a yield you are getting.

Once the work has been completed for the year, bring together the receipts and other papers related to the investment and place them with the accounting reports in a folder filed by property address. Put a fresh monthly record sheet in a file folder and keep it near your checkbook and savings passbook. That's all there is to it.

8

Disposing
of the
Investment

When you decided to make an investment in an apartment house, it was your plan to hold on to it for a number of years, to receive an adequate current return, and most importantly, to sell it ultimately to realize a long-term capital gain that was greater than alternative investment opportunities offered. Timing can be critical. It is a mistake with any investment to expect someday to discover you have made a fortune. Particularly with an investment in income property, you need to be aware of changing values and conditions and have a plan formulated to use in the event you need to dispose of the investment. There are many variables and factors to consider in being prepared for this step.

The urgency of the need to liquidate should be carefully measured against the possible gains and losses. This might not be the best asset to turn into cash, considering what you might be giving up. You need to know how you stand with the investment and what its future prospects are.

Because you have been diligently keeping your records according to the procedures and on the forms described, you can readily tell how you stand. The investment summary is all-important here.

Some of the questions to ask yourself are: what is my after-tax rate of return and how does it compare with alternatives? Have I received back all of my original cash investment? Can I meet my need for cash out of the funds built up from the investment without selling it? If I have been using accelerated depreciation, will I have a tax penalty if I sell now? How big is my equity and would refinancing rather than selling produce the cash I need? Have the repairs and maintenance become so great that the profit potential is at a minimum?

You should learn how to analyze thoroughly the financial record of the property and use the record to forecast the future. You should always stand prepared to evaluate an opportunity that comes your way against the present investment. If you do not make the most of the information you have and the skills you have developed, you will miss opportunities to increase your estate significantly.

At the end of each year, check to see if the investment is progressing as well as your original analysis suggested it would. Perhaps rents should be increased. It may be economical to undertake some preventive maintenance. This does not mean you should always fuss over it—that would be a mistake. But it will not produce the maximum return if you do not manage it intelligently. Intelligent management includes knowing always where you should make a change.

Besides an urgent need for cash for noninvestment purposes, there are other perfectly respectable reasons for considering selling. You may have made this investment as part of a plan to provide a retirement income. If that is the case, the way you dispose of the investment will be affected by how you want to use the proceeds. If you cash out you then must find a place for the proceeds. Those funds must not lie idle in a noninterest-bearing checking account. Perhaps putting the money in a savings account is the best plan. Buying government bonds is another possibility. Or, leave a lot of it in the property in the form of a mortgage and earn higher interest than the alternatives would pay. Not as secure, you say, and you are right. But if your retirement is not being financed exclusively by the liquidation, you may be able to assume a modest amount of risk in order to gain a larger return.

We are stressing the need to decide very carefully whether to sell, and before doing so, to decide equally carefully how to employ the proceeds once the sale is made. The timing and manner of sale will be very much affected by how you are going to handle the ensuing cash.

Perhaps you are so enamored of real estate investing that you want to become involved further. You feel prepared to take on a bigger project. The only problem seems to be that all your funds for investing are tied up in the first investment. Is that the end of it? Not necessarily. It may be possible to trade a smaller property in on a larger one. If you want to go after bigger things, it is possible to use your first investment as a steppingstone.

You may have found, on the other hand, that responding to demands of tenants is not your cup of tea. What are your choices? You could hire a manager and retain ownership. You could sell for a minimum cash down and continue to receive a return on your investment by way of mortgage interest. Note carefully that your status as owner or mortgagee seriously affects your income tax situation as long as there are tax benefits arising from charging depreciation and other operating expenses.

You may want to retain this property and to invest in more; but you need cash to do so. The equity in the first property may be tapped by refinancing or by a junior mortgage, thus avoiding the sale. You do not always have to sell in order to get your money out of an investment in real estate. It will cost money to refinance. There will be loan fees, new title insurance, and other expenses. Determine whether the prospective investment—for which you want the cash—is really worth the cost.

If interest rates have increased, you may want to think twice about replacing a mortgage that has a favorable rate with one that comes at a high price. Of course, the reverse situation may exist, and it will be possible to figure how much a new mortgage would save. Never overlook prepayment penalties, however, if they apply.

You may have observed a strong demand in your area for income property. It is always pleasant to be a seller in a seller's market. Don't sell just because you have a chance to sell. Where are you going to invest the proceeds? Of course, it is important to keep in touch with the market all the time—even when you are reasonably content with your investment. Be prepared to make intelligent moves.

It may be that changes are taking place in the area and the value of your property is not appreciating the way you had expected. Perhaps if you wait, things will get worse. Selling at a loss may be necessary to prevent an even greater loss.

Perhaps you bought the property as is. This is sometimes the case when the seller carries all the financing and there is no lender insisting that the property be brought up to a higher standard. You may have had some idea of doing the work yourself, to increase the value of the investment and enhance your return. Then perhaps you didn't get around to making the repairs. To have it done commercially would be uneconomical. What do you do now?

If the present mortgagee is agreeable to a new borrower, perhaps you can find a buyer who will take it over as is and assume the present loan. You may realize only part of your equity in cash; but if the buyer is responsible, the balance will be paid ultimately by way of a second mortgage or sales contract.

We have emphasized that real estate is not a short-term, in-and-out investment vehicle. Under these conditions there is a tendency to sit tight, collect the rents, do the bookkeeping, and ignore the possibility of getting rid of the property. That may lull you into a false sense of security. You may have made a mistake; the investment may not be a good one. You need to know as soon as possible whether that is the case. If it is a good investment, and you can tell as you look at your records, you still do not want to ignore the market place, because the conditions making it good may change. The solution to the problem lies in being aware, all the time, of the investment and real estate world around you. And one way to ensure that is to do an evaluation of your investment from time to time.

Interim evaluation

You made an evaluation, of course, at the beginning. The only difference is, now you are the owner, not a prospective purchaser. And you still need information. You have the benefit of the actual past history of the property. Regardless of whether you need cash, want to make another investment, or are content, you should take a set of analysis forms and prepare an evaluation.

When you have completed the analysis you will be in a better position to decide whether you should continue to own and operate the property or to liquidate it even at a loss. If you decide to put the property on the market you will have an extremely useful sales tool in the form of your set of completed analysis forms.

You may want to refer again to the example in chapter 3. You will be using an estimated sales price based — at first — on what you would like to sell it for, but you will also be facing up to the justification of that price. If the amount you use can be justified, you can proceed to offer the property for sale. The amount of cash to be realized, what you plan to do with it, and the income tax picture will assist you in knowing in advance the terms on which you prefer to sell—and to what extent you can meet the terms a prospective purchaser might offer.

Look at the fact sheet in some detail. Much of the information required is available in your own files. This may be the time to face up to the fact you have not increased rents when you should have. Some sellers say to a prospect that the rents are low and can be increased. If there is room for an increase, make it. Find out what other comparable apartments are bringing. If you have done that, you can speak authoritatively to your prospects.

Perhaps you have become acquainted with contractors who are building apartments in the area. There have been dramatic increases in construction costs. Who is to say this will not be true in the future? You should find out, in one way or another, current costs.

You may have replaced or added equipment. From your records you will be able to estimate accurately its current value. If you have notice of the assessed value for the next year and have some way of estimating a tax rate, compute the prospective property tax figures.

You have no way of knowing what a prospect may have in mind, but you can use figures you know from experience to be reasonable. You will know what the past appreciation rate has been and can reasonably estimate it for the future. If you analyzed several properties in the past, and kept the data, it would be worthwhile now to see if they are for sale again and at what prices. It is not impossible to find out at what rate property has been appreciating (or depreciating).

As a seller, you must assume the responsibility for lining up the financing. Check your loan(s) to see about prepayment penalties and assumption privileges. Perhaps you should discuss the matter with the present lender. Times and conditions change. Above all, learn what new financing might be available; watch your prepayment penalty. If possible and useful, try to obtain a loan commitment. Remember, your prospective buyer may have no ability to arrange for a loan and unless he has help he will not be able to make the purchase.

Depending upon your objectives for making the sale you may not want to take back a second mortgage unless there is no other way to make the sale. On the other hand, you may be anxious to minimize the amount of equity you realize and you will want to sell for a minimum down payment. Have a plan for financing including your participation, if any.

Closing costs

You should estimate what the closing costs will be. The amount of proration cost will be governed by the time of year the sale is made. To make it easier on the buyer, you will want to minimize as much as you can the amount of cash required. For example, don't pay any expenses any further in advance than is absolutely necessary.

. You may want to obtain a termite inspection report in an effort to anticipate what costs you will have if you have to pay for repairs called for by such a report. Regardless of the sales aspect, you may find it desirable to have that information about the property. A small amount of work done in time can save a larger expense later. Reports calling for substantial repair should not scare anyone. Sometimes recommended work is cosmetic in nature, and, if done, would not materially affect the structure or earning power of the property. That expense should be avoided.

In some states, such as California, there is a state law requiring that reports of inspection by pest-control organizations be filed with a state regulatory agency. Persons interested in the property can obtain, for a small fee, a copy of the report of any inspection made during the previous few years. Not every inspector would write the same report on a given piece of property. Some inspectors recommend work to be done that is not really necessary, and others issue a report that is not as complete as it might be. As a seller, you should learn all you can about the property; the buyer should do likewise.

If you, the seller, obtain a report, you may be able to pass the cost to the buyer if it is customary in your area for the buyer to pay for it. You may want to throw it in as a selling point.

Money spent in connection with the property will be deductible for you. Be sure, as always, to obtain and retain receipts and notes to explain. This is especially true if you fix up the property to be put on the market. Also, keep track of your travel and other marketing expenses, including advertising.

Mortgages

If the present financing is to be assumed, you already know what the monthly payments are. If you are tentatively arranging new financing, calculate the payments. If you are going to take back a second mortgage, you will have to decide on interest rate, monthly payment, and due date, if any. As for the payment, you can stipulate it to be 1 percent of the amount borrowed, as we did in our example. An alternative is to compute the payment for an amortization period such as fifteen, twenty, or twenty-five years. Include in the loan papers the provision that on a specified date the unpaid balance is due and payable in full. This gives you a due date, usually set five to ten years hence, yet a monthly payment less than 1 percent.

The shorter the estimated useful life, the larger the depreciation and the smaller the taxable income. There is also the question of whether to use an accelerated basis. Be prepared to answer questions during your selling episode.

At this point you should have all the information needed to complete the analysis. Much of the remaining work to be done is making computations with the figures recorded in the fact sheet. As you prepare this analysis, remember that if you intend to show it to a prospective buyer—a very good reason for preparing it—you will need to be able to justify the conclusions it shows.

You have some idea of what your asking price should be. Return to your original estimate of the appreciation rate and apply it. Certainly you would want to compare your property with those already on the market at this time.

Indicated economic value

Next comes one of the most important steps—computing the indicated economic value.

Here is where you give real meaning to square-foot cost figures obtained from building contractors, lenders, appraisers, or evaluation services. You will have to be careful in judging past depreciation. At this point you may want to reconsider whatever decision you reached previously about fixing up the property.

As for the gross multiplier, an important tool used in applying the market approach, from your experience and current research in the marketplace, you should know what competing properties have as gross multipliers.

From an investment point of view, capitalization of income is most important. You may get some argument from purists when you want to apply it to small apartments, but it works. Here is where you can see, graphically, what even a modest increase in rent or reduction in operating expense can do to the resulting value.

Be realistic, too, in selecting the desired yield. You should know even more about this than you did when you bought the property.

If you like, find the average of the three figures. Compare it with your asking price. If your figures are out of line you won't fool a prospect for long. Think of the confidence you can have in your asking price and terms if they are backed up by a sound analysis and evaluation.

If, at this point, you still have some doubts about setting the asking price, you should consider employing a professional appraiser. This could be well worth the cost, which may run as much as a few hundred dollars. There is always the chance that such an appraisal could result in your obtaining a higher price that more than covers the cost of the appraisal.

We have covered cash flows, yields, and estimated returns. You should have no difficulty preparing these now for presentation to a prospect. You may even reconsider your decision to offer the property. In fact, you should never make such a decision before you have plotted out what this investment will do for you if you keep it. Of course, you may be able to show yourself conclusively that you should sell.

Just because this is not a good investment for you does not mean it is not good for someone else. Each person has varying investment opportunities available. You may have chances others don't have, and it makes good sense to upgrade your portfolio. Your property, when compared with their opportunities, may present a good investment for them. Always be prepared to answer, convincingly, the prospects' query as to why you are selling.

Be sure to consider carefully what first-year deductions the buyer might have. This is of particular interest to investors seeking a tax shelter. If the present financing is being assumed, there will be less than if prepaid interest is going to be charged. You do not know what tax rate your buyer may be using—you have not met the buyer yet. If you review this analysis with him, be sure to point out the tax rates at which the amounts have been figured. He will then know whether his prospective return will be larger or smaller than your example.

After you have prepared the estimated results from the resale for a prospective buyer, calculate how you will stand if you make the sale at the asking price indicated. You should determine what your income tax picture will be according to the options you take. The manner in which you make the sale will have an impact on your tax liability. Figure out the most beneficial alternative.

If you have been using accelerated depreciation some of the depreciation expense will have to be recaptured as ordinary income, thus increasing the amount of income tax you will pay. You must have owned the property long enough for the gain to be classified as long-term. This varies from one state to another for state income tax rules; for federal, currently, it is over six months.

If you have owned the property for a very long time, or if it is old, you may have fully depreciated it, so there is no relief. The sooner you sell, the sooner you may be able to reduce your income taxes.

The tax rate to be applied to your gain from the sale is dependent upon your other income. Perhaps you are approaching retirement and soon will have a minimum taxable income from other sources. Waiting another year or so to sell may make a dramatic difference in the amount of income tax payable on the profit from this investment.

By all means, expend the effort to calculate how many dollars you will have left over after all bills are paid once the sale is complete. Then, compare these results with what you forecast when you made the original analysis and bought the property.

Now you know how you will stand if you make the sale under the conditions assumed. You have had a chance to consider seriously whether you should even sell at all. Given that the decision is still to go ahead and sell, look now at the various ways in which you could finance the sales transaction, because some will be more to your advantage than others.

Financial alternatives

Many sellers seem to prefer all cash. If you have a large equity, or if financing has become difficult, asking for all cash for your equity will probably create problems that will interfere with making a sale. More buyers have less cash, so the more cash it takes, the fewer prospects there may be. If the buyer has to obtain new financing, that could be troublesome. There may be loan fees to pay and restrictions on qualification. The selling price will be very much affected by the lender's appraisal.

If the equity is not too large, the seller could offer to take all cash and arrange for the buyer to assume the existing loans, providing the current financing can be assumed.

But there may be good reasons for not requesting all cash or for agreeing to terms that do not entirely liquidate the seller's position. If the buyer is short on cash, he may want the seller to take back a second mortgage or trust deed. There are other potential second mortgagees but a seller is a prime candidate. If the seller does not absolutely have to have all cash, he might welcome the opportunity to earn some interst on a second mortgage. He has some risk, of course. He may wish to sell the mortgage, but that would be at a discount, as a general rule. Perhaps more importantly, there is the income tax consideration.

Assuming the seller has held the property long enough to qualify for the gain to be treated as long-term, the maximum amount of income tax will be payable if he cashes out his equity.

Installment sales. A rule currently applicable to long-term capital gains when calculating federal income tax liability—state laws may vary—is taxation of installment sales. You will want to consult with the Internal Revenue Service and your tax adviser if you expect to elect this option.

The idea behind the rule is to assess equitably tax on profits from the sale of capital assets when the seller does not receive all of the purchase price at the time of sale or within the tax year. Many sales, particularly of real estate, are made on the basis of the purchaser paying a relatively small amount down and the balance over an extended period. If the seller had to pay tax right away on the total profit, regardless of how the purchase price is ultimately paid, it would be inequitable. When the sale qualifies as an installment sale, to minimize the tax the seller should receive not more than 30 percent of the contract price during the tax year in which the sale is made.

Assume the property is free and clear and sells at a profit for $100,000 with $25,000 down and the balance in monthly payments applied to a mortgage of $75,000. Assume, further, that the principal portion of the mortgage payments received in that year aggregate $4,000. So we see the seller has received a total of $29,000 of the contract price. He also has received mortgage interest which will be treated as ordinary income. The amount (excluding interest) received in the first year is less than 30 percent of the contract or sales price; income tax is assessed on the profit portion. Tax on the entire profit would be assessed if more than 30 percent was paid.

How do you compute the profit? Carefully. If we assume we bought the property for $75,000 and sell it several years later for $100,000, our profit rate is 25 percent. Once we compute this rate, we apply it in each tax year after the sale to the portion of the contract price received during the year, provided it is not more than

30 percent of the original amount. In our example, we apply the 25 percent to the $29,000 received for a taxable gain of $7,250. This will be taxed on the favorable long-term capital gain basis.

If, in our desire to cash out, we received more than $29,000 during the first tax year we would have had to pay income tax on the entire long-term gain of $25,000 in our next tax return.

In another example where there is a mortgage assumed by the buyer, we have a sales price of $60,000 and a $45,000 mortgage to be taken over by the purchaser. In this case we have sold $15,-000 worth of property. If we receive no more than 30 percent of this during the first year, we can treat the sale on the installment basis for income tax purposes. The profit rate would be the percentage of the equity that is represented by the profit. For example: assume original cost was $50,000. (This is greater than the mortgage being assumed—that is a requirement, too.) Selling for $60,-000 gives a profit or long-term gain of $10,000. The rate of profit would then be: $10,000 divided by $15,000 equals 66-2/3 percent.

To qualify for the minimum income tax and the use of the installment sale rule, the seller must not receive in the tax year more than 30 percent of the $15,000—which here would be a maximum of $4,500. Whether the seller would choose to sell for as little as $4,500 down is another matter. Perhaps you have observed that the most likely situation for which the installment sale rule would be used is where the property is free and clear of mortgages.

The taxable gain, on a long-term capital gain basis, in the first year would be 66-2/3 percent of $4,500. The $4,500 would be the total of cash down payment and principal payments on the debt owed the seller. This might be handled with a $60,000 sales price. The buyer assumes $45,000 mortgage, pays $4,500 in cash and executes a second mortgage or trust deed to the seller for $10,500 with no principal payments to be made until the following tax year (the seller's tax year).

Land contracts. One of the fears a seller may have if he does not get all cash for his equity is the risk he will not collect all that is coming to him. It is true that he can take a mortgage—first, second, or third—but he has been warned about the risk inherent there, too. Perhaps he would rest easier if he could hang on to the title to the property until the debt is fully satisfied. And indeed he can. All he has to do is sell on a sales or land contract. Let's see how that works.

Assume you are the owner and there is a first mortgage on the property. Your buyer does not have enough cash to cover your equity and you think it unwise to take a second mortgage for the deficiency. Instead, you offer to sell on a sales or land contract. You are doing this to avoid giving the buyer a deed to the property until the property is paid for.

You draw up the agreement in which the buyer contracts to pay you the purchase price, less the cash down payment, in monthly installments including interest. Upon receiving his monthly payment, you will in turn make a mortgage payment and retain the difference as payment of interest and principal on your remaining equity. Now you control the situation. If the buyer defaults, you do not have to foreclose because you still have title. Of course, to allay the buyer's concern, the land contract was recorded. Also, the buyer knows of the existence of the first mortgage. What are the problems?

The buyer may find that the seller somehow never got around to making payments on the first mortgage; then there will be a default and a foreclosure. The buyer may find himself out in the cold. His recorded land contract might provide some protection, but if the foreclosure sale brought only enough to pay off the first mortgage, our contract purchaser has trouble.

The buyer may find, after he has paid off the contract, that he cannot get a deed from the seller. The latter may have died or disappeared.

The seller may find the buyer is slow in making the payments, and now the seller has to make the first mortgage payments himself to avoid foreclosure. That is not what he bargained for.

Before the seller could legally contract with another, presumably more reliable, buyer, he would have to do something to clear the record of the original land contract. This could be done by bringing a *quiet title* action. An attorney would be needed. If the contract purchaser showed up and contested the matter, he would have to be reckoned with. Further, a considerable period of time is required for the quiet title action.

Even after the contract purchaser has defaulted he has a right to redeem the property by making up the back payments. The original seller still retains the title to the property. By this time he probably wishes he had taken a second mortgage, deeded the property to the buyer, and then sold the second to someone at a discount and banked the cash proceeds.

The foregoing has been written with the basic provisions of California real estate law in mind; it may not be quite the same in other jurisdictions. For whatever reasons, if you have trouble collecting on a land contract or a first, second, or third mortgage, see your lawyer.

Wrap-around mortgages. In a sense, the wrap-around takes the place of the sales or land contract described. If your equity is too large for the buyer, you have him execute a mortgage to you for the difference between the sales price and the down payment. The buyer takes title subject to the mortgages. Of course, the first mortgage is still unpaid and is a prior lien on the title. The amount of the wrap-around is larger than the first mortgage but it is a junior lien. Nothing can disturb the rights of the first mortgagee. The agreement between the buyer and seller provides for the payment of the first mortgage obligation. If the second or wrap-around mortgage is handled by a mortgage servicing agency, the purchaser is probably well protected, and can assume the first mortgage payments will be made. The holder of the second mortgage or trust deed is still faced with the potential default of the buyer. The buyer may prefer this wrap-around arrangement to a sales or land contract, because he should have no trouble getting a clear title when all the debts are paid.

The wrap-around mortgage has a place in fairly large transactions and is not widely used by individual buyers and sellers of small apartment properties. An imaginative private seller, however, might well find this to be a way to accomplish his objectives.

Income taxes are usually uppermost in the minds of investors. Is there a way to avoid—or to defer—paying up? Yes. There are tax-free or tax-deferred "exchanges." Let's see what is involved.

Tax-deferred exchanges. If you can find someone else who owns an apartment house, as you do, exchange properties; whatever profit one (or both) realizes will not be taxed at the time of the exchange. The properties do not have to be identical. The rules require that they be of the same general nature or "like kind." The exchange of an apartment building for an office building or a building rented for commercial purposes would be eligible.

The persons involved in the exchange must not be related. Also, you cannot exchange on the preferential basis with a corporation you control.

Be certain to notice that even though you use the proceeds of the sale of real estate to make another investment in real estate, even of the same kind, you have *not* made a nontaxable exchange. The two property owners must exchange property.

The net effect of a qualified exchange is to eliminate an income tax on the transaction at the time. When, subsequently, an exchanged asset is sold, the gain—if any—will be taxable and the basis will be governed by the terms of the previously executed exchange.

If, in the exchange, one party winds up with a cash payment in hand, there will be tax on the gain realized; but the taxable gain will not exceed the amount of cash received.

Properties of quite different values can be exchanged successfully without being subject to income tax at the time if the owners simply trade equities. For example, assume we have property A with a market value of $100,000 and a mortgage of $75,000. Property B has a market value of $150,000 and a mortgage of $125,000. The owners could exchange and defer the income tax. Here you can sell a property and use the proceeds to buy a larger piece of property and accomplish what you want. By making nontaxable trades, however, you avoid losing the buying power of your equity by having to share profits with a tax man.

If you own a fourplex and have a present equity of, say, $20,000, you may look around for the owner of an eight-unit property who would like to trade down and have fewer responsibilities. You persuade him to take your fourplex and apply your $20,000 equity to his property. If it is clear, the equity might be treated as a down payment, without any cash changing hands. You have traded up and he has traded down. You both have realized a profit if the market prices used in the exchange are greater than cost or basis; but you do not have to pay tax now—only later when you ultimately sell. Remember, the tax is only deferred, not eliminated. You may be in a lower tax bracket at some future time and would benefit by paying the tax later.

So perhaps you should be looking for an exchange rather than a sale and purchase, now that you have decided to dispose of the property.

Your reason for getting rid of the property will largely determine how you will go about selling it. If you want more income property, consider trying for a tax-deferred exchange.

Now that we have covered many of the financial alternatives facing you, there are more choices to be made.

Marketing alternatives

There is the basic choice: employ a real estate agent or do it yourself. If you go the latter route, you expect to save the amount of the commission. Any prospective buyer coming to you will also expect to save the commission because he is dealing direct. But only one of you can save the commission, and if you are particularly anxious to sell, it will be the buyer, not you.

The decision should be based on a frank appraisal of your own abilities. Can you deal effectively with strangers? Can you arrange the financing? Can you find prospects to consider the offering? Can you afford the time it takes to show the property to many people before a buyer arrives? As a general rule, if you choose a competent real estate agent, he will be well worth the cost and will probably earn it for you—so you should not feel you came out less than whole by not handling the deal on your own.

You must decide how the property is to be sold before you put it on the market. You may want to consider some of the potential marketing problems and suggested solutions.

You may have built up a substantial equity and now you find liberal financing hard to come by. There are always fewer buyers with large amounts of cash. Taking back a second mortgage may not appeal to you, perhaps because you have investment plans for the entire equity.

Condominiums. Not all condominiums are created by building a new structure. It is feasible to take an existing apartment building (or other type of property) and convert it into a condominium. Although a fourplex is a little small to justify the trouble and expense, you may want to explore the idea. Once you have made the conversion, you then have four units to sell, instead of one, and although you might prefer to find and deal with only one buyer instead of four, it may be easier to find four. Why?

An apartment tenant knows he cannot take a deduction on his income tax for rent. He has no mortgage interest or property taxes to use to reduce the tax bite. But if he buys an apartment unit that is a condominium, he then has all the rights and privileges of home ownership—but not some of the disadvantages. A condominium buyer can obtain financing comparable to that for a single-family home; and when financing is favorable, the down payment can be attractive. The major advantage over the private home is taken care of, and charged to the condominium owners.

Converting property to condominium ownership is not a job for amateurs. You can obtain guidance by talking to your banker, escrow agency, legal counselors, or real estate adviser. Larger properties are being converted every day, currently. This technique might provide the solution to your marketing problem.

Once you have decided to sell, why not see if one of your tenants would like to buy? The tenant may know of someone who would buy. A lending officer might know of someone who is anxious to make an investment in income property.

Seek out managers of real estate syndicates. Usually a syndicate is looking for large properties, but not always. Your property might fit in well with their plans.

There are some other decisions to make in preparing your marketing plan. What can be done to make the property even more attractive? Would a coat of paint speed up the sale? Be careful to spend money only if you are sure it will help.

We have stressed the importance of income in the determination of the value of income property. Should rents be increased? You do not want to drive tenants out. A vacant unit is not necessarily attractive to a buyer, because it is unlikely the buyer is looking for living accommodations. (That may not be so for a duplex, of course.) An owner should not live on the property, anyway. But perhaps there is another way to increase the income without pricing yourself out of the market.

Some structures lend themselves to remodeling. If you have one, consider seriously increasing the number of rental units by making some structural changes. True, you may reduce the size of a unit when you change it into two, for example, but the combined rent for the two smaller units will exceed what you were able to charge for one. Your expenses, including property taxes, will not ordinarily eliminate the advantage. You can increase the value of your property by having as many living units as are legal and possible.

The do-it-yourself seller. You have to find ways to let prospective buyers know you want to sell. This will mean advertising. When you were a buyer, where did you look? The local newspaper is one place. Another is the *Wall Street Journal.* Each week the Journal has a "real estate corner"; other days they run real estate ads too. Investors read this advertising carefully. Take a look yourself and get some ideas on how you might put an ad together. Do the same for the local newspaper. There will probably be a separate column for income property. Be sure your ad appears in it and not among the numerous single-family houses for sale.

In writing the ad, give the reader a reason for being attracted to your property and encourage him to respond. State a price and an indication of the financing; describe the return in one of the conventional ways, such as net or gross multiplier. Don't be secretive. This is a business proposition. State what you have and what you want. The negotiating can come only after a prospect has made contact. Include in the ad an offer to show the financial analysis you have prepared; that ought to bring responses. Remember how useful it was to you in deciding to buy in the first place?

Keep in mind you are not trying to sell a home. The prospect will be interested primarily in the financial aspect and ways to determine investment values. You will want to be able to show the inside of at least one apartment. Make appropriate arrangements with a friendly tenant (if there is one). Try to qualify your prospect before you trouble the tenant. A serious buyer will understand.

As someone who has bought a piece of income property, you know what a prospective buyer wants to know. How about preparing an information sheet to give to prospects? When you were looking, wouldn't it have been useful if sellers had stated the pertinent information on a piece of paper and handed it to you?

A prospect indicates he is interested. What do you do? Your goal will be to have him put up a deposit and sign a purchase agreement. To get ready for this activity, you should make contact with a title company or escrow agency so that you and your buyer can open an escrow. The buyer may have plans of his own. It is his money. If you have any doubts about protecting yourself, hire an attorney.

As a minimum, you should have a supply of deposit receipts or purchase agreement forms. These are provided on a complimentary basis by title companies and escrow agencies. If the buyer does not demonstrate an ability to prepare such an agreement, do it yourself. After all, you have samples to use for guidance—the one used when you purchased the property and the one illustrated in chapter 4. If you are hesitant about doing this yourself, and are not using a real estate broker, then hire an attorney who is skilled in these matters.

You must avoid being tied to a prospective purchaser for a long time, only to find the deal falls through. Basically, the prospect is making an offer to you and there should be a fairly short time period in which you will make up your mind. If you want to reject his offer, make a counter offer. Tell him the terms that would be satisfactory. The best way to accomplish this is to make out a new set of forms containing the new terms and then give him a short time in which to decide. This can bounce back and forth and consume time if you are not careful. But now there are the qualifications in the purchaser's offer.

He offers to buy "subject to obtaining financing, . . . etc." Do not agree to too long a period here. Before you accept his type of qualification, have a good idea as to whether the proposal is reasonable. For example, if current interest rates are 9 percent and he offers to buy subject to getting a loan at 6 percent, he is dreaming and you are wasting time accepting such an offer. You may also want to get some idea as to whether the buyer is likely to qualify for the financing.

A buyer who cannot make up his mind, or who tries to play one seller against another, will try to include loopholes in the offer to give him an opportunity to back out of the deal without having a good reason, from the seller's point of view. Read all offers with this in mind.

Remember, after you accept an offer, you are not able to continue to offer the property to others; and if the deal falls through, you have to start over. Reactivating the marketing momentum may be a difficult thing to do.

Who should sign the purchase contract? In many states, when the parties involved are husband and wife, it is best to have both sign all documents. In some situations, technically, if a wife did not sign the offer to buy, you might not be successful in obtaining damages for breach of contract when suing the husband, the only party you could sue. While being able to sue both husband and wife will not guarantee your success by any means, you ordinarily will be better off if both sign. When both parties feel committed because they signed the contract, you probably will have a stronger position.

Many buyers are unfamiliar with the purchasing process, are apprehensive, and are concerned they might be swindled. This feeling can be minimized if you avoid asking for the deposit or earnest money to be given to you directly. Have the buyer make out his check to a title company or escrow agent. Be sure the purchase agreement is clear on the terms for the return or forfeiture of the deposit so that future arguments will be avoided. The buyer should know that if he does everything he has agreed to do, but you fail to fulfill your obligation (such as providing clear title subject only to the liens and encumbrances agreed to), then he will get his money back. In turn, the buyer should understand that if he fails to do his part he is going to lose his deposit. That is the essence of any purchase agreement with respect to the deposit. And time is of the essence, too.

Assume you have found a buyer. An agreement has been reached, an escrow opened, and the buyer is busy arranging the financing. To conclude the transaction you will need to execute the instructions to the escrow agent. All of the details of this are covered in chapter 5 and you may want to review them.

What do you do if you cannot find a buyer? There are several choices. Perhaps the best thing to do is take the property off the market. If a prospective buyer learns that the property has been on the market for many months, he becomes suspicious. If you pursue the selling activity vigorously and cannot make a sale within ninety days, and you have a choice, it may be best to take it off the market for, say, six months or a year. Of course, if during the time you have discussed the property with prospects who did not buy, and you can find out why they are not buying, you may be able to rectify the situation and go from there. Either the property is at fault, or the buyer is deficient. It is not always possible to correct the problem with the property or change the situation for a given buyer. Finding out what is preventing the sale is important.

Depending on the motivation for trying to dispose of the property, you may find a solution in another direction. One way to get out from under the management problems — and, to some extent, the responsibility — is to lease the entire building to someone. This will be a financial advantage to the lessee and a sacrifice on your part. But if you are to give up some of the troubles, you will have to pay for the privilege. Similarly, you may want to arrange for a property management firm to take it over.

You do have some alternatives to selling, provided you do not have to liquidate the investment. Be sure to consider all options and avoid a hasty decision that may not prove to be the best.

Finally, have you fully considered potential future developments? Is it possible there is some plan for change in the area that could affect favorably your investment? Check with local building authorities, planning commission and zoning staffs, real estate people, and bankers. What is the outlook for the area? You may be trying to sell at the wrong time. Real estate is a long-term investment proposition. Has your term of ownership been long enough to produce the maximum return?

ESTATE PLANNING

CHAPTER 1

Why You Need an Estate Plan

This book is about the objectives of estate planning. You might prefer to have a treatise on how to write your own will but that would be no more practical than one on how to remove your own tonsils. You cannot do your estate planning alone but this book will help you to identify an expert and, by being well informed yourself, to get the most out of his or her talents.

This book answers three questions: Why should you create an estate plan? What kind of an estate plan should you choose? When should you review and revise your estate plan? This book deals with what you as a layman need to know.

Estate planning is a family affair. In a marriage, no matter who owns the property already acquired, the couple should share the opportunity and the challenge of developing together a better plan for the management, enjoyment, and disposition of what they own and of all that they hope to accumulate in the future. Furthermore, in most states a surviving spouse has a right to renounce a will and to claim a statutory share of the estate. This can have a damaging, if not a disastrous, consequence upon an estate plan. This option should be openly discussed and, if there is a serious possibility of its being exercised, the estate should be planned accordingly.

From the point of view of tax planning, it is usually wiser for the husband and the wife to keep their own estates separate and apart. This has an added advantage, if, unfortunately, the marriage should ultimately be dissolved.

Couples should plan their estates together. Upon the death of either party, the survivor should not have to conduct a search to discover what is owned and what should be done with it. Estate planning is an opportunity to share information and ambitions and to develop together hopes and expectations for the future.

Although the primary emphasis of this book is on the family, those who are single as well as those who are married should plan their estates.

Each of our fifty states has its own laws relating to the division of property when a person dies without a will. There are wide disparities, too, in state inheritance and estate tax laws and also in statutes relating to the administration of estates. A four- or five-volume treatise would be required to cover the idiosyncrasies of estate planning in each of the fifty jurisdictions. Necessarily, the treatment here is general, but one special word of caution must be injected. Nothing whatsoever has been said about the unique problems in estate planning that exist in community-property states: Arizona, California, Idaho, Louisiana, New Mexico, Nevada, Puerto Rico, Texas, and Washington. The omission is not an oversight but a recognition that these nine jurisdictions are not entirely in accord on community-property concepts.

I hope you will discover that you need a will, a living will, and a power of attorney. Estate planning embraces the drafting of these documents, but far more. Some of the objectives are (1) to create security during working and retiring years, (2) to provide support at death for spouse and children, (3) to minimize federal estate taxes and state inheritance taxes, (4) to design a program of gifts, (5) to reduce income taxes, (6) to insure equitable (not necessarily equal) treatment for children, (7) to maintain a family business or farm intact, (8) to design a life insurance program, (9) to designate pension and profit-sharing beneficiaries, (10) to reorganize a business enterprise, (11) to review health and casualty insurance coverages, and (12) to provide for the custody of minor children.

Tax laws are constantly changing. What is true today may not be true tomorrow. This book is a guide for determining your estate-planning needs. Meet those planning needs with well-qualified legal counsel. This will insure that your estate planning accurately reflects your needs in the light of existing tax laws.

The advantages of planning

Estate planning is the art of designing a program for the effective management, enjoyment, and disposition of property at the least possible tax cost. Tax savings should never be the primary objective, but you should plan your estate so that you, your family, and others for whom you care receive the greatest possible beneficial enjoyment of what you own. You can achieve that goal and, at the same time, minimize taxes.

Whether you are rich or poor, single or married, parent or child, male or female, you need an estate plan. In one case a man died owning only meager personal possessions and a dilapidated house and lot worth no more than $3,500. A carelessly drawn will left his entire estate to his divorced daughter for life with remainder (ownership after life tenant dies) to her seven minor children, all of whom lived 700 miles away. No one was authorized to sell the property and reinvest the proceeds. The vacant, uninsured dwelling deteriorated day by day. The cost of qualifying a guardian for each child, instituting an action for a court sale, reinvestment, and managing and accounting for the proceeds overshadowed the value of the property. A simple will leaving the entire estate to the daughter would have been a better estate plan.

In another case, a wealthy woman without children died leaving her entire estate to her husband. A few months later, he died without a will and his estate was divided among his nonresident nephews and nieces for whom neither he nor his wife cared. With an adequate estate plan, the wife by will could have left one-half of her estate in trust for her husband, with that half after his death to be added to a second trust created under the will for her nephews and nieces. Her husband could have also received the income from the second trust. Taxes would have been less and the property would have been distributed to those for whom she cared.

Again, an unmarried college graduate with accumulated savings of $20,000 died in an accident, leaving her parents and a sister. Both her mother and her father were financially secure, but they inherited her estate and, of course, it would be taxed again when it was passed on by them to their surviving daughter. A simple will leaving everything to her sister would have been far better.

As another example of a case involving no will, a farmer purchased a small, adjacent tract of land, taking title in the name of himself and his wife as tenants in common (each owning one-half) without right of survivorship (survivor takes all). By a prior marriage she had had four children. Late in life the farmer, then a widower, wanted to sell the small, adjacent tract of land, but his wife's children by her first marriage would not agree. Preferably, he should have taken title to the small tract either in his own name or as a joint tenant with his wife with right of survivorship.

A man with three minor children died without a will leaving an estate consisting principally of his home, which was encumbered by a mortgage. Under the laws of the state in which he lived, title to one-half of the home vested in his widow and the other half in his three minor children. The family could not afford to retain the residence, and yet enormous expense was incurred through the necessity of guardianships for the children plus the cost of a judicially approved sale. A simple will leaving the entire estate to the wife would have eliminated all of that trouble and expense.

In yet another case, a husband and a wife died in an automobile accident, leaving two minor children to survive them. Although their combined estates were adequate for the support of the children, neither left a will and neither had ever negotiated a contract with a member of the family or with a friend for custody of the children. An intrafamily custody dispute developed and the children were penalized further by the excessive court costs of guardianships. A will placing the estates in trust for the children and a custody contract would have constituted a more sensible estate plan.

Regrettably, for a variety of reasons very few estates are planned, and in every county in the United States, court records reveal the tragic consequences. Most of us are so concerned with living that we do not give any thought to the consequences of dying. Secondly, there has never been a widely read layman's guide to estate planning that explains the broad need for assistance in planning and outlines some of the basic techniques. Finally, there are simply not enough lawyers who are well trained in estate planning and who are compassionate enough to care about even the smallest estates.

This book is emphatically not a do-it-yourself guide. Estate planning is an art and a science beyond the mastery of any layman. But this book can help you and your lawyer to plan your estate.

CHAPTER 2

Make
a
Will

A will is the basic document of almost every estate plan. It is an instrument executed in the manner prescribed by statute whereby a person disposes of his property after his death. Ordinarily, a simple will contains only three primary provisions. First, an executor is nominated or appointed to carry out the provisions of the will. Secondly, the powers of the executor are defined. And finally the will states the person or persons who are to receive your property after all debts, funeral expenses, taxes, and costs of administration have been paid.

If you are an older male with a very small estate, an adequate will might consist of only the following words: "I leave all of my property to my wife, request that she be appointed executrix without bond, and authorize her to do everything that I could do with my property if living." Those few words in your own handwriting, followed by the date of execution and your signature, would constitute a holographic will, that is, one entirely in your own handwriting. In nineteen states, a holographic will may be admitted to probate, the judicial process of establishing the validity of a will.

A simple will like that seldom suffices. For example, it does not provide for the disposition of property if your wife should die before you. Secondly, your wife at the time of your death may be ill or otherwise unable to serve as executrix. Nevertheless, simplicity sometimes works. Former President Calvin Coolidge's will said only: "I leave my entire estate to my wife, Grace, and request that she be appointed executrix without bond."

Ordinarily, however, an adequate estate plan embraces a typed will which is far more comprehensive and which is executed in the presence of two or three witnesses who must see both the maker of the will and each other sign the instrument. Two carefully drafted wills appear in appendixes A and C.

If you have a wife and two minor children and expect to have a net estate of at least $120,000 when you die, your net taxable estate will consist at least of (1) all of the property that you own in your own name at its value on the date of your death, (2) all or some part of the property that you own with your wife as a joint tenant with right of survivorship, (3) life insurance proceeds, (4) pension and profit-sharing benefits payable to your estate, and (5) certain other assets, *less* debts, funeral expenses, and costs of administering and settling your estate.

First, you should select an executor and one or more successor-executors. The ideal executor (you may never be able to find him) will possess excellent business judgment, be a paragon of honor and integrity, have experience in estate settlement, and have a vital and continuing concern for the care, comfort, and happiness of your family.

Second, you may wish for your will to declare that all the furniture and furnishings in your house belong to your wife. A recital may remove them from taxation in your estate, but you will have some tangible, personal property of your own which you would not want to have sold but would prefer to give to your wife or to someone else. Personal letters, jewelry, automobiles, personal effects, clothing, and sporting equipment are examples of this kind of personal property.

Third, life insurance and profit-sharing and pension benefits are not disposed of by will but by a separate beneficiary designation. In those states which impose inheritance taxes, life insurance is occasionally exempt from the tax if payable to a designated beneficiary, which may include a trustee under a living trust or a trust under your will. Depending upon your situation, you may want to avoid the state inheritance tax or you may prefer to have insurance proceeds in your estate to pay debts and taxes. Lump sum pension and profit-sharing benefits generally are not subject to the federal estate tax if payable to a designated beneficiary, and here again, you have a similar choice.

With these preliminaries out of the way, you must now make a choice about the distribution of the bulk of your estate. Here, for the first time, taxes become a major consideration. The cost of dying may be a pittance or a fortune. To a great extent, the price depends on how your estate is planned. In a net estate of $120,000, the U.S. death taxes may be either $9,340 or nothing.

At one time, you could reduce your death taxes primarily by writing a will in which your wife was given either a legal or a trust estate for life in practically all of your estate with whatever might be left over at her death going to your children or other members of your family. This technique took advantage of the principle that as long as your property continued to pass under your will, death taxes would be assessed only at your death and not again at the death of your wife. Today, whenever a husband and wife have estates of approximately equal value, the best estate plan often is for each one of you to set up a life estate for the other with remainder going to your children.

A marital deduction will

Let's assume that your estate is much larger than your wife's. In your case, a marital deduction will may be the best estate-planning approach. You can leave half of your gross estate (total taxable estate, less debts, funeral expenses, and costs of administration) to your wife; that half will be free from U.S. estate taxes at your death. That half escapes tax until your wife dies. Furthermore, a $60,000 federal tax exemption is available to each of you instead of only one $60,000 exemption from tax. Then, too, because estate tax rates, like income tax rates, climb as more money is involved, when your estate is divided into two units, each half is subject to lower tax rates than would otherwise apply.

Leaving one-half of your net taxable estate outright to your wife will entitle you to the marital deduction. As an alternative, you may create an estate trust; or a power-of-appointment trust may be established. In all probability, you would choose a typical power-of-appointment trust, and here is how that works.

In your will, you appoint not only an executor but a trustee, who will probably be the same person, to manage your estate during the life of your wife. Two trusts of approximately equal value will be created. Let's call the first of these the "wife's trust" and the other we shall identify as the "family trust." You will direct the trustee to pay out of the wife's trust all of the income to your wife for life and also to pay her as much of the principal as she may need to maintain the standard of living to which she is accustomed. At her death your trustee will be directed to distribute any balance remaining in this trust exactly as your wife tells him by deed or will to distribute it. This action on her part is called the exercise of a power of appointment. If your wife does not exercise the power of appointment, however, you will direct your trustee to distribute the balance to the family trust.

Your marital deduction trust will not only save taxes but it will also give your wife an added measure of security and a valuable discretionary power. Secondly, your wife's right to distribute the principal of her trust is a valuable power in emergencies. For example, by illness or accident, one of your children may become unable to support himself. Then, too, moral equality, rather than mathematical equality may become an objective and your wife may wish to distribute a greater part of her trust to her disabled child.

You may also wish to direct your trustee, if the wife's trust assets are exhausted, to pay as much of the income and principal of the family trust to your wife as she may need to maintain her standard of living. Next, your trustee may be authorized, but not required, to distribute from the family trust income and principal sufficient for the education, maintenance, and support of each of your children, after considering other sources of income and support which each may have from time to time. After your wife's death, your trustee may be authorized to distribute all of the assets of your estate among your children at such time or times and in such amounts as he may, in his discretion, determine. Alternatively, you may require your trustee to distribute your estate to your children upon the death of your wife or upon their having reached a certain age.

Essentially, a marital deduction will such as we have been talking about makes your entire estate available to your wife as she needs it and lets the rest go to your children at the least possible tax cost.

Do not leap to the conclusion that because you have an estate of $120,000 or more you should have a marital deduction will. It is impossible to design one approach which will give the perfect answer to any given estate-planning problem. Each estate is unique.

Any particular program is dependent upon the comparative size of your estate and your wife's estate, methods of disposition, kinds of property involved, impact of both federal and state death taxes, and the fact that the property left to your wife may be consumed or donated before being exposed to a second tax. Then, too, no matter what tax savings may be involved, you may for reasons of your own not be interested in giving your wife one-half of your estate. After all, she could appoint that half to a second husband, but practically speaking, most wives care too much about their children to take property away from them to give to another man.

CHAPTER 3

Create
a
Trust

If you will add up what you own, what you expect to get by inheritance or otherwise from others, insurance proceeds and other assets, you may discover to your surprise that you are worth $80,000 or more and should consider a marital deduction will. For a variety of reasons, however, you may wish to reject that approach.

First, if you are unwilling to give your wife the power to appoint by her will one-half of your taxable estate, then forget about the marital deduction will no matter how large the tax savings you might achieve. For example, if your wife has had children by a prior marriage for whom you do not care, then you had better think twice before giving her a power to make provision for them. She could also, of course, give that part of your estate over which she has some control to a man whom she might marry after your death, but generally speaking if you have children only by your marriage, the odds are that she will permit her trust to "pour over" into theirs.

Secondly, if your wife has a large estate of her own, you had better ask your attorney to plan the two estates together. Quite often in that situation, a marital deduction provision will increase, rather than reduce, death taxes.

Finally, if you are the wife rather than the husband and if you have a large estate of your own, you may assume that your husband will remarry upon your death and you may have not the slightest interest in exposing your estate to a second wife.

If a husband plans to leave his estate in fee simple (outright) to his wife or to his adult children or to other persons free from disability, or to charities, a simple will may suffice. If, however, he wants to give someone the use and benefit of his estate for life with his properties to be divided among others thereafter, then he should consider creating a trust.

The duties of an executor are limited and temporary in character. Generally speaking, he takes possession of personal property, pays debts, funeral expenses, costs of administration, and death taxes and then distributes the estate in the manner provided by the will. Trust management begins where estate settlement ends. Generally, the same person who is appointed as executor is also appointed as trustee, which has some distinct advantages from the standpoints of both administration and taxation. Early partial distributions from an executor to a trustee are safer for the executor if he is also the trustee because he can always get a pay-back from the trust if the needs of the estate require that. Furthermore, income taxes can often be saved during administration by using a trust as a separate taxpayer.

A trust under a will is created by leaving properties to a named trustee for management with income and principal to be distributed by the trustee according to directions contained in the will. More than one trust can be created under a will and a separate trustee can be named for each trust. For example, you could appoint each of your adult children as trustee of his or her own trust.

Some of the most unsatisfactory wills ever written have left property to someone for life with the remainder to someone else. This is called a legal life estate because title is in the life tenant, for life, rather than in a trustee. For example, if you should create a legal life estate in a farm in favor of your wife with remainder to your children, all kinds of problems could arise, Would your wife have to insure buildings? If one of them burned down, would she have to replace it to the extent of insurance proceeds or would she have to supplement those with her own money to restore a building of like size and quality? Who would receive crops planted but not harvested in the year of the life tenant's death? Who, if anyone, could sell the farm and reinvest the proceeds? What would be done with moneys received from the condemnation of a part of the land for the construction of a highway or pipeline? How should taxes be prorated in the year of the life tenant's death?

Problems become more complex if an effort is made to create a legal life estate in personal property. Fixtures and equipment wear out and have to be replaced and livestock either dies or matures and must be sold. The most carefully drawn will may create or leave unsolved countless questions concerning a life tenant's right to use or dispose of property and division of income. Admittedly, a legal life estate can be created and some of these problems met but, for the most part, it is far easier and wiser to create a trust.

A child's trust

If you have two or more children, you may wish to create a family trust divided into as many equal shares as you have children, with each share being known as a "child's trust." You can direct your trustee, charging an equal portion to each child's trust, to pay your wife that part of the income and principal thereof necessary to provide for her, according to the standard of living that she is enjoying at the date of your death, and to enable her to provide as she wishes for your children. You may wish to let your wife's benefits end if she should remarry but instead it might be wiser to direct your trustee, in making distributions to your wife, to take into consideration all other sources of income and support which she might have from time to time. For example, if you should die leaving minor children, both your wife and your children might be better off if she should remarry. Admittedly, you would not want to support her second husband, but if he, too, should die or should become disabled, surely you would not want your wife starving while your trustee continued to support your children.

Next in your will, you can authorize the trustee to accumulate income to the extent that the laws of your state permit or to distribute to your children any income not paid to your wife. You may also authorize your trustee to pay expenses directly for the maintenance and education of your children out of either income or principal.

Preferably, payments to your children should be charged equally to each child's trust until all of your children have reached an age of somewhere between twenty-three and twenty-eight years. After all, if you should die after one child had completed college but before another one had entered college, it would hardly be fair to divide your estate equally among your children until all of them had first received comparable benefits from your estate.

After a particular child has reached the age level selected by you, then you may wish to authorize your trustee to supplement that child's earnings for his or her maintenance or support, provided, of course, that the trustee must first be sure to hold back enough principal for the protection of your wife and younger children. You may even want to give the trustee a power to purchase a home for a child, keeping title in the name of the trust or placing title in the name of the child. The trustee may also be authorized to make loans to the child with or without security and, if you prefer, you may make this or any other power contingent upon your trustee's obtaining advance approval of your wife.

You may wish upon the death of your wife and after all of your children have reached the age level selected by you to give the trustee the power to make partial and final distributions to your children whenever the trustee believes it to be in the best interest of the child. For example, if you have a son or daughter whose marriage is insecure or who is unable to manage property, your trustee may find it wise to keep that child's share in trust for a period of time and, perhaps, even throughout his or her life. Now, you cannot foresee the future. Later, after your children have matured, you may prefer to revise your will, making your own decision as to which shares should be paid outright and which should be kept in trust.

If you plan to will any income-producing properties to minor children, a trust is a virtual imperative. Without it, a guardian would have to qualify for each child, giving "bond" (guaranty with surety) to secure performance of his duties. Secondly, in most states, the guardian could invest only in land, government bonds, and other "legals" (a class of securities in which trustees may legally invest). In many states, a guardian would not have the right to purchase livestock to place upon a farm. Thirdly, the guardian could not use up principal even for the purpose of educating a minor without approval of the court. Of course, without judicial approval, he could not enter into a mortgage or a long-term lease. Finally, he would have to file a settlement with the court periodically. Statutes do not grant guardians the powers that can be conferred upon trustees by will. Consequently a guardian cannot be expected to earn as much for his ward as a trustee nor to have comparable freedom in taking care of the needs of minor children.

Worst of all, if you leave any income-producing assets to the child, when he or she comes of age (at eighteen or twenty-one), the child will take over the management of the assets for himself. There are very few children of that age who are capable of managing their own financial affairs. All too often, there is a temptation for an early marriage, an expensive sports car, a costly trip or a half-baked business venture.

A trust is one of the most versatile and useful of all of the estate-planning devices: Taxes are minimized, minors are better protected, and property management is simplified and improved.

Consider a living trust

Trusts are the most versatile methods known for disposing of property, but, so far, we have considered only trusts created by a will. Two basic varieties of these have been considered: (1) A wife's trust and a family trust using the marital deduction and (2) a family trust under which someone, usually a surviving wife, is given life-time benefits with division to be made thereafter to others, usually children. These two varieties and many other kinds of trusts can also be created during your lifetime. They are known as either "living" or "*inter vivos*" trusts. A living trust can be drafted so that you can amend it or revoke it at any time. Alternatively, a living trust can be made irrevocable (not subject to any change what-soever).

During recent years, the revocable living trust has had great publicity and become very popular. Actually, in many cases its use is wise and intelligent, and in many, many others it has little, if any, value whatsoever.

To create a living trust, all that you have to do is transfer property by an agreement to a trustee to be held for the use of beneficiaries in the way prescribed by the agreement. In the living trust, you can either use a marital deduction arrangement or set up a single family trust, for example, for your wife and children. If the trust is revocable, the property in the trust will continue to be a part of your estate for death tax purposes. Therefore, tax savings are seldom the motivation for creating a living trust.

Points to consider

If you have a large portfolio of life insurance, the creation of a living trust may be the best foundation for your estate plan. In many states, life insurance payable to a named beneficiary, includ-ing a trustee under a living trust, is exempt from state death taxes.

For two reasons, you are better off having all of your insurance made payable to the trustee of a living trust. First, the proceeds can be made available through the trust to your executor for the payment of debts, funeral expenses, costs of administration, and death taxes. This arrangement can be advantageous because insurance proceeds are often needed to avoid the forced sale of land, a closely held business, a home, or some other fixed asset, to obtain funds to cover estate obligations.

Second, if your life insurance is made payable to your wife, it may be exempt from state death taxes when you die, but upon her death, any unexpended portions of these funds will be a part of her estate subject to taxation. Furthermore, your trustee may be better qualified to invest and manage life insurance proceeds than either your wife or your children. In fact, if you have minor children, a guardian would have to qualify for each and a trusteeship is far more efficient than a guardianship.

Furthermore, if you die before retirement and if either your estate or a named beneficiary becomes entitled to pension or profit-sharing benefits, you should by all means consider the creation of a living trust. Whenever either profit-sharing or pension benefits from a qualified plan are payable to a named beneficiary, including the trustee of a living trust, they are totally exempt from the federal estate tax. For the same reasons that life insurance should be made payable to a trustee of a living trust, so also should pension and profit-sharing benefits be distributed in the same way.

There is a third situation in which a living trust is the best estate-planning technique. If you are an elderly person with a large estate, you can create a living trust naming, for example, one or more of your children as trustees. By placing substantially all of your property in the trust, you will be relieved of the worries of managing your property and, if your trustee does not perform to your expectations, you can always revoke the trust.

In the fourth place, the living trust is the ideal solution for a problem that is becoming increasingly common. If you live in one state and your children reside in another, they may not be eligible to qualify as executors and trustees under your will. Usually, too, a trust should be administered in the state where your beneficiaries reside. This problem can easily be solved by putting all, or substantially all, of your property in a living trust, naming as trustee either your children or a bank, for example, in the community where your children live.

Finally, a living trust avoids the delays of probate and publicity about the size of your estate and the names of your beneficiaries. If you treasure the right to privacy, a living trust is the ideal vehicle for avoiding publication of the size and disposition of your estate.

A trust, of course, does not come into existence until it has been funded, that is, until some asset has been transferred to the trustee. Life insurance is only one of the many things which can be used to fund the trust. Cash, securities, real estate, or any other asset may be used.

If you create a living trust as a part of your estate plan, you will also in all probability want to have a will leaving all of your residuary estate to the trustee of your living trust so that the bulk of your remaining estate will pour over into and be administered as a part of your living trust. A sample of a living trust appears in appendix B and of a pour-over will in appendix C.

Contrary to popular belief, the use of a living trust seldom reduces significantly either attorney fees or fiduciary fees for services rendered in the settlement of an estate. The services of both counsel and trustee in the preparation of tax returns and the management and administration of assets are virtually the same, whether your estate is disposed of by will or in part by the creation of a living trust. In some jurisdictions, however, legal and fiduciary fees are less when a living trust is used and, almost invariably, avoidance of judicial supervision eliminates bond premiums and court costs for the trusteeship.

A custody contract

If you and your wife should die in a common disaster, who would get custody of your minor children? If you are divorced and have custody of your children, who will take your place if you should die? If you are a widow or a widower with a minor child or children, who will raise them for you if you should die before they become of age?

By a will you can dispose of your property and of your body. You can appoint a trustee to manage your estate and to distribute income and principal for the support, education, and maintenance of your children. You may request, but you cannot compel, someone to accept custody and to raise them for you. What can you do?

First, if you are married, you and your wife should make a decision, to be reviewed periodically, as to whom you would like to take over your parental responsibilities. Maybe your parents or hers could and would accept the children. Another possibility is a brother, a sister, a brother-in-law, or a sister-in-law. If one of these should have children of approximately the same age, you might be able to enter into a mutual agreement under which they would assume the custody of your children or, alternatively, you would serve as custodian of their children.

Later, if you have an older child who marries, then you might want to change the custody arrangement to let that child take care of his or her younger brothers and sisters. If you do not have anyone in your family or your wife's family who could and would take over for you, there is always the possibility of your having a good and capable friend who, confronted with the same risk, would enter into a mutual custody arrangement.

You cannot expect anyone to assume the financial responsibility of raising your children. Your estate plan should be designed to create, through insurance and savings funds, sufficient support until they are of age. Social security benefits will not cover the total cost, but you can always supplement your estate by renewable term insurance to be carried in large amounts as long as you have minor children to support.

If you do not have a custody agreement, no one may volunteer, or a dispute could develop between your family and your wife's family over who should take the children. The problem could be more serious if you are divorced and do not believe that your former spouse would be a fit and proper person to have custody of your children. Admittedly, you cannot prevent him or her from trying by writing a contract with someone else, but all children are wards of the court, and the existence of a contract would be a factor which any court would consider in awarding the custody of minor children.

Your children are your most important assets. Do not forget about them when you do your estate planning.

CHAPTER 4

Powers
of
Appointment

A power of appointment should never be created without the advice of an attorney who understands fully all of the tax and legal consequences. Powers improperly designed and used can seriously penalize you and your family. And yet, with competent advice, you not only can, but should, grant powers of appointment. There is no more valuable technique in estate planning.

Here, perhaps more than anywhere else, this is not intended to be a do-it-yourself guide, but only an explanation suggesting some of the alternatives available to you.

Powers of appointment are not simply a tax-saving device, but primarily a means of disposing of your property more efficiently. Nevertheless, in most cases you can accomplish your basic objective and at the same time save taxes.

A power of appointment may be created by will, by deed, or by contract. The person who creates the power is called the "donor" and the person to whom the power is given is known as the "donee."

The "appointee" is anyone in whose favor a donee exercises the power. The property interest covered by the power of appointment is sometimes called the "appointed" property.

In considering tax aspects, we shall, for the purpose of simplicity, deal only with powers to be created now, excluding, among others, those granted prior to October 22, 1942, when the *Internal Revenue Code* was amended. At the present time, a power is "general" if it can be exercised in favor of the donee or his estate or the creditors of either and if the donee can exercise it alone, that is, without someone else with a substantial adverse interest having to join in. A general power of appointment is taxable whether exercised or not. Most of the time, a wife is given a general power of appointment in a wife's trust to take advantage of the marital deduction.

Under a "special" power of appointment, on the other hand, the donee may appoint only from a limited class of persons other than himself, his estate, and his creditors. Ordinarily, a special power of appointment permits appointment only to designated members of the family, usually children, grandchildren, and in-laws. Whereas a general power of appointment is taxable whether exercised or not, under the federal law a special power of appointment is taxable only if it is exercised. State laws differ on the tax consequences of the exercise or nonexercise of special powers of appointment.

While a general power of appointment is used most frequently in the creation of a wife's trust to take advantage of the marital deduction, it has an additional value. A wife with a general power of appointment retains greater authority over her children and she has the freedom to make unequal distributions to them. I shall never forget an estate in which a son, after the death of his father, ceased speaking to his mother and opened a business competing with the principal enterprise of his father's estate. He gave his mother every reason to use her power of appointment so that he would not receive additional benefits from that portion of his father's estate which had been placed in a trust for his mother. Repeatedly, too, I have seen examples of one of a number of children suffering a crippling disability, thus destroying his ability to support himself. In such a case, there is justification for a mother to use her power of appointment to provide for the health, support, and maintenance of her unfortunate child. Preferably, however, to avoid the inadvertent exercise of a general power of appointment, the donee, in exercising the power, should be required by deed or will to make specific reference to the instrument granting the power.

A special power of appointment, like a general power of appointment, is designed to permit the donee of the power to make adjustments in estate distribution which are needed because of events occurring after the creation of the power. For example, if you have minor children or minor grandchildren, you probably cannot, at the time the power is created, foresee their future needs. Nor is there any way for you to predict the ultimate outcome of the marriage of either a child or a grandchild. A special power of appointment enables someone else whom you trust to modify your estate plan to take care of changed conditions when they arise.

If you have a daughter, the creation of a power of appointment is especially desirable. First, you can direct your trustee to pay her income and principal necessary for the education, health, maintenance, and support of her and also of her children. If, instead, you should leave her part of your estate to her "in fee" (outright), then if she should die before her husband, he could "disclaim" (refuse to accept) under any will which she might have, and receive part of her estate by statute. Furthermore, if you are leaving a substantial estate to your daughter, she could save death taxes, perhaps, only by using the marital deduction and neither you nor she might be interested in turning over one-half of what you are giving her to her husband. On the other hand, you could give your daughter a special power of appointment which would not be taxable unless she exercised it. In default of the exercise, you could provide that the trust would continue for the benefit of her children; but you could confer upon her the right to make provision for her husband and to make an unequal distribution among her children.

Tax consequences

In the creation of powers of appointment, income tax consequences must be considered. If a son is named as trustee, the income may be taxed to him and even where he is not named as trustee, he may be subject to a tax to the extent that income is used for the support of one of his children. Certain powers in living trusts will also result in the income being taxed to the person creating the trust.

Without adverse tax consequences, you can also grant a beneficiary a power to appoint to himself in any year, out of the principal of his trust, $5,000 or 5 percent of the principal of the trust. Then if the trustee is not sufficiently generous, the object of your affection can receive, in addition to income, a part of the principal every year.

You might also want to consider giving your trustee what might be called, in a broad sense, a power of appointment to provide for your children until they reach a designated age, according to their needs, rather than according to some standard of mathematical equality. This device is known as a "sprinkling trust": The trustee may use the money where, in his opinion, it will do the most good.

Once again, using power of appointment in its broadest sense, you may authorize your wife or one of your children to appoint a successor-trustee. That procedure is particularly appropriate when at the time you are preparing your will it is impossible to foresee whether you would prefer a particular individual or a certain bank to act as trustee twenty, thirty, or forty years later.

A well designed estate plan should be a charter of freedom. By building in flexibility, you can not only save taxes but also make wiser provision for those whom you love.

5

Pick
Your Own
Fiduciary

An administrator, an executor, and a trustee—all are "fiduciaries" (persons holding property in trust). If you die without a will, the court will appoint an administrator who may or may not be qualified to manage the personal property in your estate. But he will collect assets, pay debts and expenses, and distribute the balance according to the law Ordinarily, an administrator will not have any power to deal with the real estate, not even to the extent of managing a farm during the current crop year. An executor, by contrast, can be selected by you and empowered to deal, not only with your personal estate but, also, with your real estate. Comparatively speaking, the assignment of an executor or of an administrator is of a short-term nature extending over a period of one, two, or three years. The functions of a trustee, whose services begin where those of an executor end, may extend over decades or even lifetimes.

The selection of an executor, and usually, too, of a trustee, is a challenging assignment of enormous importance. Ideally, the executor-trustee should have extensive fiduciary experience and demonstrated ability as a businessman. Integrity is vital, and of paramount importance too is a genuine and compassionate concern for the welfare of the beneficiaries of your estate. Choosing a well-qualified executor-trustee is often one of the most difficult problems in the planning of an estate.

You may be tempted to designate your spouse and to rely upon your attorney to guide the executor-trustee through the maze of responsibilities, including liquidation or operation of businesses, making elections under the *Internal Revenue Code,* preparing income and death tax returns, and keeping the estate beneficiaries informed and happy. This may work, but there are sometimes better options available. A brother, sister, adult child, or business associate is often a better choice. But a problem can arise if one of a number of children is selected to serve, especially so if the trustee is vested with discretionary powers in making distributions. He or she may be placed in an embarrassing and emotionally charged position of having to treat each brother and sister differently. Furthermore, by possessing powers to make distributions of principal to himself or to his children as beneficiaries, some income and death tax-saving possibilities may be forfeited and lost. For example, a son, while in office as trustee, can distribute principal to himself. That portion of the assets may be included in his estate when he dies and, if he uses estate funds to support his own children, he may lose the right to claim them as dependents on his own income tax return.

If an individual is appointed as executor-trustee, he may die before you do, and certainly there is a greater risk that he will die before the trust created by you terminates. The selection of a successor also becomes of vital importance. One useful alternative is to authorize a surviving spouse or one or more children to designate a successor-executor, but that power may not be exercised and someone must be designated to serve in the event of a default. In almost every will, the ultimate executor-trustee should be a bank with a well-organized and administered trust department. The bank will not die, and if you live in a metropolitan area it should be possible to identify some institution with a good record in the administration of estates and trusts.

Often, the best choice for an executor-trustee is a bank with an excellent trust department. But in smaller communities there are not many of these and there is always the risk that the trust officer, in whom you have confidence, may die before an estate and trust settlement is complete.

Fiduciary responsibilities

Before selecting anyone other than a bank as executor-trustee, consider the many things that your fiduciary must do. Preferably, except in the most simple estates, a double entry set of books should be opened. If there is a marital and nonmarital trust which cannot be combined for administrative purposes, two sets of books must be opened. If any trust allows for accumulation of income, there must be a separate account showing all accumulations, which must be segregated until they are paid out. Records must be maintained so that income and *ad valorem* (at a rate percent of value) tax returns may be prepared and beneficiaries advised of the character (whether taxable or nontaxable) of distributions made to them. The position of the trustee, especially, is not one for an amateur.

Another possibility is that of naming as coexecutors and as cotrustees a spouse or a child and a bank with a trust department either with or without some clear-cut division of responsibility between the two. For example, a wife is in a better position to determine distributions to be made to children under a sprinkling trust, whereas ordinarily, a bank is better qualified to manage a portfolio of securities.

Eligibility to serve as executor can also be a problem. In most states, a nonresident child may serve although he may be required to designate a process agent and to give bond. Ordinarily, a bank not incorporated in the state where you live will not be eligible to qualify unless, as some states permit, a coexecutor-trustee, qualified to do business in the state, is also nominated to serve. If you are a resident of one state and also own property in another state, then you should ask your attorney to examine the requirements of the foreign jurisdiction. Sometimes an ancillary executor-trustee must be designated to serve in the foreign jurisdiction, but there are ways of getting around this. For example, if you own a summer home in another state, ancillary administration can be avoided by transferring the title to this home to the survivor of your wife and yourself with remainder to your children with a power being reserved in your wife and yourself as life tenants to sell and reinvest. Another possibility is to place property located in a foreign jurisdiction in a revocable trust.

Unless your will provides otherwise, an executor and also a trustee will be required to give bond to secure performance of his duties as such. Unless there is a member of your family or a friend to sign a bond without compensation, the cost of purchasing this protection from an insurance company can become another unnecessary estate expense. Of course, unless you have complete confidence in your executor-trustee, the bonding requirement should not be waived. Ordinarily, a bank can serve as executor-trustee, pledging its corporate assets to secure its fiduciary bond in lieu of paying a premium to an insurance company for service as surety.

Empower your executor-trustee

If you are engaged in business at the time of your death, in most states neither your executor nor your trustee can lawfully carry on your business without a specific authorization. If he takes his chances and operates it, he will be liable for any losses that may result.

By his will the newspaper publisher Joseph Pulitzer imposed certain inflexible conditions which could not be complied with upon the sale of the *New York World*. After expensive litigation, the conditions were set aside, but when the *World* was sold, publication had to be suspended. Another publisher, Adolph S. Ochs, received better advice. He gave his executors and trustees broad powers of management and disposition of his interest in *The New York Times*.

A small-town druggist said nothing in his will about the operation of his store. Because the executor played it safe, the family suffered. The drugstore was gradually liquidated. When inventories were exhausted, they were not replaced. The business fizzled to a failure. With an adequate power to the executor, it could have been sold profitably as a going concern with another drugstore paying a premium to purchase the prescription file. The same will, in lieu of devising realty to a trustee, left rental properties to the wife for life with remainder to nephews and nieces. The buildings deteriorated, approaching the end of their useful life, but an expensive suit had to be filed for authorization to sell and reinvest the proceeds.

Money can be earned and expenses curtailed by granting your executor and your trustee the power to do virtually anything that you could do with your property if you were living. You should select a fiduciary whom you can trust and give him all of the powers that he needs to act. In today's complex civilization, a simple one-page will seldom suffices. Neither the common law nor the statutes of your state confer upon your executor-trustee the powers which he should have.

Ordinarily neither a will nor trust agreement needs to embrace all of the powers contained in the sample will (appendix A) and in the sample trust agreement (appendix B), but preferably each of them should contain at least the broad grant of powers which appears in the typical short will in appendix D.

If your estate is not well diversified in its investments, you may authorize your executor-trustee to retain any property which you own as original investments, although some might not be of the quality required under the laws of the state in which you live.

If you own a business it is imperative that your executor-trustee be authorized to operate and/or to dispose of that business. During administration of your estate and during administration of any trust that you may create, your trustee should be given a broad power of investment and reinvestment, including, perhaps, all forms of both personal and real property. There are many practical advantages in permitting your executor-trustee to register securities in the name of a nominee or in a "street name," as it is sometimes called. This procedure simplifies both the purchase and sale of securities and might prevent a substantial loss in a fluctuating market.

If you own or expect your trust estate to own stocks, then your executor-trustee should be authorized to vote stocks, exercise options, and participate in reorganizations. If a bank is appointed as your original or as a successor-executor and if you own stock in that bank, your executor-trustee should be authorized to both hold and acquire its own shares. But since in the election of the directors of a national bank, shares of its own stock held as trustee cannot be voted, you should include a direction as to how those shares shall be voted.

Interest rates and mortgages can be troublesome. If interest rates decline, your executor-trustee may have a problem with continuing to hold a high-interest note secured by a mortgage, which constitutes a good investment. The borrower may want to pay off and get a loan at a lower rate elsewhere. Your executor-trustee should be authorized to reduce interest rates and to release mortgages.

Often there is a troublesome question as to whether a particular disbursement constitutes a current expense or an improvement to an asset. Your executor-trustee can be empowered to charge expenses to income or to principal.

Stocks are purchased not only because of dividends which may be declared but also because of the possibility of appreciation. Your executor-trustee may be authorized to credit appreciation to either an income or a principal account. For the same purpose, he may be authorized to deduct proportionately over the term of the investment premiums paid for fixed-income investments.

Every executor-trustee should be authorized to borrow money. A loan may be needed to repair or replace an improvement or to pay debts, taxes, funeral expenses, and costs of administration. A power to borrow may avoid the forced liquidation of an asset in a declining market.

Every executor-trustee should be given the power to sell assets in your estate. What is a good investment now may not be a good investment when you die and certainly not throughout the term of any trust that you may create.

If you own land, your executor-trustee should be authorized to improve it, to subdivide it, to lease it for a term extending beyond the duration of the trust, and if there is any possibility of there being oil or any other mineral under the land, special provisions should be included for the execution of leases and unitization of properties.

Preferably, your executor should be authorized to file a joint income tax return with your surviving spouse and be given broad powers to exercise rights under the *Internal Revenue Code.* For example, if you own stock in a closely held corporation which has made or may make a *subchapter S* election (to be taxed as a partnership), your executor should be authorized to continue the election during administration of the estate and advised that when the trust created by you comes into existence, the election will be automatically cancelled unless the stock is transferred to a beneficiary who files a consent to continue the subchapter S election. He should also be given the power, when election is available, to deduct expenses on your death tax return or on fiduciary income.

These are not all of the powers which should be or could be granted to an executor-trustee. In preparing a will or a trust agreement, a careful draftsman will review the complete range of possibilities.

6

Avoid
Survivorship
Titles

For all practical purposes, there are four ways in which you might take title to your home: (1) in your name, (2) in your wife's name, (3) jointly as husband and wife, with right of survivorship, and (4) in both of your names as tenants in common. If you hold title as joint tenants with right of survivorship, then upon the death of one of you the survivor will own the entire property. On the other hand, if you hold title as tenants in common, then upon the death of one of you the survivor will own an undivided one-half interest in the property and the other one-half interest will be disposed of either by will or by inheritance as a part of the estate of the deceased.

There is seldom a sensible excuse for a joint title with a right of survivorship, but there are countless reasons for avoiding treacherous title traps. Under the U.S. Estate Tax Law, the entirety of the property held in a joint tenancy is taxed in the estate of the first joint tenant to die with the exception of that portion which a survivor can prove was paid for by the survivor. After the lapse of many years, the evidence is hard to come by, and, most frequently, the cost was paid by the husband who turns out to be the first to die. Admittedly, because of the marital deduction, one-half of the value may be excluded for U.S. estate tax purposes, but even so half or all of the value may be taxed when the first of the couple dies and the entire value will be taxed when the second dies. There is also the further risk of overqualification for the marital deduction. Thus if a substantial part of an estate is held in a joint tenancy so that more than half of the net estate goes to the survivor, the excess will not qualify for the marital deduction and therefore will be taxed in both estates. Finally, if the survivor has or inherits an estate of his or her own, then piling survivorship property on top of that will result in an exorbitant estate tax upon the death of the survivor.

Somewhat the same hazards prevail under the death tax laws of most states. In some instances the rule follows the federal practice. In others the entirety of the value is taxed in the estate of the first to die, and in still others one-half of the value is taxed in the estate of the first to die. Again, there is a risk of paying a death tax twice upon the same property. In only a few states does a survivorship title avoid taxes in the estate of the first to die.

Other tax consequences

Both the creation and the termination of joint tenancies has serious gift, estate tax, and income tax consequences, some of which are not apparent even to the well-trained attorney. Not all property placed in a joint tenancy involves the making of a gift. If title is taken in the name of a husband and wife, there are three exceptions: (1) savings or checking accounts, (2) U.S. Savings Bonds, and (3) real estate purchased after January 1, 1955. With any of these, you have the right to treat the creation of the joint tenancy as having involved a gift. If you do not, then a gift will occur only if your wife actually exercises control over the property. For example, if your wife makes a withdrawal from the joint bank account created by you, keeping a part of the proceeds, then a gift would occur. If the transfer does not come within these exceptions and, if the value of the gift exceeds $3,000, a gift tax return must be filed and the value of the gift determined by the application of tenancy by the entirety factors published by the Internal Revenue Service. For example, if a man, aged fifty, creates a joint tenancy in property worth $100,000 with his wife who is forty-five years of age, the husband will have made a gift of $44,284 and not $50,000.

Secondly, as we have already seen, the creation of joint tenancies almost invariably increases both state and federal death taxes.

Thirdly, there is an income tax consequence. If income-producing properties, such as securities or realty rentals, are placed in a joint tenancy, one-half of the income therefrom is taxed to each joint tenant. In states where, at lower rates, separate income tax returns may be filed, taxes are reduced by the husband and the wife each having separate sources of income. But this result can better be achieved by placing title exclusively rather than jointly in the name of a spouse.

Unraveling or severing joint tenancies also has gift, estate tax, and income tax consequences. In a transaction between husband and wife, there is no problem with a husband-wife joint tenancy if the person paying for the property takes it back in his own name and if the property comes within one of these three exceptions: (1) savings or checking accounts, (2) U.S. Savings Bonds, and (3) real estate purchased after January 1, 1955. Every other case involves a gift for which a gift tax return must be filed. Usually with income-producing properties, the gift involved can be minimized by converting a joint tenancy with right of survivorship into a tenancy in common.

The conversion of a joint tenancy into tenancy in common places both estates in a position to reduce estate taxes by the drafting of appropriate wills, but no one should ever create or sever a joint tenancy without the advice of competent tax counsel. You may get into trouble if you try to do it alone.

There are other compelling reasons to avoid joint tenancies. First, if you are married and have minor children, you and your spouse could be killed in a common disaster. Expensive and restrictive guardianships would be necessary for your children unless the survivor happened to have a will creating a trust for their protection.

Second, if you are married and do not have children, a question could arise as to whether you or your spouse died first in a common disaster. Jointly held property could go either to your family or to your spouse's family.

Some people, who have not considered these consequences, have carelessly called joint tenancies the "poor man's will." A better title would be the "poor man's trap."

To say this does not mean that all joint tenancies are burdened with inevitably tragic consequences. A small checking account for household purposes entails inconsequential risks and detriments.

Secondly, if an estate consists only of a home, its contents, a car and a small bank account and if there are children born of the marriage who have reached adult age, then joint tenancies with right of survivorship will avoid probate and seldom cause significantly larger death tax assessments. Then, too, if a living trust has been created, it might be wise for title in the few assets kept outside to be held jointly by husband, wife, and trustee to avoid probate. For example, title to a car could be held in the name of husband, wife, and trustee.

But joint tenancies with a right of survivorship are seldom practical and useful. Avoid them if you can, and if you have already made the mistake of creating them, seek professional advice now to get them unraveled before it is too late.

7

Your Business: Organize for the Future

If you own an interest in a retail business, a service enterprise, a farm, or a small manufacturing operation, that investment may represent your largest asset. For your estate plan, you may need to reorganize your business to save taxes, to limit liabilities, and to assure its survival in the event of your disability or death.

Almost every business is operated as a sole proprietorship, a partnership, or a corporation. In a sole proprietorship, you alone are the owner and manager, but in a partnership someone else is contributing either capital or services. Either a sole proprietorship or a partnership can be incorporated. A sole proprietorship may be interrupted by illness and ended by death and a partnership may be terminated by death or by the withdrawal of any one of the partners. The life of a corporation need never end. This fact does not mean that every business should be incorporated, but every businessman should at least consider the advantages and disadvantages of obtaining a corporate charter.

In a sole proprietorship, you are personally responsible for all of the debts of your business and your business is also responsible for all of your debts created outside of the business. If on company business, you or one of your employees should have the great misfortune to be in fault colliding with a school bus, injury and death claims in excess of your insurance coverages could total far more than your net worth.

In one case, a subcontractor entered into an agreement to erect guard rails on an interstate highway. The bid on the job was based upon quotations from suppliers and after the bid was accepted, the subcontractor issued purchase orders which were accepted by the source of supply. Unfortunately, by the time work orders were issued, the supplier could not purchase raw materials at a price equal to the contract which he had made for the delivery of fabricated materials. The supplier notified the subcontractor that no further deliveries would be made except upon the basis of a 50-percent price increase. If the subcontractor paid the higher price, the loss on the project would exceed the subcontractor's net worth. If the subcontractor bought the guard rails on the open market, the price would be even higher than the new quotation from his old supplier. If the subcontractor failed to perform the contract, the prime contractor would complete performance and sue the subcontractor for the difference between the cost of performance and the contract price. Bankruptcy was inevitable, but fortunately the subcontractor was incorporated. His loss was limited to the assets he had invested in his business.

Some of the risks of carrying on a business cannot be insured at a premium which the business can afford to pay. Incorporation is the only practical means of limiting liability. Often, too, the corporate form can be structured to reduce income taxes significantly.

If you are operating a partnership without a written partnership agreement, do you know what might happen at your death? Death dissolves a partnership, and in most states unless a court intervenes, your surviving partner or partners will have the absolute right to liquidate the partnership. If you are carrying on your business as a corporation, the stock of which is closely held, your risks are almost equally great. If you own less than a majority of the stock, the surviving stockholders can decline to elect another member of your family to replace you as an officer and can adopt a small dividend policy so that your estate will realize less than it should from your investment.

If you are in a partnership, you need a partnership agreement. If you own stock in a closely held corporation, then you need an agreement among stockholders. Many of the problems of managing a business can best be dealt with by a contract among persons associated in the business. For example, in most states unless the powers of a partner are restricted by contract, any general partner may employ or fire any employee, borrow money on behalf of the partnership, carry on the usual business of the partnership, sign contracts, and convey real estate.

Many of these same risks exist in the operation of a closely held corporation. In such, however, powers of an officer can be limited by by-laws and, too, further limitations can be imposed by an agreement among stockholders. Of course, in drafting a stock- holders' agreement, different language is used. In a partnership contract, partners agree to take certain steps and to refrain from other courses of action. In a stockholders' agreement, the stock- holder is required to vote his stock in a particular way in the man- agement of corporate affairs, but in both cases—the partnership contract and the stockholders' agreement—the same results can be achieved by similar techniques.

Why do so many partnerships fail? One of the major reasons is that many partnerships are organized upon the premise that profits and losses should be shared strictly on the basis of capital invest- ment, but in every partnership the abilities and the performances of partners differ. There is always the risk, too, that one member of a partnership will lose interest, become an alcoholic, suffer a dis- abling illness, or otherwise fail to carry his part of the load. In such event, disagreement, dispute, and dissatisfaction often begin—and may threaten to disrupt whatever plans you have made for your estate. The difficulty stems basically from a pattern of distributing profits entirely on the basis of capital investment. Such a division is fair and reasonable only in those rare instances in which the services of partners are rendered in the same proportion in which their capital has been contributed.

Division of profits

An equitable basis for dividing profits among partners is, there- fore, one of the most important matters to be covered in a part- nership agreement in order to protect your and your heirs' interests. There are many ways to meet the problem. Perhaps the most satisfactory is that of allocating a percentage of the profits to capital investments and a percentage of the profits to services. For example, it may be agreed that 50 percent of the net income of the partnership will be divided among those owning interests in the partnership in the percentage of their respective investments. The remaining 50 percent of the net income can then be divided among the partners contributing services to the partnership in proportion to the value of the work actually done by them. This basic percentage division should be predicated primarily upon the extent to which capital, as distinguished from services, will be responsible for the success of the enterprise. When the partnership agreement is first negotiated, it is far better to agree upon the initial division among the persons who are to contribute services, but there should always be some provision for changing this allocation over the years as circumstances require.

A second method of dividing profits between capital and management is to provide in the partnership agreement that salaries shall be paid to managing partners according to the job title held by each, that each partner will be elected to his job by all of the partners, and that the salaries will be reviewed and modified from time to time as necessary. The balance of the earnings, after payment of salaries to management partners, can be divided among those investing in the business in proportion to their capital contribution.

Either of these two arrangements for dividing profits can prove helpful in settling the questions which arise when a partner dies or becomes totally disabled. For example, a partner contributing services and having a capital investment would upon death or disability lose the right to draw that percentage resulting from services, but he or his estate might be permitted to retain an interest in the partnership, receiving therefrom only that part of the profits attributable to his capital invested.

Dissolution provisions

Every partnership agreement should also contain some provision for dissolution of the partnership during the lifetime of the partners. Partners, like husbands and wives, do fall out with each other. A divorce can be obtained in a bitter and expensive lawsuit, and, by the same token, a partnership can be dissolved by litigation, but only a fool would prefer a lawsuit to a well-planned method of settling differences. The largest asset of your estate could be placed in jeopardy or virtually destroyed.

Over the years any one of three situations may develop in a partnership. First, one of the partners may simply want out of the partnership. Secondly, for some excellent reason or reasons one or more of the partners may want to force another partner out. Finally there is the possibility of one or more of the partners wanting to force another out without having any good, sound business reason for the expulsion.

Many partnership agreements provide that if any partner wants to withdraw voluntarily from the partnership, then the remaining partner shall have an option to buy the interest of the retiring partner at the price set up for partnership valuation in the event of death of a partner. If you prefer to discourage voluntary retirement of partners, then it can be provided instead that the buyout shall be at some discount, such as 10 percent, of the agreed valuation basis.

It is desirable but difficult to cover the situation arising when some partners want to force one of the other partners out either with or without a good and sufficient reason. If the partnership agreement provides for the expulsion of a partner for a specific cause, then some of the causes which may be listed are these: inactivity, disability, neglect of business, breach of partnership articles, or conflicting outside interests. If causes for expulsion are listed in a partnership agreement, it is advisable to have the partnership agreement contain an arbitration clause so that an outsider may make a finding as to whether or not an adequate cause for expulsion exists. Furthermore, if you adopt a provision for expulsion with cause, it is probably wiser to provide that a partner can be forced out even then only if a premium, which may be 10 percent or more above agreed valuation, is paid to the partner being forced out.

In lieu of the arrangements described, some partnership agreements simply provide that if any partner wants out, or if any partner wants to force another out, then the entire partnership shall be transferred to those partners offering the highest price for the whole. This method, of course, often produces unfair results because a partner may not be in a financial position to protect himself in the event a dissolution occurs. The suggested alternatives are not the only possibilities, but they are the ones most frequently encountered.

A well-written partnership agreement should also cover the situation which presents itself when one of the partners becomes either totally or partially disabled and thus is prevented from performing his management duties for the partnership. Sometimes it is provided that the disabled partner shall employ, at his own expense, a person suitable to the other partners to perform his duties during the period of his absence. Again we sometimes find a provision that those partners who are able to work in the business shall then receive all of that percentage of the earnings distributable to management; but these partners must pay out of this percentage the salary of the highest paid employee of the partnership. Finally, of course, if a partner becomes disabled, the partnership can be dissolved or there can be a renegotiation of the net income percentages to be received by the various members of the partnership.

The courts have adopted most peculiar rules with reference to partnerships. One of them is that in the absence of an agreement, unequal services by partners will be presumed to have been rendered without expectation of reward. This rule emphasizes the importance of having some provision for conduct of the partnership in the event of disability of a partner. Courts do not want to take on the task of looking into the question of whether one partner has performed the more onerous duties or been more skillful or industrious than the other. If you want to take care of your rights effectively, you can do it not by looking to the courts, but only through means of a partnership agreement.

For example, in the absence of a partnership agreement, each partner has full control over partnership funds. A partner owning only a 10-percent interest in a business has full authority to make contracts, incur liabilities, and manage the business. Bearing in mind the unlimited liability of a partner for all partnership obligations, it is vitally important that every partnership agreement contain certain limitations upon the powers of a partner. Protection of your partnership investment is an essential part of estate planning and preservation.

Some of the prohibitions frequently included in a partnership agreement are these: (1) purchasing or selling real estate or any other fixed asset without the consent of copartners; (2) signing a note or contracting any other debt for the partnership without the consent of copartners; (3) guaranteeing any commercial paper on behalf of the partnership without the consent of copartners; (4) signing a partnership check payable to himself; (5) borrowing money from the firm for personal use; (6) lending any money of the firm without the consent of copartners.

Other safety provisions

Many partnership agreements contain provisions concerning the hiring and firing of employees. For example, a partnership agreement might authorize only one of the partners to engage all employees to be paid by the hour and require consent of other partners to hire salaried personnel. Some partnership agreements also require consent of partners to discharge salaried personnel.

To avoid misunderstanding, some partnership agreements define the duties of the partners quite carefully. Whenever this is done, it is easier for an outsider to determine, in the event of a dispute, whether a particular partner is carrying his assigned portion of the work load.

A partnership agreement may well contain various other miscellaneous but important provisions. It is somewhat easier to justify travel and entertainment deductions on income tax returns if they are covered by the partnership agreement. Then, too, this is the proper place to establish these allowances on a fair basis between or among the partners.

Arguments sometimes arise concerning drawing accounts and the distribution and retention of partnership profits. These matters, as well as contributions to cover partnership losses, can best be dealt with in the partnership agreement. A clause providing for an audit of partnership books on the request of any partner is also a good idea, and an especially worthwhile one in the event of the death of a partner. An arbitration clause is usually a valuable addition to any partnership agreement.

Corporate advantages

If you have incorporated or later decide to incorporate your business, you will need by-laws, corporate resolutions, and an agreement among stockholders taking care of many of the same problems that arise in the conduct of a business as a partnership. The two main reasons to consider a corporation are the limiting of liabilities, thereby conserving your estate, and the tax advantages to be gained, which will increase the value of your estate.

A corporation has a decided advantage over other types of organizations in that its creditors are limited in the collection of their claims to the assets of the corporation; they cannot reach the other assets of its stockholders. Tax considerations, however, are often paramount in determining whether a business should be incorporated or continued as a sole proprietorship or partnership.

The corporation is a separate taxpayer: It files its own income tax return with the federal tax rate now being 20 percent on the first $25,000 of net income, 22 percent on the next $25,000 of net income, and 48 percent thereafter. On your own individual tax return, you will reflect as income any salary paid to you by the corporation and any dividends which you receive from it. The corporation can deduct, in computing its net income, all salaries paid but, of course, it cannot deduct the dividends. Therefore, a tax will have been paid by the corporation on its net income and then you will be taxed again on any dividends paid to you by the corporation, with the exceptions to be discussed.

Individual income tax rates range from a low of 15 percent to a high of 70 percent. If the corporation pays out salaries to owners only as much money as they need to live on, retaining additional profits in the corporation, it is often possible that the combined earnings will be taxed at a lower rate. There are a number of ways to accomplish this objective.

First, if you incorporate a business, you can retain individual ownership of land, of improvements and, perhaps, even of fixtures and equipment. These can be leased to the corporation with the corporation being given an option to purchase. The rental, of course, will be deductible by the corporation and taxable to you. Later when profits have accumulated in the corporation, the option to purchase can be exercised and money taken out of the corporation in a form other than a taxable dividend. One word of caution here, however: If, when the option is exercised, you, your spouse, your minor children, and your minor grandchildren own together over 80 percent of the corporate stock, any gain upon the sale of depreciable property will be ordinary income rather than a capital gain.

Another way to get tax-free money out of a corporation is to organize it with what is known as a thin capital structure. For example, if $60,000 will be required to finance operations initially, 20 percent of this sum could be procured by the issuance of common stock. The remaining $48,000 could be obtained in the form of a loan. As profits accumulate, these can be used to retire the loan.

A corporation, without being subjected to a tax of 27½ percent or more upon unreasonable accumulation of surplus, can build its retained earnings to a total of $150,000. Furthermore, surplus can exceed this level as long as the funds are employed in the business activities of the corporation. When expansion no longer makes sense and after the corporation has accumulated sufficient funds for retirement of debts, exercise of options, and the financing of its operations, the corporation may make a subchapter S election (to be taxed as if it were a partnership instead of as a corporation).

Whenever you incorporate, you can transfer the assets of your sole proprietorship or of the partnership to the corporation in exchange for common stock, retaining in your business only enough in the way of assets to satisfy outstanding debts. This exchange of property for stock will be tax-free.

When you incorporate, you may wish to enter into a stockholders' agreement under section 1244 of the *Internal Revenue Code*. To do so is simply protective. If the corporation should unfortunately be unsuccessful, then the entire loss in value of the common stock can be deducted against your ordinary income. If this election is not made, your deduction would constitute a long-term capital loss only half of which would constitute a deduction, and then each year the amount of that loss which could be deducted would be only $1,000 in excess of offsetting capital gains.

Once again, this is not a do-it-yourself manual. This is only a checklist suggesting questions which you should explore. The object is not to determine whether or not you should incorporate your business or to tell you how to do it. You are only being urged to review your business to determine with the advice of counsel what the best form for its organization would be and then to prepare either a partnership agreement or a stockholders' agreement.

In estate planning, distribution of your estate at the lowest possible tax cost should not be the only objective. You must be equally concerned with building and conserving an estate to be enjoyed by you and your spouse in your retirement years.

Prepare for sale or survival

If a substantial portion of your income is derived from a business and if that business represents a significant portion of your total estate, some provision for the continuation or the liquidation of that business is a most essential part of your estate planning. Your death will create problems of (1) authority to continue the business, (2) valuation of the business, and (3) personnel to manage the business. If you are the key man in the business, you are in a better position than any one else to make a determination now for the solution of these critical problems.

If the business or your interest in the business is to be sold and if you are approaching retirement age, one solution is to sell the business during your lifetime. You may be in a better position than anyone else to negotiate satisfactory terms and price, but, of course, you will have to consider the income tax consequence. If your cost basis is low compared with the prospective sale price, the adverse income tax consequence may preclude a lifetime sale.

Some businesses are readily marketable after the death of the owner. For example, the success of a liquor store is attributable more to its licenses and location than to management. Apartments, commercial buildings, and warehouses can be readily sold at market values established by comparable sales. Established formulas exist for the valuation of insurance agencies, radio and television stations, and newspapers, but for most retail establishments the determination of market value is a difficult task and the identification of a buyer who will pay that price at what is virtually a distress sale is almost an impossibility. If you cannot sell your business during your lifetime or negotiate a satisfactory buy-and-sell agreement effective at your death, you should empower your executor-trustee to sell and/or to operate the business and give him your best advice on how to value and how to dispose of the business.

Another alternative is to give your interest in the business to members of your family during your lifetime, especially if you have a child who is interested in and capable of taking over the enterprise. This end can ordinarily best be accomplished by either incorporating the business or reorganizing an existing corporation. For example, in the organizing or recapitalizing of an existing corporation, preferred stock can be issued representing substantially all of the equity and having all the voting rights. The common stock can be given or sold to a child or children who will reap the benefits of future business success. Another possibility is to give, sell, or will to a child interested in the business the common stock with voting rights while leaving the preferred stock as a part of a trust for your wife or other children.

More often than not, a buy-or-sell agreement is the only practical solution for disposing of a business interest. The agreement is usually made among partners or among all of the stockholders of a closely held corporation, but a buy-and-sell agreement effective at death can be made between a sole proprietor and either a member of his family or a key employee. In addition to providing for disposition of the business interest, a properly prepared agreement can control the estate tax valuation of the business interest. For that purpose it must (1) be an arm's length transaction, (2) restrict the sale of the interest during the life of the seller unless first offered to the other contracting parties and, (3) either (a) give the survivor or survivors the option to buy at a price fixed by the agreement or (b) require the sale of the interest by the estate of the deceased and the purchase thereof by the other contracting parties. Alternatively, with a corporation the contract can require the corporation itself rather than its other stockholders to purchase the interest of the deceased.

The valuation of any business is a matter of opinion. No one has ever devised a formula that would be applicable to every situation. In negotiating a buy-and-sell agreement, you should remember that you may be the survivor. Because you do not know whether you will be the buyer or the seller, it is in your own interest to establish a fair and equitable basis for arriving at a price. If you should be the first to die, you want an assured purchaser at the negotiated price; and if one of your business associates should die first, then you need an assurance that you will be protected from unwanted outsiders.

You and your attorney should begin by finding out, if you can, the basis upon which similar business enterprises have been sold in recent years. For example, if your business is an insurance agency, the formula might be fixed assets plus some multiple of average commissions earned. Radio stations are ordinarily priced at fixed assets plus a multiple of annual billings. Net worth is seldom a satisfactory price basis because it is what a business earns that counts. For that reason, in many businesses the capitalization-of-earnings method is employed. The sale price can be reached by determining the average net profit of the business for a term of anywhere from three to five years preceding the date of the sale and then multiplying the average by a figure which will produce the result upon which the average profit is a fair return.

Some businessmen prefer a buy-and-sell agreement with a schedule attached on which at the end of each year the parties agree upon a new business valuation, but even if that approach is used the contract should contain a provision that if the parties fail to fix that value annually, a formula for valuation shall be used.

Finally, some contracts provide for valuation of the business by one or more experts. In some sections of the country, it is possible to identify, usually in the corporate finance department of a broker-age concern or the trust department of a large commercial bank, a man well trained in the valuation of business enterprises. The price can also be fixed by a compulsory arbitration provision.

Parties to the buy-and-sell agreement must make some arrange-ment to provide for the funds that will be needed to pay the pur-chase price. One possibility is that of allowing buyers to make the payments on an installment basis with the term being spread over a period of five or ten years, with the deferred purchase price to bear interest and with the obligation to be secured by the assets sold. Alternatively, a fund can be created in advance for the pur-pose of carrying out the contract. In the latter case, however, there is a risk that death may occur before an adequate fund has been accumulated to effect the purchase. If this risk is to be avoided, then a practical method of providing funds is to purchase insurance to fund the buy-and-sell agreement in whole or in part. Premiums on these policies are not income tax deductions, but the insurance proceeds are income-tax free.

There are a number of methods of purchasing business life insurance. If there are only two partners, each would normally want to insure the other's life in an amount sufficient to provide the purchase price set up in the buy-and-sell agreement. If there are several partners or stockholders, it is sometimes better to have the partnership or the corporation itself own the policies and pay the premiums. A third method is to use an insurance trust, which has advantages in a few situations.

One of the difficulties of a corporation accumulating earnings to fund a buy-and-sell agreement is the risk that accumulated earnings and profits will go beyond the reasonable needs of the business and become taxable at the rates imposed on accumulated, taxable income.

The importance of the buy-and-sell agreement cannot be over-emphasized. If you have been earning a salary as an officer of a closely held corporation, its board of directors may not elect another member of your family to replace you as an officer, and a small-dividend policy can be adopted so that your estate will realize very little from your investment. Upon your death, a partnership will be dissolved unless you have an agreement providing for its continuation.

8

Review Your Life Insurance

Millions of dollars are wasted on life insurance and some of that money may be yours. There are four reasons that the money may be wasted. First, ordinary life insurance (which combines pure insurance with savings) is all too often purchased when term insurance without a savings feature might offer better protection at a lower cost. Second, you may be a victim of the myth that all companies charge the same premium for like protection. Actually, the net cost of some policies is twice that of others. Third, you may purchase or carry life insurance which you do not need. Fourth, in an inflationary economy you are suffering a constant loss of the purchasing power of the dollars invested in life insurance and savings.

Life insurance can be a valuable if not essential part of your estate plan. Above all you may need coverage to provide for the care of your family in the event of your premature death. Again, life insurance may be needed to pay debts, funeral expenses, costs of administration, and death taxes. Often life insurance is the best way to fund a buy-and-sell agreement. Occasionally, life insurance serves better than anything else as a forced plan of savings. Life insurance has many other uses, too, but its primary purpose is to protect your dependents financially.

Never let anyone sell you life insurance. Buy it yourself to meet a specific need. If you do not have any dependents, you probably need little, if any, life insurance. If in the later years of your life you have accumulated an estate sufficient for the support of yourself and your wife and if you do not require insurance for some other valid purpose such as payment of death taxes, you should seriously consider converting ordinary life insurance into paid-up insurance and perhaps dropping some of your term or pure insurance. If you are married, if your wife cannot support herself, if you have minor children, and if you have only a small estate, then your life insurance requirements are probably larger than they will be at any other time in your life. As you accumulate an estate of your own and your children complete their education, your life insurance requirements ordinarily will decline with each passing year. The constant change in your own financial and family circumstances suggests that your life insurance portfolio should be reviewed at least every five years.

Consider your dependents

In reviewing your life insurance program, you should begin by defining the needs of your dependents. How much insurance is needed to increase the size of your estate to a level that will support your family if you should die now? Of course, you may or may not be able to afford as much life insurance as you should have.

After you have projected the needs of your dependents, you should determine the availability of other funds to meet their requirements. To what extent can your wife or adult children support minor children? What social security benefits will be available? Here you do not have to make a guess. From your local social security office, you can obtain a request-for-statement-of-earnings postcard to be mailed to the Social Security Administration, Baltimore, Maryland 21235. All you have to do is write on the postcard "benefit estimate, please." Your local social security office also has free pamphlets explaining the benefits to which your family will become entitled. Your local social security representative will be glad to estimate the benefits that your wife and children would receive if you should die now. Your social security benefits are a very important part of your life insurance program. You may be pleasantly surprised to find out the extent to which these will begin to meet the needs of your dependents.

Finally, you should take into consideration the other assets in your estate, including those arising out of pension and profit-sharing plans. You may also have an expectancy of inheritance or it may be that some other member of your family could and would perform a part of your obligation to support those for whom you care.

Next, you need to consider the kind of life insurance that you should buy and that decision necessitates your understanding exactly what life insurance is. The life history of a group of people can be predicted with a reasonable degree of accuracy. The combined experience of a group of life insurance companies reflects death rates per 1,000 shown in the accompanying table.

Age	Death rate per 1,000
25	1.25
35	1.40
45	3.96
55	11.00
65	27.99
75	63.36
85	149.17

If there were no costs of administering an insurance program, each of 1,000 people at age thirty-five would have to pay $1.40 per year to provide $1,000 for each person in the group who died. By age fifty-five, the cost would jump to $11 per year per person.

For term or pure insurance, you need to pay a premium equal to the risk of death at a given age level plus the cost to the insurance company of administering the program and making a profit. In a sense, term insurance is like fire insurance. If you assume that there are 1,000 homes in a town, each worth $20,000, and that only one home will burn per year, each person would have to contribute only $20 to provide a common fund sufficient to pay for that single loss.

When you buy either fire insurance or term life insurance, you pay a premium only for the actual risk of loss plus expenses and a profit to the company.

Ordinary life insurance and the many variations thereof, including endowment insurance and many others, consists of two elements: term life insurance plus a savings feature. For example, with an ordinary life policy, 12.5 cents of your premium dollar

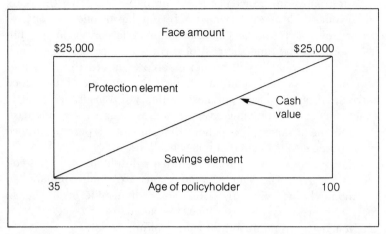

Source: Joseph M. Belth, *Life Insurance: A Consumer's Handbook;* Indiana University Press, 1973.

may pay for protection; 46.8 cents, savings; 26 cents, anticipated dividends; and 14.7 cents, the company's expenses and profit. The relationship of these elements in a $25,000 straight life policy issued at age thirty-five is illustrated in the diagram shown above.

The savings element of an ordinary life policy is called its cash value, and ordinarily that amount can be borrowed at any time from the insurance company with interest thereon. Because the cash value is constantly growing, the protection element is steadily declining. If you die, your beneficiary will receive the face amount of the policy, but a substantial part of the proceeds will represent moneys that you have saved and on which the insurance company has paid a very small rate of interest ranging from 2 to 5 percent. For this reason alone, ordinary life insurance is seldom a good investment. You can take the difference between the premium for term insurance and the premium for ordinary life insurance and invest it in a savings account producing a much larger return than you will get from a life insurance company. Admittedly, there is no income tax on the interest paid by a life insurance company on the savings deposited with it, but unless you are in a very high income tax bracket, you will make more after taxes by doing your own savings than by letting an insurance company save your money for you.

Another delightful aspect of term insurance is that the premium costs are based upon your age.

Your greatest insurance needs will probably be during the years when your children are growing up. By purchasing one-year or five-year renewable term, you can afford a much larger portfolio of life insurance. By the time the cost of term insurance becomes much higher, you probably will be better able to afford the increased premiums or perhaps you can reduce the amount of insurance carried. After all, if you purchase ordinary life insurance, that is exactly what is happening every year: as your savings increase through the ordinary life policy, the amount of pure insurance being purchased through that policy declines.

An insurance company representative will seldom try to sell you term insurance: The agent's commissions are small compared to the money he will make by selling you ordinary life insurance. In fact, with ordinary life insurance, the agent usually gets at least the first year's premium as his fee for making the sale.

After you have decided how much insurance you need and of what kind, you need to select the insurance company whose policy or policies you would like to purchase. *Best's Review, Life/Health* edition, published monthly, rates life insurance companies in terms of financial strength. Out of about 2,000 companies operating in the United States, its "most favorable" recommendation is awarded to only about 130 companies. Preferably, you should select your policies from one of these after having made a premium comparison. There are many bases of comparison; perhaps the best is the amount retained out of each premium for company expenses and profits. Among even the most highly rated companies, the most expensive policy may cost twice as much as the least expensive.

Other insurance factors

A few other comments about life insurance may be helpful. First, in purchasing and in reviewing life insurance, check the laws of your state. If there is a death tax exemption for policy proceeds made payable to a designated beneficiary, consider the possibility of creating a living trust funded by life insurance. Do not name minors as beneficiaries. A trusteeship is more efficient and flexible than a guardianship.

When you have accumulated an estate of your own sufficient to support your dependents and to pay all the costs of settling your estate, consider the possibility of converting ordinary life insurance into paid-up insurance, which means that you take a lower amount of coverage but no longer have to pay premiums. At that stage in life, some or all of your term or pure insurance may be dropped.

If you have a mortgage on your home, by all means consider buying credit life insurance or the equivalent which will pay off the loan in the event of your death. Preferably, if you live in a state where life insurance to a designated beneficiary is exempt from death taxes, you should purchase declining-value term insurance payable to a designated beneficiary rather than to a creditor.

You probably will not need certain kinds of insurance. If your wife works and helps support your children, then perhaps you do need life insurance for her; but if there is no earning power to be replaced by her death, the life insurance requirements are much smaller. You should consider only the cost of final expenses in her estate, including funeral expenses and, perhaps, the cost of hiring someone else to take care of your house and children. In most cases, however, insurance dollars can better be placed in the husband's program than in the wife's.

The premiums for accident insurance are small because the risk of death through casualty is relatively meager, but your insurance program should be based upon your needs for insurance and those certainly do not increase simply because you die an accidental rather than a natural death. If you want accident insurance, it can probably be purchased cheaper as an addition to your ordinary life or term insurance policy.

If you have ordinary life insurance, do not overlook the possibility of borrowing the cash value. At times the interest which you will have to pay the life insurance company will be substantially less than the interest or dividends which you can earn by investing the money elsewhere. Life insurance cash values are also a useful source of a loan to meet emergencies. Interest rates are often less than those charged by lending institutions.

By all means, consider the possibility of putting a waiver-of-premium rider on your life insurance policies. By so doing you provide that premiums no longer have to be paid after the policy-holder has become disabled.

Review your life insurance program every five years. Measure what you hold against the current needs of your dependents. Consider the possibility of changing a beneficiary designation. Determine whether ordinary life insurance should be converted to paid-up insurance and term coverage dropped or reduced. Do not assume that your insurance needs are static and constant. Keep your insurance program up to date.

CHAPTER 9

Think
Before
You
Give

You can save money by giving it away. Although gifts in excess of exemptions are taxable, the gift tax will probably be considerably less than the death tax. Secondly, by giving income-producing property, you will reduce your own income tax liability. But before making any substantial gift, you should do more than consider the tax consequences. For a variety of reasons, you should think twice before giving a substantial part of your estate away.

First, you should not make any gifts that will reduce your estate below the level needed for the support of yourself and your wife. Never forget that you will need income from investments after your retirement and that either you or your wife or both may suffer a long and expensive illness. Furthermore, unless your estate is substantially in excess of $120,000, tax savings from gifts may be inconsequential.

Giving to a child whose marriage may break up can prove costly. Your son's total estate will affect the alimony he has to pay and your daughter's net worth will be a factor in the alimony she can collect.

Certainly, too, you would not want to make a large gift to a child who has not demonstrated sufficient maturity and acumen to manage his or her own estate, nor should you risk a gift of an interest in a closely held business (a partnership or a corporation) to a child or a stepchild who might become alienated from you.

On the other hand, there are many compelling reasons why gifts should be made. First, if you can afford them, by all means make gifts to your children while you are living and can have the pleasure of seeing them enjoy your generosity. If you are not wealthy enough to make a major gift, you can often lend your credit to a child by becoming a cosigner on a promissory note, the proceeds of which are to be used to purchase a home or to establish a business. It is a lot of fun to see your children enjoy life while they have the time and the vitality to have the good times that you may have missed with your own struggle for survival.

The tax advantages of gifts

Second, you can achieve almost unbelievable tax savings. You can give $3,000 a year to as many people as you like without being taxed, and if your wife lets one-half of the gift be attributed to her, together you can give $6,000 a year per person without any tax. This is called the "annual exclusion." On top of that, after using up your annual exclusions, you can give away another $30,000, or with your wife, a total of $60,000 during your lifetimes, again without becoming subject to any gift tax. If you have two children, you and your wife could give them $72,000 in any one calendar year without any tax and you can give them $6,000 a year thereafter without any tax. The $30,000 allowance is known as the "specific exemption."

After you have used your annual exclusions and your specific exemptions, the gift tax rates are only three-fourths of the estate tax rates, but, better still, the property given away is removed from your highest estate tax bracket and taxed at a much lower gift tax bracket. For example, if you want to give $50,000 to each of two children, the first $72,000 is exempt from tax. The cost of giving the remaining $28,000 is only $2,040. If you should keep that money in your estate and if you die having a taxable estate in excess of $500,000, the federal estate tax (before credit for state inheritance taxes) would be not less than $35,000. Never forget that gifts come off the top of your estate on which the highest

death tax is imposed. Gifts, on the other hand, are taxed initially at
the lowest of the gift rates. You can compare the estate tax schedule
and the gift tax table in appendix E and appendix F and see for
yourself that, in all probability, any gift that you make will be subject to a lower tax than the death taxes which would be imposed if
you retained the property in your estate. Furthermore, the gift
tax that you pay removes cash from your estate which would otherwise be taxed at your death. The amount of the gift tax is added on
to the cost basis of any property transferred to the donee.

Whenever a gift is made, the tax is computed on the market
value of the donated property; but, in the hands of the donee if the
property is sold for a profit, the gift retains your cost basis plus the
gift tax. For example, if without having to pay any gift tax, you
should give your children common stock which cost you $50,000
but which has a market value of $100,000, and if your children
should sell the stock, they would have to pay a capital-gains tax.
For that reason, it is ordinarily preferable to make gifts of property
approximately equal to market value. If you do not have any
property of that kind, then the gift could well be a property which
the donee would never want to sell in any event. If the property
must be sold, it is, in some instances, better to give the property to
be sold as a gain to a donee who is in a lower income tax bracket
than you are. Certainly, assets which are selling below their costs
to you should not be used for gifts. It would be wiser to realize the
capital loss and to make a gift of the proceeds.

If one of the principal reasons for the gift is to reduce your income
taxes, then, if there is a choice of assets, those producing the greater
income might be the most desirable gifts. Although death taxes can
seldom be reduced by a gift to your wife, if you live in a state imposing state income taxes but not permitting the filing of joint
returns at lower rates, then occasionally a gift of income-producing
assets to your wife will reduce your total income tax bill. In such a
case, however, the effect upon death taxes should also be considered, and your wife certainly should also make her own will.
In fact, whenever you make a gift, the donee's will should be reviewed. It would be foolish to make a gift to children and risk
having it come back to you upon the death of a child without
leaving a spouse or children to survive.

A gift of life insurance will not deprive you of any income and will
save death taxes. It is easily valued and the present value of the
policy is much less than its maturity value. This gift also removes
the face value from the top of your estate tax bracket.

If you are reluctant to make a gift because of the gift tax involved, you can select an asset which the donee can sell and you can require the donee to pay the gift tax out of the proceeds of sale.

Another useful gift is that of an asset which can be expected to appreciate rapidly in value. For example, if you are starting a new business for which you expect phenomenal growth, you can give stock in that business before an earning pattern has been established. If that stock were retained throughout your lifetime, its value in your estate could be substantial, but by getting rid of that asset during your lifetime, you may succeed in taking valuable property out of your estate when you die.

Some gifts do not remove assets from your estate for death tax purposes. For example, if you reserve a life estate in the asset, the gift will not be effective until your death. Next, if you make a gift within three years of the time you die, the gift will be presumed to have been made in contemplation of death and may be included in your estate. In such case, it is important by letter and by conferences with your doctor, banker, lawyer, and accountant to establish living motives for your gift. For example, even if you are old, your gift motivation might be for the purpose of educating a grandchild or to enable a child to become established in a business. If your proof of living motivation is adequate, the gift would not be included even if you should have the misfortune to die within three years.

Never make a gift of over $3,000 to any one donee without the advice of counsel. First, a gift tax return must be filed. Second, you may need expert assistance in valuation of the gift. Third, the gift is an important part of your estate plan and also of the donee's estate plan. Both wills should be reviewed. Finally, if you make a gift to one child and not to another, you may want to include a provision in your will concerning advancements: In dividing up your estate among your children, you may, in effect, want to add the gift back in before making the divison and then deduct the gift from the share of the particular donee in the final settlement of your estate.

There is one other type of gift which will not save any death taxes but may have important income tax advantages. If you are supporting one of your parents, a mother-in-law, a father-in-law, or any other person, you can create what is known as a "Clifford trust," placing property in it which will earn enough income to take care of the support which you are furnishing to someone else. To accomplish your tax purposes, the trust must last for ten years or until the earlier death of the donee. Under a properly drafted agreement you do not pay an income tax on the trust income. The trust beneficiary can deduct medical expense against the income and pay tax on the balance, if any, at a lower rate. A Clifford trust can also be used for other purposes, but this one application has proven to be the most valuable of all.

CHAPTER 10

Assemble
the
Facts

Before having an estate-planning conference with your attorney, assemble all the facts concerning your estate and your family. Unless he has the most intimate details of your finances and of your family relationships, he cannot be expected to plan your estate properly. Furthermore, most attorneys charge for estate planning on the basis of the time devoted to the project. If you organize your information adequately, you will not only get a better estate plan but you will also substantially reduce its cost.

First, you should give him your complete name, nicknames, and initials which are sometimes used, together with your home and your business addresses. He will need your date of birth and preferably your medical history.

For your wife, your children, their spouses, your grandchildren, and all other dependents for whom you intend to make some provision, you will also need the complete name, address, birth date, and condition of health of each. After all, greater accuracy in names

Your Gross Estate

Types of property	(1) Husband's	(2) Jointly held Paid for by husband	(3) Paid for by wife	(4) Wife's
Liquid assets				
Cash on hand	$_____	$_____	$_____	$_____
Checking accounts	_____	_____	_____	_____
Savings accounts	_____	_____	_____	_____
Certificates of deposit	_____	_____	_____	_____
Corporate stocks	_____	_____	_____	_____
Mutual funds	_____	_____	_____	_____
Corporate bonds	_____	_____	_____	_____
U.S. Treasury bonds	_____	_____	_____	_____
Municipal bonds	_____	_____	_____	_____
Receivables	_____	_____	_____	_____
Other quick assets	_____	_____	_____	_____
Real estate				
Equity in homes	$_____	$_____	$_____	$_____
Income-producing realty	_____	_____	_____	_____
Unimproved realty	_____	_____	_____	_____
Personal property				
Autos	$_____	$_____	$_____	$_____
Sporting equipment	_____	_____	_____	_____
Furniture and household effects	_____	_____	_____	_____
Jewelry and silverware	_____	_____	_____	_____
Apparel and personal effects	_____	_____	_____	_____
Art objects	_____	_____	_____	_____
Collections	_____	_____	_____	_____
Hobby equipment	_____	_____	_____	_____

Types of property		Beneficiary Spouse	Estate	Other	
Personal insurance					
On testator's life	$_____	( )	( )	( )	$_____
On lives of others	_____	( )	( )	( )	_____
Annuities	_____	( )	( )	( )	_____

Types of property	(1) Husband's	Beneficiary Spouse	Estate	Other	(4) Wife's
Employee and retirement benefits					
Pension	$_____	( )	( )	( )	$_____
Profit sharing	_____	( )	( )	( )	_____
Other deferred compensation	_____	( )	( )	( )	_____
Stock options	_____	( )	( )	( )	_____
Savings and thrift plans	_____	( )	( )	( )	_____
Keogh retirement plans	_____	( )	( )	( )	_____
Individual retirement accounts	_____	( )	( )	( )	_____
Other	_____	( )	( )	( )	_____
Business interests					
Sole proprietorships	$_____	$_____	$_____		$_____
Partnerships	_____	_____	_____		_____
Closely held corporations	_____	_____	_____		_____
Miscellaneous					
Expectancies	$_____	$_____	$_____		$_____
Powers of appointment	_____	_____	_____		_____
Interests in trust funds	_____	_____	_____		_____
Royalties and patents	_____	_____	_____		_____
Oil, gas, and mineral interests	_____	_____	_____		_____
Other	_____	_____	_____		_____
Current Value of Total Assets	$_____	$_____	$_____		$_____

Husband's approximate gross estate (col. 1 + col. 2) $_____

Wife's approximate gross estate (col. 3 + col. 4) $_____

Gross Estate Valuation $_____ $_____

Deduct:

1. Personal and joint liabilities and debts (notes, insurance loans, mortgages, taxes owing, etc.) _____ _____
2. Funeral and last illness expenses _____ _____
3. Probate and administration expenses _____ _____

Total $_____ $_____

Approximate Adjusted Gross Estate (gross estate less above deductions) $_____ $_____

and relationships can be achieved by writing all of these out in advance, and some special provision may have to be made in your estate plan for anyone who is disabled. The more you are willing to tell your attorney about the financial status, character traits, needs, and prospects of your beneficiaries, the better the job he can do for you.

If there are any property agreements between you and either your present wife or a former wife, he will need to see these.

You may not know whether title to real estate is held by you individually, as a joint tenant, or as a tenant in common. If you have any doubt about it, it is far wiser to take every one of your deeds to your estate-planning conference. You should also examine your securities to determine how title to each one is held, and here again if you have any doubt, take every one of them to the conference. Your attorney will also definitely need to know the cost and present market value of each.

Your estate planner will also need to have all of your life insurance policies, partnership agreements, stockholder agreements, pension plans, profit-sharing plans, stock options, and deferred-compensation agreements. Preferably, before the conference, you should determine the status of your social security account.

If you hold any powers of appointment, your attorney must have a copy of each power and information concerning the appointive property. If you are already the beneficiary under a probated will or a trust, or if you have any expectancies of inheritance, this information, too, is vital.

If you have made any gifts in the past, these should be disclosed, and if gift tax returns have been filed, copies should be made available to your estate planner. Certainly you should take him copies of income tax returns for the three preceding years.

Finally, before going to an estate-planning conference, you should prepare a current balance sheet for yourself and for your wife. The form on pages 238-39 indicates some of the details required.

If you own a residence in more than one state, your attorney may wish to advise you concerning acts which you may take to establish legal residence in the state that has the most favorable income and death tax structure.

If you can, decide before your estate-planning conference what disposition you want made of automobiles, boats, trailers, household effects, hobby equipment, collections, objects of art, and personal effects. In all probability, you will want to give these to your family and not make them a part of any trust.

If you are supporting your parents, your wife's parents or anyone else, then your attorney needs to know your plans for them upon your death. You should also be prepared to share with him your hopes and expectations for your wife, children, and others for whom you care so that he may work with you in developing a plan to meet their needs. If you also plan a charitable bequest, you should take with you the full name of the institution or institutions which you want to share in your estate.

CHAPTER 11

Select an Attorney

Any attorney can write a will, but comparatively few are qualified to design an estate plan. Finding an expert is difficult. Lawyers cannot advertise their specialties although action to allow such advertising is presently being considered by the American Bar Association. The legal rating services rate attorneys on their overall abilities but not on their competence in a particular field.

There are tens of thousands of income tax, estate tax, and gift tax rulings every year. Every attorney cannot be expected to keep up with all of these, and yet unless he at least reads the advance sheets weekly which summarize each of these, he cannot hope to develop or to retain a competence in estate planning. For most lawyers, estate planning is only a small part of the total practice of law, and any particular lawyer can hardly be expected to possess an expertise in every phase of his professional practice.

Unfortunately, too, there is a common conviction that the cost of estate planning is excessive. That inaccurate view has discouraged many a person from seeking professional advice. Actually, a competent attorney can almost invariably save a client in taxes many times the cost of developing a program for his estate. If the demand for estate-planning services ever reaches its potential, many more attorneys will become versed in the art of developing plans for distribution of property to the object or objects of one's affection at the least possible tax cost.

Meanwhile, the identification of an estate-planning expert is an awesome task, but there are avenues of inquiry which should aid you in finding someone near you. *The Bar Register*, published annually, includes only those "lawyers who enjoy fine professional reputations." Not every listee in *The Bar Register* is a preeminent estate-planning specialist, nor are all those not listed without competence in this specialized field. Nevertheless, if you begin with *The Bar Register*, you have increased immeasurably in your favor the odds of your finding one of the best.

The Martindale-Hubbell Law Directory lists every lawyer in the United States and rates his legal ability with the explanation: "No arbitrary rule for determining legal ability has been formulated, but ten years' admission is the minimum required for the legal ability rating of 'a' ('very high'), five years for the 'b' ('high'), and three years for the 'c' ('fair')."

In the biographical section of the same publication, subscribers may publish cards reflecting legal education, public offices held, association memberships, and publications. An attorney whose credits reflect that he has published or lectured in the field of estate planning may be your best choice. Both *The Bar Register* and *The Martindale-Hubbell Law Directory* are available in law school libraries.

If you are fortunate enough to live near a law school, a member of the faculty may be able to help you identify an estate-planning expert. Trust officers of banks are certainly in an excellent position to know those who are best qualified, but in smaller towns particularly, there are few expert trust officers and many of these are tempted to recommend whoever happens to be general counsel for the bank. Some probate judges and some probate clerks are experienced enough to differentiate between lawyers who write wills and attorneys who specialize in estate practice.

You should not hesitate to ask your prospective counsel to show you his library. If he does not have a complete loose-leaf service (eleven volumes, more or less) on income taxes, gift taxes, and estate taxes, he will probably be a very poor choice. Preferably his library or another to which he has access should also contain all of the federal tax decisions.

Almost every estate-planning expert subscribes to, reads, and retains in his office copies of *Trusts and Estates* magazine and one or more treatises on estate planning. You should not hesitate to ask to borrow recent issues of the magazine and one of the estate-planning books. If none of these publications are available, you had better try to find an attorney someplace else.

In a small town, you can go to a probate clerk's office and examine wills recently admitted to probate. The attorneys who are still writing one- and two-page wills should be stricken from your list of prospects. You may be surprised to discover how easy it is for you to determine which members of the bar are the more sophisticated draftsmen.

Doctors, at least, have been wise enough to identify specialties within their profession and those who have passed their board-qualifying examinations are probably adequate practitioners of their respective specialized arts. Unfortunately, for the public, an infallible technique has not been developed for singling out the attorneys who are specialists in any particular field, except patent and trademark specialists.

CHAPTER 12

A
Legal
Checkup

Have you had a legal checkup lately? Most of us have a dental examination annually, an eye examination every few years, and a complete physical examination at least occasionally. Health is more important than property, but wisdom dictates the preservation of both. Estate planning, as, hopefully, you have discovered, is far more than employing someone to write a will. It is the art of designing a program for the effective management, enjoyment, and disposition of your property at the least possible tax cost, not only at your death but also during your lifetime.

As a part of your estate planning, you may want to ask your attorney to give you a complete legal audit. That would include not only your life insurance, but also your fire insurance, casualty insurance, and health insurance programs. Have you ever made a list of your risk-of-loss exposures and compared these with your insurance coverages? The odds are that you will discover some enormous gaps. For example, on your automobile policy, are you carrying adequate liability coverage? All too many policies are written with limits of only $10,000 per person and $20,000 per accident, but judgments of $100,000 or more are becoming exceedingly common. For an amazingly small additional premium, you can increase your liability limits for bodily injury to $100,000 per person and $300,000 per occurrence. It is better to spend insurance dollars to achieve protection against major losses than in any other way.

Furthermore, your coverage of automobile-property-damage liability should also be increased. If you were to be involved in a collision with a bus, a truck, or any vehicle with a valuable cargo, the usual $5,000 or $10,000 coverage would be grossly inadequate. Once again, for a small additional premium, you can increase your property-damage-liability coverage to $50,000 or $100,000 per accident.

In an automobile policy, collision coverage (which takes care of damage to your own car) is relatively expensive, but if you can afford to pay the small losses yourself, you can reduce the premium materially by increasing the deductible amount (the portion of the loss to be borne by you) to at least $500. For a small cost, automobile coverages can include medical payments to each person injured, additional family protection coverages, and protection against losses caused by an uninsured motorist.

If you are engaged in the practice of any profession, you should carry a professional liability policy, and here again it is often possible to reduce the premium cost by providing for a deductible amount; the loss to be borne by you. A comprehensive liability policy should be purchased also by every farmer. If you are engaged in business, you should have a comprehensive general liability policy, a workman's compensation policy, and, possibily, business interruption coverage. These policies should be reviewed, too, upon a legal audit.

Today, the risk of loss by fire of a home, apartment, or business building is best covered under a multiperil policy which takes care not only of loss by fire but of many losses to persons and property occasioned by other casualties. With inflation increasing the cost of replacement of any structure, the amount of fire coverage should be reviewed annually.

On a homeowner's or other multiperil policy, liability limits can be increased to $100,000 per person and $300,000 per occurrence for a nominal additional premium. If you use your home also for some office activities, an endorsement covering that use should be included on your homeowner's policy. A mysterious disappearance endorsement and credit card endorsement are also good buys.

An umbrella policy

If you do not have, you should certainly consider purchasing an "umbrella" policy to supplement all of your individual policies. After your underlying liability coverages have been exhausted by a claim, an umbrella policy protects up to a limit of perhaps $1 million or more. For example, if you are carrying an automobile liability of $100,000 per person and $300,000 per occurrence for bodily injury liability and if claims against you exceeded those amounts, then your umbrella policy would take care of the catastrophic excess. The umbrella policy would supplement your liability on your automobile policy, your professional liability, your comprehensive liability, your homeowner's policy, and all other underlying coverages. Small commercial risks are now written with $500 as the minimum three-year premium. Personal coverage for executives and professionals may be only $270 for three years with a $1-million limit and $540 for three years with a $5-million limit.

In health coverage, the average layman has neither the training nor the experience to compare available coverages and measure the reasonableness of premium cost. Exceptions, exclusions, waiting periods, and durations of coverage limit the benefits of many of the policies being sold. If you are unwilling to seek professional guidance on what policy to buy, you had better stick to Blue Cross-Blue Shield for basic protection and then supplement that with a major medical or a catastrophic coverage which takes care of 75 percent or more of the cost of a major illness over and above a deductible amount, which usually is covered by Blue Cross-Blue Shield.

A legal checkup often includes a review of leases. Whether you are renting a house, an apartment, or a storeroom, the odds are that your lease can be improved by a supplemental lease, amended lease, or renewal lease.

If you carry automobile collision insurance, you may know that in the event of an accident, your insurance company will settle your loss with you and then take an assignment of your right to sue the operator of the other vehicle involved in the accident. In effect, your insurance company takes over your right to recover from the person who hit you. This arrangement applies to other types of insurance. For example, some years ago, a tenant conducting a grocery business negligently caused the premises to be destroyed by a fire. The landlord's insurer promptly paid the landlord, accepted an assignment of right to recover, sued the tenant for the loss, and recovered.

Almost every fire results from negligence. Of course, legal liability insurance can be purchased to cover this risk, but unfortunately the premiums are substantial. This risk of loss can be eliminated by the simple process of obtaining a waiver of indemnity rights. In many states, a mutual waiver may be included in a lease without any increase in the cost of the insurance carried by the landlord or the tenant. If, however, a lease does not contain a waiver-of-indemnification right, then both the landlord and the tenant need to protect themselves by carrying legal liability insurance.

Every existing lease and every new lease that is written should contain the following provision:

> The Lessor waives and releases its right of indemnity against the Lessee for damages to its property (by fire or other casualty) occasioned by the negligence of the Lessee, its agents or employees, to the extent that the Lessor receives actual payment therefor under the Lessor's insurance policies. The Lessee waives and releases the Lessee's right of indemnity against the Lessor for damages to the Lessee's property (by fire or other casualty) occasioned by the negligence of the Lessor, its agents or employees, to the extent that Lessee receives actual payment therefor under Lessee's insurance policies.

Many insurance policies permit this agreement without notice to the insurance company, but preferably both the landlord and the tenant should advise their own insurance carriers that leases do contain the recommended clause.

The preparation of income tax returns is a seasonal affair and under the pressure of meeting a filing deadline, the tax preparer often does not have sufficient time to render tax-planning advice. In a legal checkup, an attorney can render tax-planning advice and often in reviewing past income tax returns he can discover a possible tax refund claim.

If you are engaged in a business, an attorney can render valuable advice on the best form of business organization for you and on many subjects relating to the conduct of your business, including, for example, group health and life plans and pension and profit-sharing plans.

If you have not had a legal checkup recently, you have overlooked an impressive opportunity for the more effective management, preservation, and disposition of your property at the least possible tax cost.

CHAPTER 13

A Power of Attorney and a Living Will

A power of attorney is a written instrument by which you, as principal, appoint an attorney-in-fact to act as your agent and confer upon him the authority to act in your behalf. A power of attorney may be either general (giving your attorney-in-fact power to do almost anything on your behalf) or special (giving your attorney-in-fact only the power to do one or more specific things). Death cancels a power of attorney and you can call it off at any time during your life. You may also appoint a successor to act in the event of the death or disability of your original appointee.

You should grant a power of attorney to someone although you may retain the power of letting it be delivered only when your appointee needs to act in your behalf. For example, you may grant a power of attorney to your wife (husband), your brother (sister), your son (daughter), or a business associate, leaving the power with your attorney to be delivered to the appointee only in the event that your attorney-in-fact needs to act.

If you should have a heart attack, someone should be authorized to sign checks to pay bills, borrow money if necessary, and file insurance claims. If you plan to be away from home for two weeks or longer on a vacation or a business trip, something might arise in your absence which should be dealt with immediately. Later on in life, you may have the misfortune of becoming senile or weak and disabled. Here again, someone should have the authority to take care of your business for you.

In some jurisdictions, incompetency terminates a power of attorney. If you should live in one of those, you may wish to create a revocable living trust while you are possessed of your senses.

Powers of attorney should not, of course, be handed out indiscriminately. There is always a risk of abuse. Ordinarily, this can be avoided by leaving a power of attorney with your attorney or your banker to be delivered only if in his judgment circumstances are such that you would want it to become effective.

You may also wish to consider executing a living will. Today, with devices, a patient who has no chance whatsoever of survival can be kept alive by artificial means. If you do not want this to happen to you, then execute a living will such as this one:

To My Family, My Physician,
My Clergyman, My Lawyer:

If the time comes when I can no longer take part in decisions for my own future, let this statement stand as the testament of my wishes:

> If there is no reasonable expectation of my recovery from physical or mental or spiritual disability, I request that I be allowed to die and not be kept alive by artificial means or heroic measures. Death is as much a reality as birth, growth, maturity, and old age—it is the one certainty. I do not fear death as much as I fear the indignity of deterioration, dependence, and hopeless pain. I ask that drugs be mercifully administered to me for terminal suffering even if they hasten the moment of death.

This request is made while I am in good health and spirits. Although this document is not legally binding, you who care for me will, I hope, feel morally bound to follow its mandates. I recognize it places a heavy burden of responsibility upon you, and it is with the intention of sharing that responsibility and of mitigating any feelings of guilt that this statement is made.

This the _____ day of _____, 19_____.

Witness:

As yet there is no state in which the courts have recognized the right of an individual to let himself die, let alone the right of another to make that decision for him. Nevertheless, a living will delivered to your family, your physician, your clergyman, and your attorney may persuade them to honor your wishes.

You may also wish to consider leaving part or all of your body to research and educational purposes. In over twenty states, legislation requires provision on an automobile driver's license for a space in which the driver may indicate whether or not he wishes to make an anatomical gift, to take effect upon death. The National Kidney Foundation, 116 East Twenty-seventh Street, New York, New York 10016, also has available a form of bequeathal which does not name a specific recipient and which is legally valid in all fifty states. If you bequeath all or part of your body for scientific and educational purposes, you should ask your family physician and members of your family to notify the proper medical institution by telephone, immediately after your death.

14

A Letter to Your Executor-Trustee

Your executor-trustee is going to need all the information that you have assembled for your attorney and more. After all, he is going to take your place in carrying on your business, managing your investments, and making financial provision for your family. With your will, you should have a current balance sheet, all of your life insurance policies, partnership agreements, stockholders' agreements, pension plans, profit-sharing plans, stock options, and deferred-compensation agreements. Do not forget to revise the balance sheet regularly, preferably every year.

If you own an interest in a closely held business the disposition of which is not controlled by a buy-and-sell agreement, by all means tell your executor whether you want the business retained or sold. If it is to be kept in your estate, your executor will need your advice as to which of your key employees can run it, or as to how to find a competent manager. If it is to be sold, you will know how the business should be valued and where to locate prospective purchasers.

If your will gives discretionary power to your executor-trustee in the distribution of income and principal, he will need complete and specific information about your family. For example, to illustrate the detailed information which you should give him, you might want to say in one letter that you have given a child a car upon graduation from college or upon marriage and that you want each other child to be given a car at that same stage in life. You might want to point out that you have paid for an expensive wedding and reception for one daughter and that your other daughter should have the same things done for her.

Your letter or letters are not to be mailed during your lifetime but to be left with your will for delivery only to your executor at your death. You can change the letters from time to time as circumstances require.

If you have a child who is a spendthrift, warn your executor to be careful and prudent in distributions to him or to her. If you have a son or daughter whose marriage is in jeopardy, be frank with your executor about that. If you have a son or a son-in-law who could never make a success of a business venture, tell your executor never to make a loan for that purpose.

If your will authorizes your trustee to make distributions to your wife for her support and maintenance after considering other sources of income and support which she may from time to time have, explain to your trustee exactly what you mean. Tell him, for example, that if your widow remarries, you certainly do not want to support a second husband. On the other hand, if he, too, should die or become totally disabled, ask your executor to begin again making distributions to your widow. After all, you would not want her starving while your children were well provided for.

There are many things about your family that you would not want to include in a will, which is to be recorded in the courthouse. Then, too, over the years your children, their spouses, and your grandchildren will mature. You will view them differently with each passing year and your changing attitudes should be reflected in letter revisions as required.

In writing letters to your executor to be kept with your will, your objective should be to keep him currently advised of everything which he could conceivably need to know about your assets, your liabilities, and the members of your family. With your advice, he can do a much better job of taking your place.

15

Further Checks for Your Estate Plan

After your attorney has completed a first draft of your entire estate plan and before you sign anything, check every document carefully. First, and above all, make sure that your property is to be distributed according to your wishes and instructions. After all, the primary purpose of a living trust, a will, life insurance endorsements, and pension and profit-sharing designations is to protect and provide for those for whom you care. Secondly, make sure this primary objective has been accomplished at the least possible tax cost. Has advantage been taken of the marital deduction if it is needed? Will your property continue to pass under your will for more than one generation?

Make certain that your executor-trustee has been given adequate power to act without having to seek the advice and consent of a probate court. Paper is cheaper than lawsuits. Do not risk appointing a well-chosen executor-trustee who cannot perform adequately because you have failed to give him authority to act.

Per stirpes

Child	Child	Deceased child	
1/3	1/3	Grandson	Granddaughter
		1/6	1/6

Per capita

Child	Child	Deceased child	
1/4	1/4	Grandson	Granddaughter
		1/4	1/4

In reading your will, you may come across the phrases *per capita* and *per stirpes*. If the words *per stirpes* are used, then the children of a deceased child will receive their parent's share. The words *per capita* require an equal division to each person irrespective of relationship.

Occasionally, a grandfather or a grandmother will want a division among grandchildren on a *per capita* rather than a *per stirpes* basis, but this sometimes creates two problems. First, each child as distinguished from the grandchildren usually believes that a distribution should be on a *per stirpes* basis. Secondly, if a *per capita* distribution is used, the will or trust agreement must contain a provision stating the time at which the class closes. The common law incorrectly assumes that people can continue to have children as long as they live, and therefore the members of a "class," composed of grandchildren, could not be determined until the date of death of the last of your own children. This difficulty can be met by stating a year or an event upon which a class will close and beyond which no further members of the class will be admitted.

Most wills direct an executor to pay just debts and funeral expenses, but an executor would take care of these responsibilities anyhow. You may wish, however, to direct your executor to have a monument or a marker erected at your grave and you should certainly be more precise about the payment of debts. For example, is a loan on a life insurance policy to be paid out of the policy proceeds? Is the mortgage on a home, a rental property, a car, or some other asset to be paid out of that particular property or with the proceeds from some other asset of your estate?

Preferably every will should contain a provision concerning the payment of death taxes. U.S. estate taxes are imposed against your estate and must be paid by your executor out of the assets of your estate. In the final distribution, however, who should bear the burden of these taxes? Should the U.S. estate taxes be treated as if the

assessment constituted a debt of your estate, or should the beneficiaries of your estate, in effect, bear a proportionate part of those
taxes depending upon what each receives?

State inheritance taxes generally are imposed upon the right to
receive. The executor has an obligation to pay these taxes but, in
most states, he is required to charge the state inheritance taxes to
the particular beneficiaries. Here again, is that what you want or
do you prefer that state inheritance taxes also be treated as a
debt of your estate? If any death taxes must be paid out of the
property left to your wife outright or in trust to obtain the marital
deduction, then you will not obtain the full advantage of the marital
deduction under your will. The will in appendix A contains one
kind of a tax clause which can be used in a marital deduction will
in an estate of $1,000,000 or less. In larger estates it is often wiser
to let a portion of the taxes be paid out of the marital trust.

Common disaster clause

In all probability, your will should have a common disaster
clause. It is possible that you and your wife might die in an accident
so that it would be difficult if not impossible to determine which of
you died first. In most states you may declare in your will that your
wife shall be deemed to survive. This declaration will give you the
benefit of the marital deduction even though a coroner might be in
doubt as to which death occurred first. Secondly, in states imposing
an inheritance tax and granting exemptions based on relationship,
the state death tax would also be less if your wife were presumed to
have survived you. Conceivably of course, for nontax reasons, you
might prefer instead a presumption that you survived your wife.

Make sure that your will does not violate the rule against per-
petuities. Under this rule, a fee-simple interest or absolute title
must vest not later than twenty-one years after any reasonable
number of lives in being, at the time of the creation of the interest.
For example, you cannot create a valid trust for grandchildren
until each has reached the age of twenty-five unless your will provides that the trust, in any event, will come to an end twenty-one
years after the death of the last of your descendants living on the
date of your death. A rule-against-perpetuities clause appears in
the model will in appendix A.

Conceivably, taxes can be saved by including "income in respect
of a decedent" in the family trust instead of in the wife's trust in a
marital deduction will. Income in respect of a decedent consists of
income which someone dying has earned but has neither collected

nor accounted for on the final income tax return to be filed for him. For example, such income would embrace gains on installment sales, a bonus received after a cash-basis taxpayer's death, an award upon a claim being litigated when the decedent died, and, for a cash-basis taxpayer, interest earned but not received and dividends declared but not paid at the time of death. Income in respect of a decedent is taxed on returns filed by the executor, but the executor may claim as a deduction against the income, the estate tax paid as a result of income in respect of a decedent. If income of this character should be included in the wife's marital trust, there would be no estate tax credit to claim as a deduction on the income tax return filed by the executor.

In most states, the statutes require the probate court to appoint appraisers. The executor is under a duty to see that an appraisal is made and to file settlements with the court periodically. These statutes were adopted primarily for the protection of creditors. In a solvent estate with an executor of integrity these are unnecessary expenses which can in some states be avoided by a provision in a will relieving the executor from the duty of obtaining an appraisal and for the responsibility of filing settlements. In practice, settlements are not audited by many courts. Your family will be better protected by a requirement that an annual accounting be made to each current income beneficiary who shall have, perhaps, sixty days within which to make an objection.

After you have approved and signed your will, ask for a copy of it which you may take home with you. The original should be placed in your lockbox or in your attorney's lockbox. If, at some time, you want changes made in your will, make notations on your copy and take that to your attorney. Words inserted on an executed will can invalidate the will.

Review your estate plan

Ask your attorney to review your will whenever there is a change in either state or federal tax law that might affect your estate planning. Some members of the bar keep on file cards an abstract of each will in the office so that this service can be performed for every client quickly and economically.

But your attorney cannot possibly know of all of the things that may happen in your life. If any of the following events occur, you should review the potential effect on your estate planning to determine whether your will or trust should be amended or revised in its entirety:

1. Special circumstances relating to a child, e.g., special needs, such as education, health, or business.
2. Adoption of a child
3. Birth or death of a child
4. Birth or death of a grandchild
5. Marriage or divorce of a child
6. Death of a spouse
7. Increase or decrease in personal wealth
8. Receipt of substantial inheritance or gift
9. Making of a substantial gift
10. Purchase of life insurance
11. Participation in a new pension or profit-sharing plan
12. Move to another state
13. Marriage or divorce

In many states either marriage or divorce invalidates any existing will. Some states permit the execution of a will in anticipation of marriage, but the will must specifically cite that fact. Marriage or divorce will drastically change your testamentary plans.

In a divorce proceeding, alimony, payable under the court's decree or under a written agreement incident to the divorce, may or may not be taxable income to the wife and deductible by the husband. Furthermore, whenever there is a property settlement as a part of a divorce proceeding, a transfer of assets, which have appreciated in value, may be a taxable capital gain. Payments for support of children may or may not be deductible by the husband, again depending, in part, upon the divorce decree or the support agreement.

If you or any one of your descendants should adopt a child, the question of whether or not that child can take under your will can best be resolved by a codicil to your will or by a total revision of your will. Obviously the birth or the death of a child or a grandchild could affect your estate planning. Certainly your will should again be reviewed. The marriage of a child or the divorce of a child could also necessitate a revision in your estate plan.

If your wife dies, your will should be reviewed immediately. For example, a marital deduction will can no longer serve to reduce taxes; and, without a wife to support, you may find it advisable to accelerate a program of gifts to your children. If, after the death of your wife, you should decide to remarry, not only will you need a new estate plan, but preferably that estate plan should embrace a prenuptial agreement. When each party to the remarriage has children by a prior marriage, family difficulties may be minimized by property agreements made in advance of the marriage.

A substantial change in your personal wealth might also prompt a change in a program of giving to children and a revision in your will or trust to take advantage of an alternate approach for the reduction of taxes. Of course, if you receive a substantial inheritance or gift, or make a major gift to someone, once more your estate plan should be reviewed. Such increase or decrease could constitute a substantial change in your net worth, which might call for a total revision of your estate plan.

If you purchase additional life insurance or become a participant in a new pension or profit-sharing plan, again you should consult with your attorney. These additional assets must be coordinated into your estate plan.

If you move to another state, you will encounter a different set of laws which will be applicable if you should die without a will, and, in all probability, if your wife should renounce your will in the other state, a different consequence would ensue. State laws also affect the type of administrative powers which should be granted and the impact of state death taxes upon your estate plan. It is also more economical to probate a will if the witnesses to the will live in the same state in which you reside.

In every family special circumstances develop from time to time that require the revision of an estate plan. The decision of a child to attend graduate school, the disability of a member of the family, or a business success or reverse could make it advisable for you to review and revise your estate plan.

A will speaks as of the moment of your death. It should be kept current with the changes in your property ownerships, with your family relationships, and with state and federal tax laws.

An act of Congress, a statute adopted in your home state, or a judicial decision may have a disastrous effect upon a well designed estate plan. Such events occur so frequently that you should not discredit the attorney whom you consult because his conclusions differ from the recommendations made here.

16

Support a Charity

In this topsy-turvy world of taxes, you can make money by giving money away. To take one extreme example, if a taxpayer in a 70-percent bracket gives stock having a market value of $5,000 to a qualified charity, he will save $3,500 on his U.S. income tax return and perhaps $300 on his state income tax return. If the stock cost him $1,000 and if he should sell it realizing a long-term capital gain of $4,000, he would, depending upon other factors, have to pay U.S. income taxes of, perhaps, $120. After paying these taxes, he would have $3,480 left; but, if he had made the gift instead, he would be $3,800 ahead. Thus he could net $320 by making a $5,000 gift. The $5,000 gift has removed an asset from the estate which would be subject to death taxes if the gift were not made.

Admittedly, that is an extreme example: Very few taxpayers can show a profit on a charitable gift. But the purpose of the illustration is to emphasize the tax savings which you can make by making major gifts in the form of appreciated property rather than in cash.

Gift tax laws have become encrusted with complexities. A comprehensive analysis is beyond the scope of this survey, but something must be said about the available alternatives.

Under the Tax Reform Act of 1969, contributions made to certain charities may now be deducted up to 50 percent of adjusted gross income after disregarding any net-operating loss. For most taxpayers, this means simply that they can deduct as contributions one-half of their income before they have reduced it by exemptions and itemized deductions. The 50-percent limitation applies to contributions to religious groups, schools, hospitals, government units, and certain other organizations such as the Red Cross, community chest or fund, public museums, and libraries. Contributions to certain other charities, and this does not concern the average taxpayer, are subject to a 20-percent limitation. Gifts in excess of the limitations may be carried over and deducted in later tax years.

Every taxpayer who makes a gift of appreciated property gets a tax deduction, but the entire gift may not be deductible that year. Any gift of appreciated property is subject to a 30-percent rather than a 50-percent maximum unless the individual elects, as he should, to carry the excess over to later tax years.

For most of the contributions which you make during your lifetime, you need to know only that you will realize a tax benefit by giving appreciated property rather than cash. There will be a 30-percent limitation if you use appreciated property, but the excess above this can be carried over and deducted in later years.

If you give paintings, works of art, or other tangible, personal property to a qualified charity, your deduction will be reduced by one-half of your long-term capital gain unless the donee is able to use the property in a way related to its exempt purpose or function. For example, a gift of a painting to an art museum would not have to be reduced by one-half of the capital gain applicable if a sale had occurred.

Another interesting exception is that if you give "ordinary income property" to a charity, the deduction will be limited to your cost basis. Ordinary income property is property, which, if sold by you, would result in ordinary income or a short-term capital gain. Inventory, crops raised, or livestock produced would come within this classification.

Charitable alternatives

Private educational institutions are primarily dependent upon contributions for their survival. There are a number of ways in which you can make gifts to these and other organized charities and obtain at the same time tangible tax benefits.

You can reserve a life estate in a personal residence or a farm, giving the remainder to a charity upon your death. Under a special rule for valuing a deductible remainder interest in a personal residence or a farm, you will be entitled to a significant charitable deduction on your income tax return.

As an alternative, you can create a "charitable remainder trust." Essentially, this action consists only of an arrangement with a charity under which it pays income to you or to you and your wife on the amount of your gift as long as you live, with the gift then belonging to the charity. Any charitable organization will be glad to furnish you all of the necessary forms and explanations. There are, however, three varieties of charitable remainder trusts and a brief explanation will show you some of the advantages of each.

An "annuity trust" provides for the payment of 5 percent or more of the fair market value of the property placed in trust. A "unitrust" provides for the payment of 5 percent or more of the net fair market value of the trust assets, valued annually. In other words, whereas the annuity trust provides a percentage on the initial fair market value, the unitrust provides for a percentage on the fluctuating market value. The third type of charitable remainder trust is a "pooled-income fund." Essentially, this is a trust administered by the charitable organization with the trustee making investments of contributed property in a diversified portfolio of securities which resembles, in some respects, a mutual fund. A subscriber to a pooled-income fund receives income earned by the fund during one or more lives; the property thereafter goes to the charitable organization.

The pooled-income fund has the broadest appeal. If you purchase an interest by the use of appreciated stock or real estate you do not incur any capital-gains tax upon the transaction, but your charitable deduction would be determined on the basis of the market value of the securities transferred. The tax deductible portion of a pooled-income fund is a higher percentage of the total gift value than any other life income plan. For example, if you are aged sixty and your wife aged fifty-eight, the deductible portion of a $10,000 pooled-income investment would be about $3,250.

If you have $10,000 or more in highly appreciated property and want to increase your income, you could trade your property to the charity for a high-income unitrust which would pay out the net income earned by the trust assets, but not more than a stated percentage of the market value of those assets as valued each year. In the present market, an organized charity can invest in high-quality bonds yielding 7 percent or more. The income would be taxable to you as ordinary income. For example, if you gave $20,000 in stock which had a cost to you of $12,000, the charity would sell the stock and invest the proceeds in high-quality bonds with a net yield of 7 percent or better. Assuming that you and your wife are aged sixty and fifty-eight respectively, you would get a tax deduction of about $3,720. You would not have a capital gain on the sale of the stock. The annual income from the donated assets might jump, for example, from $400 (2 percent of market value) to $1,400 (7 percent of $20,000). Upon your death, the existence of this trust would increase the tax-free marital deduction share of your estate to your wife, and only her remaining interest in the life income of the trust would be taxable. The contribution would effectively remove the balance of the gift from taxation at your death.

For the high-bracket taxpayer, there are still more interesting possibilities. If you are interested in tax free income, you can transfer to the charity property which has neither appreciated nor depreciated in value in exchange for a tax-exempt unitrust. The charitable organization would sell your gift and invest the contribution in tax-exempt bonds which might yield about 5 percent. If you are in a 42-percent income tax bracket, 5 percent tax-exempt income is equal to almost 9 percent of ordinary income. At the lower yield of 5 percent, your tax deduction for the contribution will be larger than under some other unitrust plans. If you and your wife are aged sixty and fifty-eight respectively, the deductible portion of a $10,000 gift would be $3,000. Once again, upon your death the existence of the trust would increase the tax-free marital deduction share of your estate to your wife and only her remaining interest in the life income trust would be taxable. The contribution would effectively remove the balance of the gift from taxation at your death.

If you are a high-bracket taxpayer with $50,000 or more in highly appreciated stock or real estate, you might trade it to a charity for a straight unitrust. Your charitable deduction will be computed on the market value of the contribution, but you will not have to pay any capital-gains tax. When the property is sold by the charity, the capital gain will not be taxable immediately either to you or to it. But, if some of the gain is later paid out to you to meet the required yield of your contract, that portion of the payment will be reported by you as long-term capital gain rather than as ordinary income. In this type of unitrust, the charity ordinarily will keep your contribution invested in growth stocks which characteristically have a low-dividend yield. This serves two purposes. With little ordinary income to distribute, most of the yield to you will be long-term capital gain. Secondly, investment in growth stocks makes it likely that the market value of the trust assets will increase, which also increases the amount payable to you. Most charities will guarantee to pay you 6 percent of the market value of the assets each year. In making this payment, the charity will first distribute ordinary income (such as dividends and interest), then realized long-term capital gain, and finally, if necessary, return of principal. You will carry each type of distribution through to your own tax return.

For example, if your gift is $50,000 in stock which cost you $20,000, the trust will pay you 6 percent of the market value of the assets each year, and invest the proceeds in growth stocks yielding, perhaps, 1 percent on market value. If you are sixty and fifty-eight, and if you are both to be beneficiaries, the tax deduction will be $12,000. Income in the first full year will be $3,000 (6 percent of $50,000), consisting of $500 ordinary income and $2,500 long-term capital gain. If the trust grows 4 percent in the second year to $52,000, the yield in that year would be $520 ordinary income and $2,600 capital gain. If the assets continue to grow at a rate of 4 percent per year (after the annual yield to the beneficiary), their value would be about $65,000 in the seventh year, and the income to the beneficiary in that year would be $650 ordinary income and $3,250 capital gain. (In the 42-percent bracket, $3,250 of capital-gain income is better than $54,400 of ordinary income on an after-tax basis.)

This example illustrates the benefits of increasing income to you (assuming growing market value), and the fact that much of the income would be taxed at favorable capital-gains rates. Because of this, the 6 percent yield from the unitrust will equal 7 or 8 percent of ordinary income on an after-tax basis.

Upon your death, the existence of the trust would increase the tax-free marital deduction share of your estate to your wife, and only her remaining interest in the life income from the trust would be taxable. The contribution would effectively remove the balance of the gift from taxation at your death.

A charitable remainder trust can be used to great advantage in a will. For example, take the case of a childless couple. For an adjusted gross estate of $240,000 or less, one-half of the estate can be placed in a power-of-appointment trust for the wife. The remaining $120,000 can be placed in a 6-percent charitable annuity trust which will be created for the wife. If she is sixty-nine years of age or older and, if he, being sixty-four years of age or older, should be survivor, the value of the life estate would be less than 50 percent of the assets placed in the annuity trust. Therefore, less than $60,000 would be subject to taxation, and of course this would be offset by the $60,000 exemption. A similar will could be written for the wife if she had property of her own.

If the childless couple should be worth more than $250,000, the same plan would work equally well, but of course there would be subject to taxation approximately one-fourth of the adjusted gross estate in excess of the $60,000 exemption. The tax saving will be astronomical in large estates.

17

Don't
Die
Intestate

To die intestate is to die without a will. If you have a will, you can appoint an executor to settle your estate. If you die without one, the court will appoint an administrator to serve instead. In most states a statute establishes an order of preference, but disputes often develop among children as to which one of them shall serve. You should exercise your right to select the person to settle your estate.

Every administrator appointed by a court must give bond with surety thereon to guarantee performance of his duties. If there are minor children a guardian must be qualified for each and, again, a bond must be posted. This additional trouble and extra expense far exceeds the cost of drafting most wills.

The powers of the administrator, derived from statute, are seldom adequate to permit settlement of your estate efficiently and economically. In most states securities cannot be sold without first incurring the expense of obtaining a court order.

If you die without a will, your real estate will go by statute to your heirs and not to your administrator. If there are minors involved, the real estate cannot be sold without a court order, and if all of your heirs are of age, all of them must agree upon the operation or sale of your assets.

The greatest danger of dying without a will is that the laws of your state will determine how your property is to be divided; that division will seldom be exactly what you would want. For example, in some states if you die without a will, one-half of your property will go to your spouse and one-half to your children. If you have a small estate, you would probably prefer that your entire estate go to your wife, and certainly you would not want any of it to go to minor children whose rights would be dependent upon the qualification of a guardian.

In other states the statute might provide that one-half of your personal property would go to your spouse and one-half to your children, with your spouse having, however, only one-third interest for life in the real estate. This division of realty is totally impractical.

Typically if a person dies without leaving a spouse or a descendant to survive him, one-half of his estate will go to his mother and one-half to his father, but if either of them has died, then the entirety will go to the survivor. Often this results in death taxes being imposed upon property distributed to aged parents with the tax being assessed again when the parents die and leave the property to their other children.

In a few states, the Uniform Probate Code has been adopted. It is far better than most other intestacy laws, but far from perfect. No one can design a uniform house which would be suitable to every family in the United States, and yet that is what every law of intestacy attempts to do with property: to make the same distribution no matter what the situation.

Under the Uniform Probate Code, your property would pass to your wife if you had neither issue nor parents surviving. If you should die with issue of your marriage to your surviving spouse, the first $50,000 plus one-half of the balance would go to her and the other half to the issue. If there are issue, but one or more of them are not also issue of the surviving spouse, then your estate would go equally to your surviving spouse and to all of the issue without the first $50,000 passing to your surviving spouse.

The Uniform Probate Code and other laws of intestacy cover all of the other possible variations including death without leaving a spouse, issue, parent, brother, or sister to survive. Some states give adopted children the same rights of inheritance as natural children. Some states give a preference to relatives of the whole blood over relatives of the half blood. There is an enormous variation in the treatment of illegitimate children.

"Only the wealthy need wills" is a false saying which overlooks the fact that the less property you have, the more important it becomes to distribute that property properly. The assets of a multimillionaire will take care of all his loved ones no matter how the assets are divided by statute. Furthermore, only by careful estate planning can you be assured that your property will be distributed to those whom you love at the least possible tax cost.

A Marital Deduction Will

I, John Doe, of _____ (town, state), hereby make this my last will revoking every will heretofore made by me.

ARTICLE 1. I appoint my wife, Mary Doe, Executrix of this will and Trustee of my estate and request that no bond be required of her as such. In the event of the death, default, disqualification, resignation, or removal of my wife, I authorize my wife to appoint a Successor-Executor of this will and Trustee of my estate and to require, or not to require, the execution of a bond. In the event of the failure of my wife to exercise this power of appointment and in the event of the death, default, disqualification, resignation, or removal of the appointee, I appoint my brother, Charles Doe, Executor of this will and Trustee of my estate and request that no bond be required of him as such. In the event of the death, default, disqualification, resignation, or removal of my brother, I appoint the National Bank of _____, as Executor of this will and Trustee of my estate. The word "Executor," whenever used herein, shall be deemed to refer to my Executor or to my Executrix, which-ever shall be acting as such.

ARTICLE II. I direct my Executor to pay all of my just debts and funeral éxpenses, to have a monument or marker erected at my grave, and to pay out of my residuary estate, which is disposed of in Article VI, all estate, inheritance, transfer, and succession taxes payable by my estate or payable on the legacies given herein, and my Executor shall make no claims against any person receiving any money or property including the proceeds of insurance policies includable in my gross estate for death tax purposes on account of such taxes being assessed because of such money or property.

ARTICLE III. I hereby declare that all of the household and homestead furniture and furnishings of every kind and character, including (but without being limited to) furniture, rugs, silver, chinaware, linens, paintings, and all other similar articles which have been utilized by my wife and me in our home belong to and are the exclusive property of my wife.

ARTICLE IV. I bequeath all of my personal letters, jewelry, automobiles, personal effects, and clothing to my wife if she be living on the date of my death, but if she predecease me, then to my children equally, *per stirpes.*

MARITAL TRUST

ARTICLE V. If my wife survives me, I devise and bequeath to my Trustee to be held as a part of the marital trust that fraction of my residuary estate which will reduce the federal estate tax falling due because of my death to the lowest possible amount, with the calculation to be made as if death taxes are not payable out of the marital share. Any property distributed in kind to the Trustee shall be distributed at the lower of (1) its value at the time of dis-tribution and (2) its adjusted income tax basis, provided, however, that if a beneficiary of my estate shall be the Executor-Trustee thereof, the selection of the property to be allocated to this trust shall not be made by the Executor-Trustee but by that person or institution next eligible to qualify as Executor-Trustee under this will. Subject to the foregoing, the Executor or the successor, as the case may be, shall have absolute discretion in selecting the property to be allocated pursuant to this provision without any duty to make a ratable apportionment of values, provided, however, that the assets selected and transferred must qualify for the marital deduc-tion, and provided further, that my Executor shall have the power to transfer to the Family Trust hereinafter created (and also to treat during administration of my estate as if transferred to the Family Trust) all of the assets of my estate which shall constitute income in respect to a decedent within the meaning of the Internal Revenue code provided that such a transfer can be made without loss of all or any part of the marital deduction within the meaning of the Internal Revenue code. This portion of my estate shall be held in trust upon the following terms, provisions, and conditions and for the following uses and purposes:

Section A. Commencing with the date of my death, my Trustee shall pay to my beloved wife quarterly or oftener if she shall request it, all of the income of this trust during her life, and upon her death, my Trustee shall have the right to pay out of the income or principal of this trust, the funeral expenses for my wife.

Section B. In addition to the net income, my Trustee in the exercise of its uncontrolled discretion shall pay to my wife as much of the principal of this trust as my Trustee shall deem needful or desirable for her comfortable support and maintenance including medical, surgical, hospital, or other institutional care so that my wife shall receive income and principal sufficient to maintain her station in life and the standard of living that she is enjoying at the date of my death.

Section C. Without reference to whether or not my wife survives me, my Trustee shall pay principal and any undistributed income of this trust unto such persons and in such estates, interests, and proportions as my wife by will shall appoint, provided, however, that any appointment must make specific reference to this power. In all other respects, my wife, in the exercise of this power of appointment, shall not be limited in any manner but, in all respects, the power shall be general and absolute and shall include specifically the power in my wife to appoint to her estate. If my wife shall fail to exercise the power of appointment herein granted as to any property in this trust, then upon her death (whether before or after my death), any property remaining in this trust not effectively appointed shall be poured over into and become a part of the Family Trust hereinafter created.

Section D. In the administration of this trust, my Trustee shall have and exercise all the rights and powers hereinafter granted to my Trustee provided only that there shall be, and there is hereby, excepted and excluded therefrom any and all of the powers hereinafter created which might or could cause or result in a loss of the marital deduction under the federal estate tax law; and provided further that this trust shall be administered separately and apart from the trusts hereinafter created unless my wife shall request that, for the purposes of administration only, the trusts created by this will be combined; and further provided that this request shall not be honored if, by reason of a joint administration of the various trusts herein created, the marital deduction provided for in the federal estate tax law shall be lost or forteited.

Section E. If there is no sufficient evidence as to the order of our deaths, my wife shall be presumed to have survived me and this will shall be construed upon that assumption and basis.

FAMILY TRUSTS

ARTICLE VI. I specifically refrain from exercising any power of appointment which I may have under any will, contract, trust agreement, profit-sharing agreement, or otherwise, and I devise and bequeath all of my other property, real, personal, and mixed in which I have or I or my estate shall hereafter acquire any interest, present or future, vested or contingent, to my Trustee to hold in trust for a period no longer than the lives of my wife and my descendants living on the date of my death and twenty years and eleven months thereafter upon and for the following uses and purposes:

Section A. The property in this trust shall be deemed to consist of (a) all of the property originally in this trust and (b) all the property received from the marital trust created in Article V or from any other source, and my Trustee shall divide on a *per stirpes* basis the property in this trust (as thus calculated into as many equal shares as I shall have children living ten months after my death, and children dead with issue surviving ten months after my death), and shall set up a separate trust for each child then living and one for the issue as a group of each deceased child, with each share being known as a "Child's Trust" and with the shares as a whole being identified as the "Family Trust," provided, however, that the shares of this trust may be held and administered together with the Trustee being under a duty only to make a separate accounting for and a separate income tax return for each of the separate shares or separate trusts.

Section B. The Trustee, out of the Family Trust, charging an equal portion to each Child's Trust, shall pay to my wife that portion of the income and principal thereof necessary to provide for here according to the standard of living that she is enjoying at the date of my death and to enable her to provide as she wishes for our children, provided, however, that the Trustee shall not make any distribution of principal to my wife until she shall have exhausted all of the income and principal of the marital trust and provided, further, that the Trustee in its discretion shall take into consideration the individual estate of my wife and any and all other sources of income and support which she may from time to time have.

Section C. If in any year all or any part of the income of the Family Trusts created by this Article shall not be paid to my wife, such income may be accumulated insofar as it may be lawfully accumulated and added to the principal of the trusts created by this Article or, alternatively, such income may be distributed in the manner provided by subsequent sections of this Article.

Section D. Provided only that a sufficient reserve of principal can be and is maintained for discharge of the benefits provided for my wife, the Trustee, out of the Family Trusts, charging an equal portion to each Child's Trust, shall pay each of my children income and principal sufficient for the maintenance and education of that child until that child has reached the age of twenty-three years.

Section E. Provided only that a sufficient reserve of principal can be and is maintained to provide for the protection and security of my wife under previous sections and articles of this will, my Trustee may pay each child that part of the income and principal of that Child's Trust necessary to supplement his or her earnings for his or her maintenance and support. My Trustee, out of a Child's Trust, may also advance a portion of the principal thereof to the beneficiary of that trust for the purpose of purchasing a home or alternatively the Trustee may purchase a home as Trustee for the use and benefit of that child with the purchase to be made out of the principal of that Child's Trust and with the title to be held by the Trustee until such time as the Trustee deems it wise to place title in the name of that child. My Trustee, out of a Child's Trust, may lend a portion of the principal thereof to the beneficiary of that trust for any purpose deemed sufficient by my Trustee, with such loan, if any, to be made upon such terms and with such security, if any, as the Trustee may require.

Section F. Before making any loan or distribution of principal as otherwise authorized by Section E hereof, my Trustee shall be required to obtain from my wife, if living, advance approval of any proposed distribution of principal. Subject only to this limitation, absolute power is granted to my Trustee not only to relieve my Trustee from seeking judicial instruction, but to the extent that my Trustee deems it to be prudent, to make determinations freely in favor of liberal distributions to current income beneficiaries. In each instance, the rights of all subsequent beneficiaries shall be subordinate, but my Trustee shall not be answerable to any of the lifetime beneficiaries nor to any subsequent beneficiary for anything done or omitted in favor of a current income beneficiary; but no current income beneficiary shall have the right to compel any such favorable treatment.

Section G. Upon the death of my wife and upon the attainment of the age of twenty-three years of all of my children, my Trustee shall pay to each child at such time or times and in such amounts as the Trustee in its unlimited discretion shall deem such distribution to be in the best interest of such child the income and principal of that Child's Trust. The power granted to my Trustee to make and also to defer making a distribution, various partial distributions, and a final distribution of the principal of each Child's Trust shall not be subject to modification or interpretation by any court but shall be deemed as broadly discretionary as the power I might possess myself if living. Inasmuch as the needs of each of my children and their respective abilities to care for property shall differ, the Trustee is not only authorized but expected to follow, if advisable, a different pattern of distribution for each child.

Section H. If any of my children die before this trust terminates leaving widow, widower, descendants, spouses of descendants, or widow or widower of deceased descendants living at the date of said deceased child's death, my Trustee shall pay his or her share of the income and of the principal to his widow, her widower, and/or to such of his or her descendants, spouses of descendants and widow or widower of deceased descendants as said deceased child shall by will appoint, provided, however, that any daughter of mine shall not have the right to appoint to her widower or to any widower of any of her descendants anything other than an estate for life or until his remarriage, whichever shall sooner occur, and in the event of any such appointment, the Trustee may invade the principal of my estate for the benefit of the descendants of any daughter exercising the power of appointment without reference to the fact that such invasion of principal will diminish the life estate benefits.

Section I. If any of my children die before this trust terminates without having exercised the power of appointment provided for in Section H hereof, my Trustee shall distribute this child's trust to his children equally per stirpes, but if any of my children die before this trust terminates without leaving descendants at the date of said deceased child's death and without having exercised the power of appointment provided for in Section H hereof, my Trustee shall distribute this child's trust equally among the remaining trusts established for my family under this Article.

Section J. If pursuant to this will, a person under twenty-three years of age other than one of my children shall become entitled to a devise or bequest, such devise or bequest shall become and be impressed with a trust and held in trust by my Trustee until that particular person attains the age of twenty-three years, and I direct my Trustee to spend for each such person as much of the income and principal of that trust as is necessary for that person's education, maintenance and support until that person is twenty-three years of age; whereupon, my Trustee shall pay to that person the principal and any undistributed income of his or her trust.

Section K. If at any time or from time to time any beneficiary hereunder shall be under twenty-three years of age, the Trustee is to make payments in its sole discretion in any one or more of the following ways: (a) directly to such beneficiary, (b) directly in payment of the expense of support, maintenance, education and welfare of such beneficiary, (c) to the legal or natural guardian of such beneficiary, (d) or to any relative or guardian of the person of such beneficiary who shall have custody and care of the person of such beneficiary. The Trustee shall not be obligated to see to the application of the funds so paid, but the receipt of such payee shall be full acquittance to the Trustee, and all such distributions may be without the intervention of any guardian or any court, provided, however, that the Trustee in its discretion may require an accounting and take such steps as it may deem requisite to assure and enforce the due application of such money to the purpose for which it is intended.

ARTICLE VII. Notwithstanding any other provision of this will, all of the property of my estate shall be finally distributed not later than twenty years and eleven months after the date of death of the last survivor of my descendants living on the date of my death and at the expiration of such period, if any part of my estate remains undistributed, the same shall immediately vest in and be distributed to the persons then entitled to receive the income from the trust estate in the proportions to which they are so entitled.

ARTICLE VIII. Certain of my life insurance policies may be made payable to my testamentary trustee, thereby exempting those proceeds from state inheritance taxes. My Trustee may lend all of any portion of these life insurance proceeds to my Executor.

ARTICLE IX. My Executor shall not be required to file an appraisal with any court and neither my Executor nor my Trustee shall be required to make an accounting or to file any settlement with any court unless requested by a current income beneficiary of my estate. Within four months after the close of each fiscal year of my estate, the Executor or the Trustee thereof will render a written account of the administration of the trust estate to current income beneficiaries thereof. The written approval of such accounting by a majority of all current income beneficiaries (the parent, guardian, or conservator acting on behalf of any beneficiary who is a minor or otherwise incompetent) shall be final and binding as to all matters stated in said account or as shown thereby upon all persons (whether or not in being) who are then or thereafter may become elgible to share in either the principal or the income of my estate. The failure of any beneficiary to object in writing to the acting fiduciary to such an account within sixty days after the receipt of the same shall be final and binding to the same extent as if the written assent were given as hereinbefore provided.

ARTICLE X. I empower my Executor, any successor Executor, my Trustee and any successor Trustee:

Section 1. To allot, assign, care for, collect, contract with respect to, convey, convert, deal with, dispose of, enter into, exchange, hold, improve, insure, invest, lease, manage, mortgage, grant and exercise options with respect to, take possession of, pledge, protect, receive, release, repair, sell, sue for, and in general, to do any and every act and thing and to enter into and carry out any and every agreement with respect to the trust estate or any part thereof as the trustee would have the right to do if it were the individual owner thereof and as it may deem in the best interest of the beneficiaries of the trust, without being limited in any way by the grant of specific powers hereinafter made.

Section 2. To retain, without liability for loss or depreciation resulting from such retention, original property, real or personal, for such time as to it shall seem best, although such property may not be of the character prescribed by law or by the terms of this instrument for the investment of other trust funds and although it represents a large percentage of the total property of the trust estate; and to dispose of such original property by sale or exchange or otherwise as and when it shall deem advisable and receive and administer the proceeds as a part of the trust estate; and, if non-income-producing property is retained, then upon the sale, exchange or other disposition of such property, to make a reasonable apportionment of the proceeds between income and principal so as to make up for the loss of income during the period of retention of the unproductive property.

Section 3. To continue and operate any business which I may own or in which I may be financially interested at the time of my death, whether as sole proprietor, partner or shareholder for such time as it may deem to be for the best interest of my estate; to delegate such duties and the requisite powers to any employee, manager, or partner as it may deem proper without liability for such delegation except for its own negligence; to employ in the conduct of any such business, not only my capital investment therein at the time of my death, but also such additional capital out of my general estate as it may deem proper; to borrow money for any such business, either alone or along with other persons financially interested in the business, and to secure such loan or loans by a pledge or mortgage not only of my property or interest in the business, but also of any part of my property outside the business as my executor or trustee may deem proper; to lend money out of my estate or out of any trust hereby created to any business in which my estate or any trust hereby created is financially interested; to organize either by itself or jointly with others, a corporation to carry on any business; to contribute all or any part of my interest in any business as capital to any such corporation; to accept stock in the corporation in lieu thereof and if it deems advisable to provide for different classes of stocks and and bonds; to sell any business and any interest in any business or any stock or other securities representing my interest in any business as and when and upon such terms as shall seem to it to be for the best interest of my estate; to liquidate, either by itself or jointly with others, any business or any interest in any business at such times and upon such terms as shall seem to be for the best interest of my estate; and generally, to exercise with respect to the continuance, management, sale or liquidation of any business or business interest I own at the time of my death, all the powers which I myself could have exercised during my lifetime.

Section 4. To invest and reinvest and keep the trust estate invested in any kind of property, real or personal, including by way of illustration, but not of limitation, livestock, common and preferred stocks, voting trust certificates, bonds, notes, debentures, mortgages, shares or interests in investment trusts, shares or interests in common trust funds, investments that yield a high rate of income or no income at all, and wasting investments, without regard to the proportion any such investment or investments of a similar character may bear to the total trust estate or whether or not such investments are in new issues or in new or foreign enterprises, and without being limited to the classes of investments in which trustees are or may be authorized by statute or case or rule of court to invest trust funds, intending hereby to authorize the Trustee to act in such manner as it shall believe to be for the best interest of the trust estate, regarding it as a whole, even though particular investments otherwise might not be proper.

Section 5. To cause the securities or other property (other than accessable securities) which may comprise the trust estate or any part thereof to be registered in its name as trustee hereunder or in its own name, or in the name of its nominee without disclosing the trust, or (in the case of securities) to take and keep the same unregistered and to retain them or any part of them in such manner that they will pass by delivery; but no such registration or holding by the trustee shall relieve it of liability for the safe custody and proper disposition of such trust property in accordance with the terms and provisions hereof.

Section 6. To vote any corporate stock belonging to the trust estate through its officers or by proxy, with or without power of substitution, and to execute proxies to one or more nominees, provided, however, that if any bank shall be acting as the Executor-Trustee of my estate and if any of the stock held in my estate shall include common stock of the same bank, then said stock must be voted in such manner as the then current income beneficiary or beneficiaries, as the case may be, shall direct.

Section 7. To reduce the interest rate on any mortgage constituting a part of the trust estate.

Section 8. To consent to the modification or release of any guaranty of any mortgage which it holds in the trust estate or in which it has a partial interest.

Section 9. To determine what expenses, costs, taxes and charges of all kinds shall be charged against income and what against principal, and its decision with respect thereto shall be conclusive upon all parties.

Section 10. To treat as principal or as income or partly as one and partly the other, as to it shall seem best, all realized appreciation in the value of stocks and bonds, securities or other property forming a part of the trust estate, resulting from the sale or other disposition thereof, and its decision with respect thereto shall be conclusive upon all parties.

Section 11. To determine whether premiums on investments

shall be charged against principal or income or apportioned between them and whether discounts on investments shall be credited to principal or income or apportioned between them; to establish sinking funds for purposes of amortizations already started and distribute the sinking fund between principal and income or allocate all to the one or to the other as to it shall seem best.

Section 12. To treat stock dividends, dividends payable in the stocks or bonds of another company, extraordinary cash or noncash dividends, and liquidating dividends as income or as principal or partly as one and partly the other as to the Trustee shall seem best, and its decision with respect thereto shall be conclusive upon all parties.

Section 13. To make division or distribution in money or in kind or partly in money and partly in kind, including securities, real property, and undivided interests in real or personal property, making the necessary equalizations in cash, at values to be determined by the Trustee, whose judgment as to values shall be binding and conclusive upon all parties at interest.

Section 14. To collect, receive and receipt for the rents, issues, profits, and income of the trust estate.

Section 15. To institute, prosecute, defend, compromise, settle, pay and discharge all actions for or against the estate or arising in connection with the administration thereof, including inheritance taxes, estate taxes, gift taxes and income taxes, and to give or receive appropriate receipts, releases, acquittances and discharges, and the decision and acts of the Executor or Trustee shall be binding and conclusive upon all parties at interest.

Section 16. To borrow money for the benefit of the trust estate and to secure the loan by pledge or mortgage of the trust property and to renew existing loans.

Section 17. To sell publicly or privately, for cash or on time without an order of court, upon such terms and conditions as to it shall seem best, any property, real or personal, included in the estate, and the purchaser shall not be required to see to the application of the proceeds.

Section 18. To improve, manage, protect, and subdivide any real estate comprising the trust estate or any part thereof; to dedicate parks, streets, highways, or alleys and to vacate any subdivision or part thereof, and to resubdivide the same as often as desired; to contract to sell, to grant options to purchase; to sell on any terms, to convey either with or without consideration; to convey said premises or any part thereof to a successor or successors in trust and to grant to such successor or successors in trust all of the title, estate, powers, and authorities vested in the Trustee; to donate, to dedicate, to mortgage, pledge or otherwise encumber any such property, or any part thereof; to lease any such property, or any part thereof, from time to time in possession or reversion, by leases to commence *in praesenti* or *in futuro*, and upon any terms and for any period or periods of time, not exceeding in the case of any single demise the term of 198 years, and to renew or extend leases upon any terms and for any period or periods of time, and to amend, change or modify leases and the terms and provisions thereof at any time or times hereafter, to contract to make leases and to grant options to lease and options to renew leases and options to purchase the whole or any part of the reversion and to contract respecting the manner of fixing the amount of present or future rentals; to partition or to exchange said property, or any part thereof, for other real or personal property; to grant easements or charges of any kind, to release, convey or assign any right, title or interest in or about or easement appurtenant to any property or any part thereof; and to deal with any such property, and every part thereof in all other ways and for such other considerations as it would be lawful for any person owning the same to deal with the same whether similar to or different from the ways above specified, at any time or times hereafter.

Section 19. To sell outright or to lease or grant the right to mine or drill and to remove from any real property held hereunder gas, oil, sand, gravel, rock, and other minerals, irrespective of whether or not any such right is to continue longer than the duration of the trust created hereunder, and should any of the above rights be exercised, any bonus, royalties, rentals, or proceeds of sale shall be allocated to the income or principal or partly to the income and partly to the principal as may in the sole discretion of my Executor or in the discretion of my Trustee be deemed to be just and equitable.

Section 20. To execute and deliver oil, gas, and other mineral leases containing such unitazation or pooling agreements and other provisions as the Trustee shall think fit; to execute mineral and royalty conveyances; to purchase leases, royalties and any type of mineral interest; to execute and deliver drilling contracts and other contracts options, and other instruments necessary or desirable in engaging actively in the oil, gas, or other mining business, all of the foregoing to be done with such terms, conditions, agreements, covenants, provisions, or undertakings as the Trustee shall think fit.

Section 21. To employ and compensate, out of the principal or income of the estate as to it shall seem proper, agents, accountants, brokers, attorneys in fact, attorneys at law, tax specialists, and other assistants and advisers deemed by it to be necessary for the proper settlement or administration of the estate, and to do so without liability for any neglect, omission, misconduct, or default of any such agent or attorney provided he was selected and retained with reasonable care; provided, however, that I request but do not require that my Executor-Trustee employ in the settlement of my estate and in the administration of the trust under my will that attorney who shall last have represented me prior to my death in matters relating to my estate.

Section 22. To exercise any power herein granted with reference to the control, management, investment, or disposition of the estate or any part thereof, either as Executor or as Trustee, and without having to declare in which capacity it is acting.

Section 23. To hold and retain the principal of the trust estate undivided, if more convenient to do so, until actual division becomes necessary to make any distribution; to hold, manage, invest, and account for the several shares or parts thereof, as a single trust estate, making the division thereof only upon the books of account by proper entries; and to allocate to each a share, a part or proportionate part of the receipts and expenses; provided that no such holding shall defer the vesting in possession of any estate.

Section 24. To pay the beneficiary entitled to the next successive estate dividends declared but not paid and interest or other income accrued but not received.

Section 25. To file joint income or gift tax returns with my spouse for the periods prior to my death; and in its sole discretion to pay any part or all of the taxes, interest, or penalties for such periods and for periods for which joint returns were filed prior to my death. Any decision made by the Executor-Trustee shall be conclusive on all persons.

Section 26. To exercise any right available under the Internal Revenue Code to elect the manner in which any partnership, corporation, or other business unit shall be taxed, and, if necessary, in order to place an election into effect or in order to preserve an election which has been made, then to sell if it so elects any partnership interest or shares of stock from the trust estate for cash or for a note to any beneficiary or beneficiaries of my estate.

Section 27. To budget the estimated annual income and expenses of the trust in such manner as to equalize so far as practicable periodic income payments to beneficiaries.

Section 28. To transfer any asset from one of the trusts under this will to any other trust under this will by purchase, sale, loan or exchange at values to be determined by the Trustee whose judgment as to value shall be binding and conclusive upon all parties at interest, and upon such terms and conditions as to it shall seem advisable.

Section 29. To deduct costs and expenses incurred in the administration of my estate either to reduce the income tax liability of my estate or the federal estate tax liability thereof so that, in the judgment of my Executor-Trustee, the smallest combined federal estate tax and federal income tax shall be paid by my estate and the beneficiaries thereof without regard to the effect of such action upon the comparative values of the trusts created hereunder, and my Executor-Trustee shall not be required to make any compensating adjustments in either the income or principal of the several trusts created hereunder.

Section 30. To exercise any and all of the rights, powers, and discretions granted by this will without giving prior notice to any person and without first obtaining an order of court therefor.

Section 31. To do all other acts which, in its judgment, may be necessary or appropriate for the proper and advantageous management, investment and distribution of my estate.

ARTICLE XI. Notwithstanding any provision of this will hereinbefore made, my Executor may distribute the income earned by my estate during administration thereof in the manner hereinafter set forth, provided, however, that the duration of this power shall be for the lesser of the two following periods: (1) From the date of my death until the final audit of the United States Estate Tax Return filed in my estate, or (2) from the date of my death until the end of the fourth fiscal year after the date of my death, with the first of the four fiscal years to be deemed to commence upon the first day of the month in which my death shall occur:

First, my Executor shall pay to my widow not less than the income earned on the marital trust created for her benefit by this will.

Secondly, my Executor shall pay to my widow any additional income of my estate which in my Executor's discretion may be needed by her for her comfortable maintenance and support.

Finally, all the remaining income of my estate may be either (1) accumulated in whole or in part and added to the principal of my estate, or (2) distributed in whole or in part to all or any of the current income beneficiaries of the Family Trusts created by this will, and my Executor shall not be under a duty to make a ratable distribution thereof, but instead shall have the right to make distributions according to the respective needs of the current income beneficiaries according to my Executor's discretion.

The discretionary rights granted to my Executor shall not be subject to modification or interpretation by any court for any cause whatsoever.

The word "income" as hereinbefore used shall be that sum equal to taxable income as computed by my Executor for United States income tax purposes, plus income, if any, upon tax free municipals, and this definition shall not be modified as a result of any audit made by the Internal Revenue Service of any fiduciary income tax return filed in my estate.

I, John Doe, residing in _____ (town, state), being now in good health of body and mind and not acting under duress, menace, fraud, or undue influence of any person whatsoever, do make, publish, and declare this my last will and testament, and do hereby expressly revoke all other and former wills and codicils to wills heretofore made by me.

IN WITNESS WHEREOF, I have hereunto set my hand this _____ day of _____, 19 ___.

_____

The foregoing instrument, consisting of this and ___ preceding pages, was, at the date hereof, signed, published and declared by John Doe to be his last will and testament in the presence of us, the undersigned, who, at his request and in his sight and presence, and in the sight and presence of each other, have hereunto subscribed our names as witnesses thereto, having also together seen the said testator's name written by him at the conclusion of the will on page ___.

_____ residing at _____
_____ residing at _____
_____ residing at _____

A Revocable Living Trust

The parties to this trust agreement are John Doe, donor, and Charles Doe, trustee, both of _____ (town, county, state), WITNESSETH:

ARTICLE I

A. The donor has executed this trust agreement as a part of a comprehensive plan for the comfort and support of his wife and children in the manner hereinafter provided.

B. The donor has deposited with the trustee certain policies of insurance on the donor's life which are described in Schedule A attached hereto.

C. From time to time further property, including policies of life insurance, may be deposited with the trustee hereunder; and the donor intends to direct by the provisions of his last will that the residue of his probate estate shall pass to the trustee of this trust for administration hereunder after the donor's death.

ARTICLE II

A. The original trustee acknowledges receipt of the insurance policies listed in the schedule annexed hereto.

B. The trustee and his successor in office will hold, manage, invest, and reinvest all property described in the schedule annexed and all property hereinafter deposited by the donor during his lifetime and accepted by the trustee, and all of the proceeds of said property, upon the uses and for the purposes hereinafter set forth.

C. The acting trustee will accept and administer hereunder whatever part of the donor's probate estate is to be paid to the trustee hereunder to be so administered.

D. The original trustee and its successor or successors will use its best efforts to collect when due and thereafter will administer in accordance with the terms hereof the proceeds of all policies of insurance made payable to the trustee hereunder. Neither the trustee nor any successor shall have any responsibility, however, except as above specified as to such policies, nor as to the premiums thereof nor the interest on any loan thereon; and the insurance companies which shall have issued such policies shall have no responsibility in the premises other than to pay the proceeds of the said policies when they shall become due and payable to the trustee.

E. The trustee shall not be required to make an accounting or to file any settlement with any court unless requested by a current-income beneficiary of the estate. Upon the request of any current-income beneficiary, the trustee shall file a settlement with a court of competent jurisdiction. Within four months after the close of each fiscal year of the trust, the trustee will render a written account of the administration of the trust to the current-income beneficiaries of the trust. The written approval of any such accounting by a majority of all current-income beneficiaries (the parent, guardian, or conservator acting on behalf of any beneficiary who is a minor or otherwise incompetent) shall be final and binding as to all matters stated in said account as shown thereby upon all persons (whether or not in being) who are then or thereafter may become eligible to share in either the principal or the income of said trust estate. The failure of any beneficiary to object in writing to the trustee to such an account within sixty (60) days after the receipt of the same shall be final and binding to the same extent as if the written assent were given as hereinbefore provided.

F. Upon written request by the donor, the trustee will assent to or join in the execution of any instrument presented to it by the donor and designed to enable the donor to avail himself of any of the rights reserved to him by the provisions of Article IV of this instrument.

ARTICLE III

The donor agrees with the trustee that upon the request of the trustee he will execute and deliver to the trustee such further instrument, or instruments, as such trustee may hereafter deem necessary or convenient to vest the title of the trust assets in the trustee or to evidence the legal title of the trustee thereto.

ARTICLE IV

A. During his life (except during any period of adjudicated incompetency) the donor shall have the full right to be exercised from time to time by a writing, or writings, signed and acknowledged by him to be effective when delivered to the trustee hereunder:

1. To revoke this instrument entirely and to receive from the trustee all of the trust property remaining after making payment or provision for payment of all expenses connected with the adminis- tration of this trust to the date of revocation.

2. From time to time to alter or amend this instrument in any and every particular.

3. From time to time to change the identity or number, or both, of the trustee hereunder.

4. From time to time to withdraw from the operation of this trust any part or all of the trust property.

B. With respect to all policies of insurance at any time deposited hereunder by the donor and made subject to the terms of this trust, he reserves full right and authority, to be exercised by him in the manner and during the periods hereinabove in Section A of this Article IV specified:

1. To sell, assign, or hypothecate any or all of said policies.

2. To exercise any option or privilege granted by said policies, including the right to change the beneficiaries of any policy.

3. To borrow any sum from the insurer or any individual, part- nership, corporation, or association.

4. To recieve all payments, dividends, surrender values, benefits, or privileges of any kind which may accrue on account of said policies. To freely inspect and to withdraw from this instrument any or all of said policies.

If, because of illness, adjudicated imcompetency, or for any other reason the donor shall be incapable of managing his affairs, then during all such periods the trustee may exercise one or more or all of the rights hereinabove in this Section B of Article IV enumerated, and may make use of any part or all of the income or principal of the trust property for the purpose of maintaining said policies of insurance or any or all of them in full force and good standing, or alternatively, may surrender one or more of said policies and convert the same into cash.

C. During the life of the donor (except during any period of adjudicated incompetency) the trustee shall pay over to him or to his written order whatever part or parts or all of the income and of the principal of the trust fund he shall from time to time and in writing direct.

If the donor shall, because of prolonged illness, or for any other reason be incapable of managing his affairs, then during all such periods the trustee may use, apply or expend for his direct or indirect benefit, or for the direct or indirect benefit of his wife, or for the direct or indirect benefit of one or more of his living children or for the direct or indirect benefit of one or more of said persons, whatever part, or parts, or all of the income and principal, or both, of the trust fund the said trustee shall think best.

During all periods of the donor's adjudicated incompetency, if any, the trustee shall have and exercise all of said powers of payment, use, application and expenditure of income and principal hereinabove described.

D. Neither the committee nor the guardian of the donor nor any other person other than the donor himself, except as otherwise herein provided, may exercise any of the rights reserved to the donor by the provisions of this Article IV.

ARTICLE V

The trustee shall hold all of the property in this trust for a period no longer than the life of the donor's wife and his descendants living on the date of his death and twenty years and eleven months thereafter upon and for the following uses and purposes:

A. The property in this trust shall be deemed to consist of all of the property originally in this trust and all of the property received from any other source, and the trustee shall divide on a *per stirpes* basis the property in this trust as thus calculated into as many equal shares as the donor shall have children living ten months after his death and children dead with issue surviving ten months after his death, and shall set up a separate trust for each child then living and one for the issue as a group of each deceased child with each share being known as a "Child's Trust," (for example, John Doe, Jr.

Trust, Joseph Doe Trust, and Susan Doe Trust) and with the shares as a whole being identified as the "Children's Trust." The shares of this trust may be held and administered together with the trustee being under a duty only to make a separate accounting for and a separate income tax return for each Child's Trust.

B. The trustee out of the Children's Trust charging an equal portion to each Child's Trust shall pay to the donor's wife that portion of the income and principal thereof necessary to provide for the donor's wife according to the standard of living that she is enjoying at the date of the donor's death and to enable her to provide as she wishes for the donor's children, provided, however, that the trustee in its discretion shall take into consideration the individual estate of the donor's wife and any and all other sources of income and support which the donor's wife may from time to time have.

C. If in any year all or any part of the income of the Children's Trust created by this section shall not be paid to the donor's wife, such income may be accumulated insofar as it may be lawfully accumulated and added to the principal of the Children's Trust created by this section or, alternatively, such income may be distributed in the manner provided by subsequent subsections of this section.

D. Provided only that a sufficient reserve of principal can be and is maintained for discharge of the benefits provided for the donor's wife, the trustee out of the Children's Trust, charging an equal portion to each Child's Trust, shall pay each of the donor's children income and principal sufficient for the maintenance and education of that child until that child has reached the age of twenty-five years.

E. Provided only that a sufficient reserve of principal can be and is maintained for discharge of the benefits provided for the donor's wife, the trustee may pay each of the donor's children out of that Child's Trust quarterly or monthly that part of the income and principal of that Child's Trust necessary to supplement his or her earnings and for the purpose of providing adequately for his or her maintenance and support. The trustee, out of a Child's Trust may also advance a portion of the principal thereof to the beneficiary of that trust for the purpose of purchasing a home, or alternatively, the trustee may purchase a home as trustee for the use and benefit of that child, with the purchase to be made out of the principal of that Child's Trust and with the title to be held by the trustee until such time as the trustee deems it wise to place title in the name of the child. The trustee out of a Child's Trust may lend a portion of the principal thereof to the beneficiary of that trust for any purpose deemed sufficient by the trustee, with such loan, if any, to be made upon such terms and with such security, if any, as the trustee may require.

F. The trustee upon receiving a written direction from the wife of the donor shall be under a duty to distribute out of a Child's Trust to the beneficiary of that trust that portion of the income and principal thereof which the donor's wife shall direct to be distributed and such direction shall be honored from time to time as received by the trustee from the donor's wife.

G. Upon the death of the donor's wife, the trustee shall pay to each child, at such time or times and in such amounts as the trustee in its unlimited discretion shall deem such distribution to be in the best interest of said child, the income and principal of that Child's Trust. The power granted to the trustee to make and also to defer making a distribution, various partial distributions, and a final distribution of the principal of each Child's Trust shall not be subject to modification or interpretation by any court but shall be deemed as broadly discretionary as the power that the donor would possess if living. Inasmuch as the needs of the donor's children and their respective abilities to care for property shall differ, the trustee is not only authorized but expected to follow, if advisable, a different pattern of distribution for each child.

H. Absolute power is granted the trustee not only to relieve it from seeking judicial instruction, but also to the extent that the trustee deems it to be prudent to make determinations freely in favor of liberal distributions to current-income beneficiaries. In each instance the rights of all subsequent beneficiaries shall be subordinate, but the trustee shall not be answerable to any of the lifetime beneficiaries nor to any subsequent beneficiary for anything done or omitted in favor of a current-income beneficiary; but no current-income beneficiary shall have the right to compel any such favorable treatment.

I. If any of the children of the donor die before this trust terminates leaving widow, widower, descendants, spouses of descendants, or widow or widower of deceased descendants living at the date of said deceased child's death, the trustee shall pay his or her share of the income and principal to his widow or her widower and/or to such of his or her descendants, spouses of descendants and widow or widower of deceased descendants as said deceased child shall by will appoint, provided, however, that the donor's daughter, Susan Doe, shall not have the right to appoint to any husband that she might have anything other than an estate for his life or until his remarriage whichever shall sooner occur, and in the event of any such appointment, the donor's trustee may invade the principal of the donor's estate for the benefit of the descendants of the donor's daughter, Susan Doe, without reference to the fact that such invasion of principal will diminish the life estate benefits.

J. If any child of the donor having a power of appointment under the preceding provision does not appoint his or her share of this trust by will, or if any attempted appointment shall be invalid, the trustee shall pay and distribute his or her share of this trust to his or her children *per stirpes.*

K. If any of the children of the donor die before this trust terminates without leaving descendants living at the date of said deceased child's death and without making a valid exercise of the power of appointment provided for, the trustee shall pay his or her share of the income and of the principal of this trust equally to the other children of the donor *per stirpes.*

L. If, pursuant to this agreement, any person other than a child of the donor shall become entitled to a portion of this trust as a beneficiary thereof, such share shall become and be impressed with a trust and held in trust by the trustee until that particular minor attains the age of twenty-five years and the trustee shall spend for each person under the age of twenty-five years as much of the income and principal of that trust as is necessary for that person's education, maintenance, and support until that person is twenty-five years of age, whereupon the trustee shall pay to that beneficiary the principal and any undistributed income of his or her trust.

M. If at any time or from time to time any beneficiaries hereunder shall be under twenty-five years of age, the trustee is to make payments in its sole discretion in any one or more of the following ways: (1) directly to such beneficiary, (2) directly in payment of the expense of support, maintenance, education, and welfare of such beneficiary, (3) to the legal or natural guardian of such beneficiary, (4) or to any relative or guardian of the person of such beneficiary who shall have custody and care of the person of such beneficiary; except, however, as and to the extent that such distribution shall be herein otherwise expressly directed. The trustee shall not be obliged to see to the application of the funds so paid, but the receipt of such payee shall be full acquittance to the trustee, and all such distributions may be without the intervention of any guardian or any court, provided, however, that the trustee may require an accounting and take such steps as it may deem requisite to enforce the due application of such money to the purposes for which it is intended.

N. With respect to the establishment and administration of each trust above described, the donor declares that the trustee shall have full power and authority to allocate property to each trust either in cash or in kind or partly in cash and partly in kind, and the action of the trustee in this respect, particularly with respect to the value of any such property, shall be binding on all persons if made reasonably and in good faith.

The trustee without the advice, consent, or approval of any court and without regard to the effect of its determinations upon the beneficiaries shall have the right in its capacity as executor under the donor's will or as trustee under this trust agreement to value assets and to elect whether deductions shall be claimed on the estate tax return or on income tax returns. The donor requests, but does not require, that determinations be made by the executor or by the trustee for the purpose of minimizing the total of combined estate, inheritance, and income taxes upon the donor's estate and the beneficiaries thereof.

ARTICLE VI

This trust shall not be permitted to fail for want of a trustee. In the event of the default, death, disqualification, resignation, or removal of the original trustee, then the donor appoints George Doe of _____ (town, state), as successor trustee and in the event of the default, death, disqualification, resignation or removal of George Doe as successor trustee, the donor appoints William Doe of _____ (town, state), as successor trustee. In the event of the default, death, disqualification, resignation, or removal of William Doe as successor trustee, then the donor requests the appointment of that successor trustee nominated by the donor's wife whether the nomination be made by deed or will. In exercising this power of appointment, the donor's wife may appoint either an individual or a corporation and may make the appointment so that the appointee shall be relieved from the requirement of giving bond or required to give bond. If for any reason the donor's wife shall fail to exercise the power hereby granted or if any attempt by her to exercise this power shall be invalid and also in the event of the death, default, disqualification, resignation, or removal of her appointee, the donor appoints the _____ National Bank of _____ trustee of the donor's estate. It shall not be necessary for any trustee designated herein to be appointed by any court or give bond before any court although it shall have the right to seek such recognition of its fiduciary capacity if it so desires.

Neither the original trustee nor any successor trustee nominated herein shall be required to give bond as such, and any corporate trustee whether designated by this trust instrument or appointed by a court shall not be required to do any more than to pledge its corporate effects to secure the bond executed by it.

Notwithstanding the other provisions of this Article, if either of the donor's sons shall at any time be acting as trustee, then the acting trustee shall not have the power to distribute to himself or to themselves individually any portion of the principal of his trust excepting only that part thereof needful or desirable for the respective beneficiary's comfortable support and maintenance including medical, surgical, hospital, or other institutional care so that the beneficiary shall receive income and only that part of the principal, if any is necessary, that may be sufficient to maintain his standard of living that he is enjoying on the date of the donor's death.

ARTICLE VII

Neither the original nor any successor trustee shall be required to qualify as such before any court, but shall assume and hold office solely by reason of the authority contained in this trust agreement. Any trustee at any time serving hereunder may resign as trustee by delivering to the successor trustee an instrument in writing containing such resignation.

ARTICLE VIII

Each trust created hereunder shall in any event terminate twenty years and eleven months after the death of the last survivor of such of the beneficiaries hereunder as shall be living at the time of the execution of this agreement, and thereafter the property held in trust shall be discharged of trust and distributed to the persons then entitled to the income and principal thereof as if all classes had closed and interests vested according to the terms of this agreement on that date.

ARTICLE IX

This trust has been created under the laws of Any State and its validity, construction and administration shall be determined by the laws of that state.

ARTICLE X

The trustee and any successor trustee shall have the right, power, and authority to receive either from the donor or from any other person by deed or will any other property to be added to this trust.

ARTICLE XI

The trustee and any successor trustee shall have all of the following powers:

(Use a complete set of powers such as appears in the preceding will.)

WITNESS the signatures of the parties hereunto as of the _____ day of _____, 19 ___.

_____

John Doe

_____

Charles Doe

State of_____

_____ (county)

I, _____, a Notary Public in and for the County and State aforesaid, hereby certify that the foregoing Trust Agreement was produced before me in my said county by John Doe and Charles Doe and was by them and each of them signed and acknowledged to be their free and voluntary act and deed.

Given under my hand and notarial seal this _____ day of _____, 19_____.

_____

Notary Public,   (county, state)

A Pour-Over Will

I, John Doe, of _____ (town, state), hereby make this my last will revoking every will heretofore made by me.

ARTICLE I. I appoint my wife, Mary Doe, Executrix of this will and Trustee of my estate and request that no bond be required of her as such. In the event of the death, default, disqualification, resignation, or removal of my wife, I authorize my wife to appoint a Successor-Executor of this will and Trustee of my estate and to require, or not to require, the execution of a bond. In the event of the failure of my wife to exercise this power of appointment and in the event of the death, default, disqualification, resignation, or removal of the appointee, I appoint my brother, Charles Doe, Executor of this will and Trustee of my estate and request that no bond be required of him as such. In the event of the death, default, disqualification, resignation or removal of my brother, I appoint the _____ National Bank of _____, as Executor of this will and Trustee of my estate. The word "Executor," whenever used herein, shall be deemed to refer to my Executor or to my Executrix, whichever shall be acting as such.

ARTICLE II. This will and the John Doe Revocable Living Trust hereinafter referred to shall be construed as if the two instruments constituted a single document.

ARTICLE III. I direct my Executor to pay all my just debts and funeral expenses, to have a monument or marker erected at my grave, and to pay out of my residuary estate all estate, inheritance, transfer, and succession taxes payable by my estate or payable on the legacies given herein, and my Executor shall make no claims against any person receiving any money or property including the proceeds of insurance policies includable in my gross estate for death tax purposes on account of such taxes being assessed because of such money or property.

ARTICLE IV. I hereby declare that all of the household and homestead furniture and furnishings of every kind and character, including (but without being limited to) furniture, rugs, silver, chinaware, linens, paintings, and all other similar articles which have been utilized by my wife and me in our home belong to and are the exclusive property of my wife.

ARTICLE V. I bequeath all my personal letters, jewelry, automobiles, personal effects, and clothing to my wife if she be living on the date of my death, but if she predeceases me, then to my children equally *per stirpes*.

ARTICLE VI. Certain of my life insurance policies may be made payable to my testamentary trustee, thereby exempting these proceeds from _____ (state) inheritance taxes. My Trustee may lend all or any portion of these life insurance proceeds with or without interest to my Executor.

ARTICLE VII. If there is no sufficient evidence as to the order of our deaths, my wife shall be presumed to have survived me and this will shall be construed upon that assumption and basis.

ARTICLE VIII. I specifically refrain from exercising any power of appointment which I may have under any will, contract, trust agreement, profit-sharing agreement, or otherwise, and I devise and bequeath all of my other property, real, personal or mixed, in which I have or I or my estate shall acquire any interest, present or future, vested or contingent, and excluding only interests which I have a right to appoint, to the acting trustee under a certain instrument of revocable living trust heretofore executed by me on _____, and entitled "John Doe Revocable Living Trust" to be held and administered by the Trustee in accordance with the terms thereof as stated in said instrument of revocable living trust as originally executed but as from time to time hereinafter amended.

ARTICLE IX. If for any reason said John Doe Revocable Living Trust shall not be in existence at the time of my death, or if for any reason a court of competent jurisdiction shall declare this testamentary transfer to the trustee of said revocable living trust to be invalid, then I hereby declare that the estate disposed of by this will shall be held, managed, invested, and reinvested in exactly the manner described in the said instrument of revocable living trust for the period beginning with the date of my death, giving effect to all the then existing amendments to said trust if it shall be legal so to do, but, in any event, giving effect to said trust as now in effect by the same Trustee and the same successor Trustee therein named and defined who are to serve hereunder without the necessity of providing sureties on their bonds and for that purpose I do hereby incorporate that same instrument of revocable living trust by reference into this my last will. I also declare that said revocable living trust was signed not only before a notary public but before two witnesses before whom I executed said revocable living trust as if it constituted also a last will and testament so that, in effect, this instrument can be construed as a codicil to said John Doe Revocable Living Trust.

ARTICLE X. I empower my Executor and any successor Executor, my Trustee and any successor Trustee to have and enjoy all of the powers granted to my Trustee under the John Doe Revocable Living Trust and in addition thereto but without limitation thereon, the following express powers:

Section 1. To allot, assign, borrow, care for, collect, contract with respect to, convey, convert, deal with, dispose of, enter into, exchange, hold, improve, insure, invest, lease, manage, mortgage, grant and exercise options with respect to, take possession of, pledge, protect, receive, release, repair, sell, sue for, and in general to do any and every act and thing and to enter into and carry out any and every agreement with respect to my estate or any part thereof as the Executor would have the right to do if he or it were the individual owner thereof, and as may be deemed by my Executor to be in the best interest of the beneficiaries of my estate; and this grant of power shall be construed to embrace specifically all of the powers granted to my Trustee in said John Doe Revocable Living Trust, and shall not be limited in any way by the grant of specific powers hereinafter made.

Section 2. To file joint income or gift tax returns with my wife for the period prior to my death and, in her sole discretion, to pay any part or all of the taxes, interest, or penalties for such periods and for the periods for which joint returns were filed prior to my death, with any decision made being conclusive on all persons.

Section 3. To make sales and to make and receive loans to and from said John Doe Revocable Living Trust, even though the person serving as Trustee under said trust shall be the same as the fiduciary under this will.

Section 4. To make any election under the Internal Revenue code requisite to enable the earnings of a corporation to be taxed as a partnership, or, alternatively, the earnings of a partnership to be taxed as a corporation, and my Executor is specifically directed to review this question and take any action requisite in connection therewith within thirty (30) days after my death.

ARTICLE XI. My Executor shall not be required to file an appraisal with any court or to make any settlement, final, partial, or otherwise, with any court. In lieu thereof, within four months after the close of each fiscal year of my estate, the Executor shall render a written account of the administration thereof to the current-income beneficiaries thereof. The written approval of such accounting by a majority of all current income beneficiaries (the parent, guardian, or conservator acting on behalf of any beneficiary who is a minor or otherwise incompetent) shall be final and binding as to all matters stated in said account or as shown thereby upon all persons (whether or not in being) who are then or thereafter may become eligible to share in either the principal or the income of my estate. The failure of any beneficiary to object in writing to the acting fiduciary to such an account within sixty (60) days after receipt of the same shall be final and binding to the same extent as if the written assent were given as hereinbefore provided.

ARTICLE XII. Notwithstanding any provision of this will or of the John Doe Revocable Living Trust, all of the property of my estate shall be finally distributed not later than twenty years and eleven months after the date of death of the last survivor of the group composed of my wife and my descendants living on the date of my death, and at the expiration of such period if any part of my estate remains undistributed, the same shall immediately vest in and be distributed to the persons then entitled to receive the income from the trust estate in the proportions to which they are so entitled.

I, John Doe, residing in _____ (town, county, state), being now in good health of body and mind and not acting under duress, menace, fraud or undue influence of any person whatsoever, do make, publish, and declare this my last will and testament, and do hereby expressly revoke all other and former wills and codicils to wills heretofore made by me.

IN WITNESS WHEREOF, I have hereunto set my hand this _____ day of _____, 19_____.

_____

The foregoing instrument, consisting of this and _____ preceding pages, was, at the date hereof, published and declared by John Doe to be his last will and testament in the presence of us, the undersigned, who, at his request, and in his sight and presence, and in the sight and presence of each other, have hereunto subscribed our names as witnesses thereto, having also together seen the said testator's name written by him at the conclusion of the will on page _____.

_____ Residing at _____
_____ Residing at _____
_____ Residing at _____

A Typical Short Will for a Man With a Wife, Adult Children, and a Small Estate

I, John Doe, of _____ (town, state), hereby make this my last will revoking every will heretofore made by me.

ARTICLE I. I appoint my wife, Mary Doe, Executrix of this will and request that no bond be required of her as such. In the event of the death, default, disqualification, resignation, or removal of my wife, I appoint my brother, Charles Doe, Executor of this will and request that no bond be required of him as such. In the event of the death, default, disqualification, resignation, or removal of my brother, I appoint the _____ National Bank _____, as Executor of this will. The word "Executor," whenever used herein, shall be deemed to refer to my Executor or to my Executrix, whichever shall be acting as such.

ARTICLE II. I devise and bequeath my entire estate to my Executor to be distributed by him to my wife, if living, but if she predecease me, to my Children equally *per stirpes*.

ARTICLE III. I empower my Executor, and any successor Executor to allot, assign, care for, collect, contract with respect to, convey, convert, deal with, dispose of, enter into, exchange, hold, improve, insure, invest, lease, manage, mortgage, grant and exercise options with respect to, take possession of, pledge, protect, receive, release, repair, sell, sue for, and in general, to do any and every act and thing and to enter into and carry out any and every agreement with respect to my estate or any part thereof as the Executor would have the right to do if it were the individual owner thereof and as it may deem in the best interest of the beneficiaries of my estate.

I, John Doe, residing in _____, being now in good health of body and mind and not acting under duress, menace, fraud, or undue influence of any person whatsoever, do make, publish, and declare this my last will and testament, and do hereby expressly revoke all other and former wills and codicils to wills heretofore made by me.

IN WITNESS WHEREOF, I have hereunto set my hand this _____ day of _____, 19_____.

_____

The foregoing instrument, consisting of this and _____ preceding pages, was, at the date hereof, signed, published and declared by John Doe to be his last will and testament in the presence of us, the undersigned, who, at his request, and in his sight and presence, and in the sight and presence of each other, have hereunto subscribed our names as witnesses thereto, having also together seen the said testator's name written by him at the conclusion of the will on page _____.

_____ Residing at _____
_____ Residing at _____
_____ Residing at _____

Estate Tax Table

Amount of taxable estate		Estate tax (before credits)			Estate tax (after maximum state death tax credit)		
From A (in thousands)	To B (in thousands)	Tax on A	+	Percent of excess over A	Tax on A	+	Percent of excess over A
$ 0	$ 5	$ 0		3%	$ 0		3%
5	10	150		7	150		7
10	20	500		11	500		11
20	30	1,600		14	1,600		14
30	40	3,000		18	3,000		18
40	50	4,800		22	4,800		21.2
50	60	7,000		25	6,920		24.2
60	90	9,500		28	9,340		27.2
90	100	17,900		28	17,500		26.4
100	140	20,700		30	20,140		28.4
140	240	32,700		30	31,500		27.6

Amount of taxable estate		Estate tax (before credits)		Estate tax (after maximum state death tax credit)	
From A (in thousands)	To B (in thousands)	Tax on A	Percent of excess over A	Tax on A	Percent of excess over A
$ 240	$ 250	$ 62,700	30	$ 59,100	26.8
250	440	65,700	32	61,780	28.8
440	500	126,500	32	116,500	28
500	640	145,700	35	133,300	31
640	750	194,700	35	176,700	30.2
750	840	233,200	37	209,920	32.2
840	1,000	266,500	37	238,900	31.4
1,000	1,040	325,700	39	289,140	33.4
1,040	1,250	341,300	39	302,500	32.6
1,250	1,500	423,200	42	370,960	35.6
1,500	1,540	528,200	45	459,960	38.6
1,540	2,000	546,200	45	475,400	37.8
2,000	2,040	753,200	49	649,280	41.8
2,040	2,500	772,800	49	666,000	41
2,500	2,540	998,200	53	854,600	45
2,540	3,000	1,019,400	53	872,600	44.2
3,000	3,040	1,263,200	56	1,075,920	47.2
3,040	3,500	1,285,600	56	1,094,800	46.4
3,500	3,540	1,543,200	59	1,308,240	49.4
3,540	4,000	1,566,800	59%	1,328,000	48.6%
4,000	4,040	1,838,200	63	1,551,560	52.6
4,040	5,000	1,863,400	63	1,572,600	51.8
5,000	5,040	2,468,200	67	2,069,880	55.8
5,040	6,000	2,495,000	67	2,092,200	55
6,000	6,040	3,138,200	70	2,620,200	58
6,040	7,000	3,166,200	70	2,643,400	57.2
7,000	7,040	3,838,200	73	3,192,520	60.2
7,040	8,000	3,867,400	73	3,216,600	59.4
8,000	8,040	4,568,200	76	3,786,840	62.4
8,040	9,040	4,598,600	76	3,811,800	61.6
9,040	10,000	5,358,600	76	4,427,800	60.8
10,000	10,040	6,088,200	77	5,011,480	61.8
10,040	—	6,119,000	77	5,036,200	61

Gift Tax Table

Amount of taxable gifts (after all exemptions and deductions)		Tax on amount in A	Percent of excess over A
From A (in thousands)	To B (in thousands)		
$ 0	$ 5	$ 0	2¼%
5	10	112.50	5¼
10	20	375	8¼
20	30	1,200	10½
30	40	2,250	13½
40	50	3,600	16½
50	60	5,250	18¾
60	100	7,125	21
100	250	15,525	22½
250	500	49,275	24
500	750	109,275	26¼
750	1,000	174,900	27¾

Appendix F *(continued)*

Amount of taxable gifts (after all exemptions and deductions)		Tax on amount in A	Percent of excess over A
From A (in thousands)	To B (in thousands)		
$ 1,000	$ 1,250	$ 244 275	29¼
1,250	1,500	317,400	31½
1,500	2,000	396,150	33¾
2,000	2,500	564 900	3 ¾
2,500	3,000	748,650	39¾
3,000	3,500	947,400	42
3,500	4,000	1,157,400	44¼
4,000	5,000	1,378,650	47¼
5,000	6,000	1,851,150	50¼
6,000	7,000	2,353,650	52½
7,000	8,000	2,878,650	54¾
8,000	10,000	3,426,150	57
10,000	—	4,566 150	57¾

APPENDIX G

Saving Taxes With the Marital Deduction

Adjusted gross estate	U.S. tax life estate will	U.S. tax, marital deduction will	Difference
$ 120,000	$ 9,340	$ 0	$ 9,340
200,000	31,500	9,600	21,900
300,000	59,100	35,000	24,100
400,000	87,700	63,000	24,700
600,000	145,700	118,200	27,500
800,000	206,900	175,400	31,500
1,000,000	270,300	233,000	37,300
2,000,000	626,600	540,600	86,000
4,000,000	1,522,400	1,253,200	269,200